NOV 24 1993	DATE DUE	
DEC 11 1993		
APR 0 8 1997		
OCT 0 1 1998		
APR 0 9 1999		

James Baldwin

· THE LEGACY ·

Edited by Quincy Troupe

A TOUCHSTONE BOOK
Published by Simon & Schuster Inc.
New York London Toronto Sydney Tokyo Singapore

SIMON AND SCHUSTER/TOUCHSTONE
Simon & Schuster Building
Rockefeller Center
1230 Avenue of the Americas
New York, New York 10020

Designed by Sheree L. Goodman
Manufactured in the United States of America

10 9 8 7 6 5 4 3 2 1

10 9 8 7 6 5 4 3 2   Pbk.

Library of Congress Cataloging in Publication Data

James Baldwin : the legacy / edited by Quincy Troupe.
    p.   cm.—(A Touchstone book)
  Bibliography: p.
  1. Baldwin, James, 1924–1987.   2. Baldwin, James,
1924–1987—Interviews.   3. Authors, American—20th
century—Biography.   4. Civil rights workers—United
States—Biography.   5. Afro-Americans—Civil rights—
History—20th century.   I. Troupe, Quincy.
PS3552.A45Z73   1989
818′.5409—dc19   89-4126
                                                        CIP

ISBN 0-671-67650-4
      0-671-67651-2 Pbk.

*Acknowledgments for use of selections
appear on pages 266–67.*

TO DAVID BALDWIN
AND THE BALDWIN FAMILY

· CONTENTS ·

Foreword: James Baldwin at the
   Welcome Table by Wole Soyinka   9
   Preface by Quincy Troupe   19

· I ·

AMAZING GRACE   27
Celebrating Jimmy by Clyde Taylor   29

· II ·

FRIEND AND BROTHER   39
A *Brother's Love* by Maya Angelou   41
Jimmy in the House by William Styron   43
Baldwin by Mary McCarthy   47

7

"Vous Êtes Swing" by Verta Mae Grosvenor   51
Dinner at Jimmy's by Caryl Phillips   59
The Last Days by Pat Mikell   65

• III •

WRITER   73
Life in His Language by Toni Morrison   75
"The Way Love Never Dies" by Eugene B. Redmond   79
I Hear Music in the Air: James Baldwin's Just Above My Head by
Eleanor W. Traylor   95
An Appreciation by Mel Watkins   107

• IV •

WITNESS AND ADVOCATE   125
"Jimmy!" by Amiri Baraka   127
Dialogue in Black and White (1964–1965) by James
Baldwin and Budd Schulberg   135
*An Interview with Josephine Baker and James
Baldwin (1973)* by Henry Louis Gates, Jr.   161
*"Go the Way Your Blood Beats": An Interview with James Baldwin
(1984)* by Richard Goldstein   173
The Last Interview (1987) by Quincy Troupe   186
James Baldwin by Chinua Achebe   213

• V •

SELECTED WRITINGS   219
Notes of a Native Son by James Baldwin   221
Introduction to *The Price of the Ticket* by James Baldwin   243

Bibliography   257

Foreword:
James Baldwin
at the
Welcome Table

IT was not false modesty, and least of all was it a dread of mortality, whose lengthening shadow would be made palpable, flattered with a vote of consent—but when a black American colleague telephoned me early in 1987 with a proposal that James Baldwin and I make a "time capsule" for posterity, I felt very uneasy. He suggested a free-ranging "historic recording," debating any subject. It would be videotaped and made available to libraries. I was then in New York for a production of my play at Lincoln Center. "Here," the voice went, "we have the unique presence of two of the foremost black writers on the globe—one from the mother continent, the other from the Black Diaspora. We owe it to duty," he pleaded, "to preserve their thoughts, the mutual interplay of their ideas for future generations."

I hedged. The immediate obstacle was clear enough—I was in the middle of rehearsals and that is not the best time for a guaranteed flow of lofty thoughts or the testing of ideas against the time-honed soundboard of an intellect like Baldwin's. Theater directors know how the mind is tyrannized by rehearsals—sudden flashes of alternative blockings, costume details, musical interpolations, textual extrapolations, etc. As a playwright himself, Baldwin would understand. I had been assured that he was quite at ease with the idea of the time capsule, so I undertook to speak to him: my first conversation with him in over twenty years and, lamentably, my last. I lied to him that, in principle, I was equally enthusiastic, but—the studio bookings just had to be shifted. He understood, as I expected any man of the theater would—and agreed to place himself at my disposal.

More telephone calls. I was running out of excuses. New dates were set for studio bookings. The producer added his voice; the moderator expressed his enthusiasm. Next came invitations to come over to my interlocutor's apartment for a relaxed prerecording session, when we could survey the territory of the proposed debate. I now had to confess my unease about the entire project. I could not enter into the spirit of such a self-conscious—as it seemed to me—exercise. A conversation or debate that came up naturally, in a more mundane course of interaction, accidentally acquiring greater permanence or accessibility than the usual reels of tape in a broadcasting studio—that I could understand. But to set out deliberately to record "for posterity"—this somehow went against the grain. I felt, and confessed that I found something "artificial" about it.

It was, alas, the last conversation I would ever have with James Baldwin.

But I did meet James Baldwin again!

I heard him, watched his watchful eyes and listened with his intensely alert ears in the company in which he was so much at ease, so compassionately his own unique being. No, not in his second (and permanent) place of exile but paradoxically, in his first, St.-Paul-de-Vence in the south of France. It happened this way.

My friend and colleague, Professor Henry Louis Gates, had spoken often of James Baldwin's home in St. Paul. He had visited and interviewed him there quite a number of times and indeed was now busy trying to turn this retreat into a home for the James Baldwin Foundation.

"Skip" Gates had also informed me earlier of the existence of a play, in manuscript only, which James Baldwin had written virtually on his deathbed. The play was based, in part, upon an actual event—a late night August dinner in the gardens of his home at St. Paul, attended by Skip (then a journalist at *Time* magazine in London), his wife, Sharon Adams, Josephine Baker (whom Skip had brought over from her home in Monaco), Cecil Brown, and three of Jimmy's friends who were living in St. Paul. It was the first time that Baker and Baldwin had seen each other in decades; it would be their last. *The Welcome Table* was James Baldwin's last theatrical work.

In April, 1988, visiting St. Paul with Skip, I obtained the playscript from him and read it. It was not the personal genesis of the work that made it, for me, such a poignant piece. It was the tangible personality of the work.

James Baldwin's intense, restive and febrile persona hovered, it seemed, over the pages, pulsated through the mannerisms, wiles and vulnerabilities of his manipulating and manipulated guests, a somewhat withdrawn ghostly host. I felt that I was listening, after all, to Baldwin's annotations to the dialogue which we never held, lightly touching on the paradoxes of human relationships, of emotions, of the treachery of memories, but consistent in its homage to that elusive quality which Baldwin had elevated to nearly the First Principle of the meaning of human existence—love.

In the ambiguities of Baldwin's expression of social, sexual, even racial and political conflicts will be found that insistent modality of conduct, and even resolution, celebrated or lamented as a tragic omission—love. And herein lies the subjective unease which has been my portion from the bounty of Baldwin's creative ethic and its production.

From his first published work, *Go Tell It on the Mountain*, to the uncompromising, near-deification of love in *Giovanni's Room*, through numerous essays on the politics of race and even reconstructions of traumatizing events such as *Blues for Mister Charlie*, there is this near-evangelical commitment to the principle that rules all being—love sought, denied, distorted, waiting in the wings or hovering on the wing, a veritable *deus ex machina*, lacking only a landing permit from a blinkered humanity that hesitates at the door of salvation.

It is not, of course, crude preaching—on the contrary. Urbane is the word. James Baldwin's humanity was the product of an urbane intellect, an intellect that was self-conscious almost to a fault, one which took for its province the entire gamut of emotional ambiguities, then proceeded to fashion a life-ethic from its very contradictions: love, acceptance. If a subjective aspect of sexuality rose to the fore, it can be understood within Baldwin's own findings—that it is within the sexual expression of love (or the search for love) that the ambiguity which is yet another characteristic of human (and social) relationships is most cogently revealed.

This elevation of a minority preference to the altar of the universal is of course a creative choice in whose cause some of Baldwin's most involuted, inner-quarrying writing will be found. *Giovanni's Room* stands as supreme example. At such moments, Baldwin appears to attempt to do for the minority of humanity what D. H. Lawrence also tried to do for his equally mythified Everyman-and-Everywoman (minus the bourgeois prude). The difference perhaps is in Baldwin's insistence on the value, *Love*, in contrast to Lawrence's erotic imperative. This commitment necessarily complicates works whose subjects render love not merely marginal but almost gratuitous, contextually.

This is a most appropriate occasion to introduce *The Welcome Table*, which, like *Giovanni's Room*, does not attempt to venture beyond the intricate loom of private relationships into the prejudicial terrain of race or politics, except as these intrude on the conversation.

A journalist arrives to interview a famous star. The interview, plus its earlier photo session, serves as the play's structure-motif of self-revelation and exposure. Even the journalist, Peter, submits to the compulsion of the meddlesome profession. All partake of the rites of revelation in spite of the reticent, withholding self, a needful act of exorcism. Haunting or elusive variants of love constitute their common humanity.

For the actress-singer, Edith, the enigma of a vanished lover. Then, a cousin's mothering love—disinterested? How truthful is affection even between sisters—and in this case, cousins who merely grew up together? The questions pile up. A painful drama of childhood and immature infatuation recalled. When does innocent sibling envy turn into acts that transform the entire existence of the object of such love-hate?

Edith, the celebrity centerpiece, focus of admiration, curiosity and envy, now has herself a young lover who in turn has a male lover. A world of ambiguity is compressed even into stage directions. Laverne, the cousin, kisses Edith on the cheek. The kiss provokes a "carefully controlled shrinking against this touch," to which, however, Laverne "does not react." An ambience of teases, of pregnant gestures which are never fully delivered of meaning, only of the very flux of possibilities. Androgynous utterances complement the same quality of gestures. "We've just confessed our love for each other," jokes Edith to the same cousin, the "other" being the worshiping servant, Angelina. But it is no more than domestic banter—or is it?

And again what is the nature of friendship between Edith and yet another guest-tenant of that same menagerie, the widowed Regina, slowly drinking herself to death? "What are we going to do about her?" asks Edith's lover, Rob. The question provokes a riposte from Edith, this time focused on Rob's acknowledged homosexual friend, Mark— "What are we going to do about *him?*" Regina on her part has "wondered about love" ever since her wedding day. "I really should have married you," she laughs—or *confesses?*—to Edith.

And so it goes on, the musical chairs of past and present relationships.

"Love is where you find it." "Love isn't something you can take back to the store for a refund." Daniel, the ex-Black Panther, now a would-be playwright, also shares in this love—the welcoming arms of hospitality, the breath that he has newly learned to take, the Welcome Table that embraces them one and all, including the embittered, racist Madame LaFarge whose birthday is the immediate occasion for their all getting together.

Yes, in Baldwin love is often, even obtrusively, "where you find it." Against a projection of the memory of tortures, castrations, burning flesh, the horrors of Algerian colonialism, Latin American repression and externally induced destabilization, lynchings and Nazi horrors, love like Laverne's emerald—"the only piece of jewelry you really care about"—is always flashed, a lucent talisman even in incongruous situations. "Every time I see you flash that emerald, I know that you are trying to resuscitate *Miss Laverne*. I know that she is endangered, but not dead."

The journalist narrates his encounter with a Nazi conscript in the context of dormant Fascist revivalism, yet the fundamental abjuration of love, which is the metaphysical reality that defines the history and experience of Nazism, is not relived or spoken of in the starkness of its own identity. Marginalized, a mere casual inflection, is this menace freshly pronounced by Nazi sympathizers who swear to pick up where Hitler had left off. The core of the experience for Baldwin is the human contact. Ultimates in inhumanity provide the opportunity for flashing the lone emerald: their purpose is to annunciate its indestructibility, the sole salvage whose glimmer constantly redeems the human personality and restores the psyche.

> Well, the point is that, in the course of the interview [with the ex-engineer in Nazi uniform] this man and I, who had never met before: the atmosphere between us changed. It was electrical. It was beautiful. We became friends. We are still friends.

When love, friendship, empathy and even their muted correlatives recur as capstones of the structures of relationships, with such devotion and exclusivity, and often on shifty grounds, the commodity becomes suspect. This is the difficulty I personally encounter in Baldwin's work. The language of its exposition then verges on preciosity especially when, in its attempts to plumb emotive depths, imperatives of social conduct become suffocated and can actually be heard to struggle for breath—as in *Blues for Mister Charlie*.

"Love is as old as thunder, and it strikes like lightning." Ah yes, but where what we see striking like lightning is actually the law of the lynch mob, the tar-and-feather, and physical castration, the flash of the emerald talisman becomes a blinding distraction and the generosity of the visionary a ponderous weight on the shoulders of lesser beings. To such, James Baldwin appears to eke out the inadequate humanity of the individual, and with means which stretch the limits of creative license. Love becomes unfocused; it is expressed, defined, even by its lack of focus, as a pantheistic hymn to that which is lost but surrounds one, which touches but is never grasped, which is individual-specific and yet questions its own form, flesh or gender:

> He must have changed. He may be dead. He may be a junkie. He may be a dealer. He may be on Death Row. Or he may be the round fat black raisin sweating his hour in the sun, President of a Black Free Enterprise up and coming business. He may have been tortured to death in South Africa. He may be fighting in South America, or in Palestine—ah! he might be you. Yes, I might not recognize him if he were as close to me as you are—but he would think that he recognized *me*. . . .

This is Edith, speaking of her lost lover, the most significant love of her life, indeed, the focus of her tragic experience. And in *The Welcome Table*, nowhere does the title sound more pertinent—love as a board of welcome, and to all comers or perhaps to none in particular; certainly there are no disqualifications. This constitutes the terrain of discomfort. Edith's song of universal embrace of nostalgia and elegant ennui is a cry of the *salon* which, suitably decorative at the Welcome Table, savages our grasp of reality when a kin balm of a laxity of emotions is evoked in *Blues*.

For in *Blues* we confront an event of racial murder—that of Emmett Till in 1955. The drama is winnowed through the humanist sensibilities of the playwright and is turned into a compassionate study of human relationships which, of course must first be "fabricated." Black victims of racial murder and dehumanization were simply members of the "invisible" race, and Baldwin's creative mission was partly to shred this cloak of invisibility and render the victim here as a sentient being in all his human complexity. This "fleshing out" however remains, for Baldwin, incomplete, without a corresponding ability in the victim to respond to the humanity of the other, his assailant and destroyer, thus piloting both through a carefully contrived set of interactions, essential to the thematic core. Against the social fact that, to his aggressors, the victim's individuality was nonexistent, Baldwin justly asserts that individuality, but it is also dependent on the innate humanity (albeit warped) of the aggressor. Few writers are capable of this largeness of compassion; few can write with a grace which matches the graciousness that permits an "alibi" for the enemy of one's kind. Baldwin's legacy embraces this liaison of art and the mission of compassion, a unique quality that first seduces, then poses its subtle challenge to the reader's moral complacency.

Was James Baldwin a writer capable of the expression of anger? Of moral anger for example. Of a truly lacerating, righteous rage against human folly or cruelty?

I met James Baldwin thrice in his lifetime. The most memorable was in the early sixties, in London, that is, during the period of black revolt in the United States, at the height of a new self-awareness of a condemned race and its expression in a language of violence on the streets, in the arts, especially in poetry and theatre. The controversial journal *Encounter* was then edited by an expatriate American, Melvin Lasky, who, perhaps because of his own "exile status" (as Jew and American), found a correspondence between what was taking place among the blacks of the United States and the race towards independence then occurring on the African continent. AMSAC, the American Society for African Culture, was born about this time, partly financed, as it turned out later, by a foundation with a rather dubious origin, the same foundation which largely sponsored the *Encounter* magazine. Whatever the labyrinthine motives of that foundation were, no one remembers today. Suffice it that it was through this linkage that American writers, intellectuals, artists and musicians—Gwendolyn Brooks, James Baker, Odetta, Nina Simone, Peter Lawrence, Langston Hughes, Mercer Cook, Sam Allen, Saunders Redding . . . and of course James Baldwin, came to interact physically, intellectually and creatively with their African counterparts—Chinua Achebe, Eldred Jones, Malangatana, Peter Abrahams, Cyprian Ekwensi, Dei-Anang, Es'kia Mphahlele, and so on. These physical encounters took place not only in the United States and in Africa, but also in Europe, in large formal sessions and in small informal exchanges, which either "happened" in the offices of *Encounter* magazine in London, or over lunch in one of Melvin Lasky's favorite restaurants.

My first meeting with the diminutive prose stylist took place, I recall, in the office of the editor, with the poet Stephen Spender providing what we might call the European leaven. The conversation, which ranged over African and American culture, Negritude, and *Culture*, took place naturally against the background of the black American restive assertion. What I recall most about James Baldwin's quite animated contributions was the paradox of the *intensity* of his beliefs in the racial question, and the suppression of its inherent subjectivity for him as a black man. He spoke as a convinced universalist— no, perhaps cosmopolite describes it more accurately—who, while he passionately contested the diminution of his humanity in American racism, did not, for instance, see culture as an instrument of combat. I obtained the impression that Baldwin saw Art and Culture as individual entities in their own right, as universal property which betrayed and impoverished their own nature when appropriated by one section of humanity against the other, even in its own self-defense.

I recall this encounter vividly because of Baldwin's reversal of position two or three years later. He returned to the States and made what appeared to be one of the strongest denunciations of American racism of that period and one which also fully endorsed the cultural resistance which was then at its height. The anger was authentic, and the deployment of language was a sharp departure from the Baldwin of the famous essays. The question that came to my mind was: was this a complete transformation or a response to a specific phase in the American social struggle?

I am convinced that it was the latter. James Baldwin's was—to stress the obvious—a different cast of intellect and creative sensibility from a Ralph Ellison's, a Sonia Sanchez's, a Richard Wright's, an Amiri Baraka's, or an Ed Bullins'. He was, till the end, too deeply fascinated by the ambiguities of moral choices in human relations to posit them in raw conflict terms. His penetrating eyes saw the oppressor as *also* the oppressed. Hate as a revelation of self-hatred, never unambiguously outward-directed. Contempt as thwarted love, yearning for expression. Violence as inner fear, insecurity. Cruelty as an inward-turned knife. His was an optimistic, grey-toned vision of humanity in which the domain of mob law and lynch culture is turned inside out to reveal a landscape of scarecrows, an inner content of straws that await the compassionate breath of human love.

"If I hurt you, I also hurt myself." At the Welcome Table in the Great Beyond, I have no doubt that we shall find Jimmy seated between some Grand Master of the K.K.K., Governor Wallace and the Scottsboro boys, enjoying a wise laugh at the former's unease, applying to their self-inflicted wounds the soothing balm of his imperishable, celestial prose.

—Wole Soyinka
Abeokuta, Nigeria

O N November 13, 1987, I flew
Air France from Paris to Nice to visit the distinguished American
writer James Baldwin. There were several reasons for my visit, the first
being that Jimmy Baldwin was an old friend who quite generously and
without fail had always been there with his encouragement and help
throughout my writing career. I wanted to interview him for the autobiography of Miles Davis that I was writing with Mr. Davis, his
longtime friend, and I wanted to be with him because I had heard
that he was quite ill. I thought that such a meeting might prove
significant for us both. So, for all of those reasons, I was looking
forward to spending time in the south of France with Jimmy and his
brother David.

Upon boarding Air France flight 1401, the first sound I heard over
the buzzing of passengers' voices was the haunting saxophone of John

Coltrane, one of the great musicians of this or any other century. The effect of hearing his music wafting through the plane cabin like incense brought a smile to my face because it was both exhilarating and comforting to hear this extraordinary musician acknowledged in this way, and tears because he could never be recognized in this way in his place of birth. On that gray November morning I thought of James Baldwin, Richard Wright, and others who would never be honored in the United States as they were abroad, simply because they were black. On the flight down to Nice, this thought profoundly saddened and troubled me. But by the time I had arrived at Nice's Côte d'Azur airport my spirits had been lifted considerably, no doubt due in large measure to the sun-splashed beauty of Nice but also to David Baldwin, who was there at the airport to greet me. With him was Lucien Happersburger, the painter who had known Jimmy for so long. (His essay, "Stranger in the Village," was written while visiting Lucien in Switzerland as was *Go Tell It on the Mountain*.) I was soon to find out that it is almost impossible to be down in the company of these two affable and luminous human beings.

After I collected my bags and on the way out of the airport, David informed me quite matter-of-factly that Jimmy had cancer and that the prognosis was that it was terminal. "At the most," he said, "the doctor gives him about a month." I was stunned, knocked off balance by the finality of the news and also by David's casual manner. I looked at Lucien, searching for some sign of grief, but he only shrugged and said, "That's the way life is; we all have to go someday." Then David said that they had decided to have an upbeat attitude about everything so that Jimmy's last days could be as normal as possible. David also told me that Jimmy had not been told that his cancer was terminal, although they both believed that he probably knew. He said that he was telling me this to prepare me for the way Jimmy looked. "He can't walk," David said. "We have to carry him everywhere and dress him. He sleeps a lot and weighs about eighty pounds, down from his usual one thirty-five. I don't see how it's possible for him to lose any more weight. Anyway," he went on, "that's why I'm telling you now, so that you won't look shocked when you see him. Just try to act upbeat, like you normally are." I said, "Okay."

As we left the airport to travel to the mountain to the village of St.-Paul-de-Vence where Jimmy lived, David turned to me and said, "Quincy, you can't imagine all the things that I have been through for the last few months since I've been here. Man, it's been rough. But I'm happy you're here, so let's try to have some fun." At that moment, I could see the unspeakable grief etched in the mask that was not his face.

On the winding drive up the mountain to Vence, through the quaint little villages that reminded me of Haiti, David asked if I would do him a favor; he asked me to conduct an in-depth interview with Jimmy. That interview is included in its entirety in this volume. Because of Jimmy's rapidly deteriorating condition, David knew that this would be the last opportunity for Jimmy to air his final thoughts and observations. I felt honored by his request. Although it was what I had hoped to do, I hadn't expected the situation to be as grave as it was.

After recovering from this shock, I asked David if there was anything else that I might do. He then suggested my helping to do a kind of celebration of Jimmy's life. I said I would, though I didn't know at the time what form that celebration would take.

We drove up the mountain sharing tall tales, jokes, and lies to lighten our heavy load. We stopped at a café for a couple of rounds of coffee and cognac before continuing to St.-Paul-de-Vence and my almost certain to be sad and happy reunion with a great and dear friend.

The village of St. Paul was founded in 1009. The old section sits behind the fifty-foot-high walls that completely surround it. The cannons that project from the walls are now rusty tourist attractions, as are the ramparts which were once used to spot enemy soldiers. Marc Chagall lived here, as did Pablo Picasso, Georges Braque, and Simone Signoret. Today Yves Montand can be seen playing *la boule* on any sunny day with his fellow villagers in front of the Café de la Place on rue Charles de Gaulle. Across the street is the internationally renowned restaurant and inn La Colombe d'Or, celebrated as much for its cuisine as for its rich and famous clientele and its priceless art collection. Canvases by Picasso, Matisse, Miró, Léger, and many others adorn the walls.

Just down the hill, negotiated by a narrow, twisting road, is the three-hundred-year-old farmhouse of James Baldwin. The red and white St. Paul city-limits sign spots the front-gate entrance of James Baldwin's home. There is history in the sign being placed precisely where it is. A few years back a group of St. Paul residents, upon noticing that the Baldwin house sat just outside the limits of the village, secretly moved the sign one late night so that when you enter the village of St. Paul it is seemingly with the blessing of James Baldwin, who has lived there for nineteen years.

To reach the two-story, light-brown stone and stucco house which sits off the main road of la Route de la Colle, one must negotiate a narrow cobblestone path umbrellaed by trees. Entering this comfortable home, one is immediately struck by the commanding view from the dining room windows. The scene opens out onto the valley below, now dotted with expensive villas; it is a beautiful, serene, peaceful setting.

The house was sold to him by St. Paul's most prominent local historian, the late Madame Jeanne Fauré, whose book *Saint Paul: une ville royale de l'ancienne France sur la Côte d'Azur,* is considered the definitive local history. Madame Fauré, like the wife of the late owner of La Colombe D'Or, Tintine—the two of them the most prominent and powerful women in St. Paul—came to deeply love and respect James Baldwin. Both women, who disliked each other intensely, had embraced him as a member of their families, had tolerated each other because of him, and had made Jimmy's stay in St. Paul even richer and more pleasant.

When I was taken to see Jimmy, who had been moved from the ground-floor wing of the house where he slept and worked to another bedroom that was very dark, I was shocked by his frail and weakened condition. I quickly hugged and kissed him on the top of his head. I held him close for a long moment, partly because I loved this man and also because I didn't want him to notice the overwhelming sadness that had welled in my eyes. But remembering David's admonition to "act normally," I quickly pulled myself together and told him how happy I was to see him. He smiled that brilliant smile of his, his large eyes bright and inquisitive like those of a child. He told me in a very weak voice that he was convalescing and tired but would come out to greet me properly in about two to three hours. Then those bright luminous owl eyes burned deeply into mine as if seeking some clue, some sign that would give him a hint as to the seriousness of his condition. How much did I know that he didn't know? those eyes seemed to be asking me. They probed for a moment and then released me from their questioning fire. I was relieved when David led me out of the darkened room. I will never forget that image of Jimmy weakly sitting there, the feel of his now wispy hair scratching my face when I hugged him, the birdlike frailty of his ravaged body and the parting telescopic image of him dressed in a red and green mackintosh robe that all but swallowed him, his large head lolling from one side to the other as Lucien lifted him to put him to bed.

David informed me that I would be sleeping in Jimmy's old work area, where the great French artist Georges Braque had once slept and worked. His ground-floor studio and bedroom was sunny and expansive and opened out onto a beautiful garden with a workbench set under an umbrella where he could write. Flowers and fruit trees were in abundance. Four or five cats scurried and darted around the garden, sometimes making sly but futile attempts to slip by the barrier of my foot to gain entry to the studio and bedroom.

There are so many articles in the house that caught my attention, most notably the many paintings and sculptures, especially the colorful paintings of the late African-American expatriate painter Beauford Delaney, who had been one of Jimmy's best friends. There were two other pieces that I believed said much about the political commitment of the man. One, a black pen-and-ink drawing of Nelson Mandela against an orange background accompanied by a poem, was framed and hung over the dining-room fireplace, the prominent place in the house. The other was an assemblage, created by David. The items in this montage were of distinct interest individually, but when viewed as a composite, they made an obvious and stunning political statement. The centerpiece was the Honneur Patrie of the République Française Ordre National de la Légion d'Honneur (France's Legion of Honor), which was awarded to James Baldwin in January 1987 by François Mitterrand. Underneath the framed citation on the mantelpiece and placed on each side were a sword and an old hunting rifle, both pointing toward the certificate. Framed by these two pieces and sitting on the mantel were a black-and-white photograph of Jimmy, an abstract steel sculpture of an Indian pointing a bow and arrow, two crystal inkwells, a figure resembling a guitar, and an oversized ink pen pointed directly toward the Legion of Honor citation. Later, when I asked David about the significance of the montage, he said, "It was my hommage to my brother."

I see him in a very similar way.

James Baldwin was much more than a superb writer who created an immensely influential and personal language; he was also a genuine world celebrity whose face and name were as recognizable as those of famous athletes, heads of state, or any film or pop music "star" who lived in this century. But his celebrity extended far beyond his great influence in literature.

In many ways Baldwin, like Martin Luther King, Malcolm X, and President John F. Kennedy, represented—along with many others far less renowned—the spirit of change that affected all our lives so dramatically during the 1960s. And none who lived through the experience of that period have ever been the same since, whether black or white, conservative or liberal; all were put on notice, and their view of the world, their view of themselves and others, their political, social, cultural, and economic views—whether left or right—were incalculably altered.

Throughout this period James Baldwin represented a spirit, a progressive and moral consciousness that was a symbol of what was good and right in this country, a country he always referred to as "these yet to be United States." His was an outspoken voice that disturbed many with its unrelenting crusade to bring to light all that was evil and unjust in our society and which, he felt, if allowed to go unchecked would ultimately destroy the beacon light of what this country professes to stand for—the freedom of the individual guaranteed by a system of law: in short, what is meant by the word "democracy."

James Baldwin was hated by many for his brilliant, on-the-mark sermonizing of this truth. But he was revered by an even greater number, who knew in their hearts that his point of view was ultimately healing and morally correct.

I loved Jimmy. To be in his company and listen to him hold forth on the seemingly inexhaustible topics he had at his command was part pleasure and part honor. Jimmy's voice in "the flesh" was almost identical to the voice he utilized in his transcendent, fiery, and eloquent essays, rich in the nuances of the black minister (which he *was* early in his life). It seemed almost effortless, this instrument that was his voice, so seamlessly flowing, natural—both in its written and spoken forms—easy with the rhythms of American, black, oral tradition. There is not a doubt in my mind—and I daresay in the minds of countless others—that the voice of James Baldwin was that of a genius. It was the vehicle with which he approached glory; it was a miracle of expression. The "Baldwin sentence" was muscular, compelling, flexible, musical, original—his own invention. But it was *what* he said that finally hypnotized us with such powerful seduction.

The interview was conducted over a period of two days, whenever Jimmy's physical condition allowed. He had to be carried by David to his favorite chair, a large, soft, stuffed orange one next to the dining room table. From this place he had a panoramic view of the St. Paul valley and the surrounding mountains he loved so dearly. Our conversations ranged over such topics as the American economy, yuppies, Ronald Reagan, Toni Morrison, Norman Mailer, Miles Davis, Ralph Ellison, music, his life—growing up and now. Always candid, direct, he was as earthy and "street" and "down" as he was intellectually challenging. It was the last interview James Baldwin sat for. He could not finish our last session because of the pain that overwhelmed him.

One of the last things he expressed to me after apologizing for being too weak to complete the last part of the interview was his hope that I and other writers "would continue to be witnesses of our time; that we must speak out against institutionalized and individual tyranny wherever we find it. Because if left unchecked it threatens to engulf and subjugate us all"—the fire *this* time.

The inspiration for this book did not originate with me, but came from Jimmy's brother David. It is a celebration of the life, the vision and, yes, the death of our good and great, passionate, genius witness of a brother, James Arthur Baldwin.

Clyde Taylor's piece, written expressly for this book, introduces its motif. Other pieces commissioned for the book are works by Mary McCarthy, Mel Watkins, Eugene B. Redmond, and Pat Mikell's moving account of Jimmy's final days. William Styron's remembrance was first published in *The New York Times Book Review* along with the funeral remarks by Maya Angelou, Toni Morrison, and Amiri Baraka. Chinua Achebe's, also written after Jimmy's death, was delivered at a commemoration ceremony at the University of Massachusetts in Amherst; Jimmy taught at Hampshire College at Amherst on occasion. The other selections are excerpted from various publications and date back as early as the 1960s.

Jimmy's writings are prodigious and varied. Those included here testify to the breadth of his career and the scope of his ambitions. He was—and remains in the living words of his books—one of the greatest and most unrelenting "witnesses," of this or any century, a wise and gentle, flawed but profoundly good and correct human spirit.

—Quincy Troupe
New York City

· I ·

AMAZING GRACE

In the private chambers of the soul, the guilty party is identified, and the accusing finger there is not legend, but consequence, not fantasy, but the truth. People pay for what they do, and still more, for what they have allowed themselves to become. And they pay for it simply: by the lives they lead.

—JAMES BALDWIN

CELEBRATING JIMMY
▪ by Clyde Taylor ▪

Clyde Taylor writes widely on black literature, film, and culture. An Associate Professor in English at Tufts University, he is also Associate Editor of Black Film Review. *He is currently a Ford Foundation Fellow at the DuBois Institute, Harvard University.*

THEY came that Tuesday, December 8, 1987, to say farewell to Jimmy Baldwin, a name, voice, and face they had grown to know and love as part of their own growth. To satisfy the obligation of one's presence, pay one's respects, was the uppermost motive that brought them. Black people have redefined the ritual marking death as "celebration of life." But if the ritual of the celebration is to signify at all, then the life is the question that the ritual must answer.

An undeflectable pall sits at the "celebration" of a black man in America. It spreads from the knowledge, oversimply, that he did not die and will not be buried in "Africa." Translated, this means that whatever the gameness of his spirit, he did not, could not uncover his most refined meaning among the scheme of errors laid out before his birth. *Ogun,* the first kidnapped Africans must have prayed, *let me not die in this forsaken land. But if I do, return my spirit to the ancestors.*

For many reasons, not least of which was Jimmy Baldwin's own force brought to the redefinition and self-discovery of Africans in America—being quite possibly for his times their most essential interpreter—this question had to be addressed by new and thoughtful responses.

Among the five thousand celebrants who overflowed the Cathedral of St. John the Divine at Amsterdam and 112th Streets known as the largest Gothic cathedral in the world, many dressed to the nines, many in their everydays, it was a commonplace that Jimmy Baldwin of Harlem had changed their lives. But having changed it, how was it again changed by his leaving? His passing came most unwelcomed. Everybody could see it coming. His slight self grew frailer by the years. Word of illnesses and missed speaking engagements had trickled from Amherst. One of the last times I had seen him was to exchange a few words on College Avenue in Berkeley, just outside a liquor store at eleven-thirty in the morning.

It had been wrenching, his dying in Southern France—a turn of events he hardly suspected, or let on that he suspected—someplace we could not imagine well enough to gather over imaginatively. At the wake on St. Nicholas Avenue that Monday night there was little comfort looking for the appropriate place to be among rooms divided between two different mourning parties. Jimmy looked thinner, almost toylike, and grayer in the casket, but still Jimmy. It was a mess. Sixty-three years old. Way out of time by any scheme of reckoning.

Even at the family house on the West Side there was a strained, casual unreadiness. The Baldwins encountered a stranger in their halls like a familiar neighbor, spoke as though picking up an old conversation. In the sitting room where an offered drink was welcomed, the family nestled in a space somewhere between resting and alertly tending the tiniest details of each other's comfort, lounging the time out and away from themselves. Which was also what was happening at Mikell's, where at the door the sign over his picture said, "We are closed tonight in honor of our dear friend Jimmy Baldwin," and friends, some from long distances, chatted around the occasion.

The disorder of his departure, the sense of an accidental interruption of the flow of life nowhere more restless than on the Upper West Side, struck again, Tuesday noon at St. John's, as a confusion of focus when a double file of black-dressed honorary pallbearers passed by my pew. Familiarity out of context, the shock of half-recognition: they passed by like a moving group photo of black talent and genius assembled for some unimaginable event. Friends; and faces I could deceive myself I "knew" for having seen so often: Maya Angelou and Toni Morrison, Baraka, Odetta, Max Roach, Ellis Haizlip, Paule Marshall, Lerone Bennett, Louise Meriwether, Joan Sandler, Quincy Troupe, Verta Mae Grosvenor, Ossie Davis, Toni Cade Bambara, Clarence Williams, Rosa Guy, Arthur Moore, Wilfred Cartey, Richard Long, Gwendolyn Brooks, Howard Dodson, and others I didn't recognize or have time to. A choral procession of portrait faces and iconic associations too many to digest spun my mind into scattered orbits. Their seating at one arc of the broad circle, the symbolic heart of the house, made the first punctuation that marked the occasion momentous.

The drums of Babatunde Olatunji and his ensemble, in white akbadas with half sleeves, broke the waiting silence, heart-thumped the body-shaped cathedral into conscious life. Their sound resonated through this awesome structure, its huge columns rising toward dimly lit Gothic arches whose elaborate, figured moldings rested easily within the building's symmetry. To the question of "Africa" a rhetorical answer had been resoundingly announced. "Africa" was here, "Africa" had come to witness this formal revelation of one complete life.

I silently thanked Eleanor Traylor, literary critic, ritualist, and inner member of the extended Baldwin clan for her spare, profound, perfect ceremonial design. If Jimmy's story was also the story of this mass of believers in him, mostly black, then it was right that it begin in the Africa of Olatunji's drums. History was re-created as drama and pageant when the body of that quickened moment, beating cavernously, was intersected by a slow procession of the Baldwin family down the age-long aisle, led by the dean of the cathedral and an Anglican choir in white tunics over burgundy robes, carrying large crosses and candlesticks, singing an anthem. A ritual narrative was unfolding, of syncretisms and cultural interpenetrations out of which black identity—Baldwin's more deeply than most—had been imprinted. In this ordering of events, with African rhythmic gnosis framing white Christian logos, one could read redress of those moments recorded in *Notes of a Native Son* when Baldwin faced the authoritative cathedrals of Europe armed only with a few Bessie Smith disks for cultural comfort. After the ferment of black rediscovery and after Jimmy's luminous confessions of his perpetual self-discovery, no gifted young black American, this pageant seemed to be saying, need ever again stand with deference before the monuments of Western civilization.

Attention honed in on the family just seated at another arc of the circle, while the host church cadre anonymously sang, prayed a few words of welcome, and tactfully rustled out of the circle. Thoughts and eyes sought Jimmy's mother, Mrs. Berdis Baldwin, now in tears as Odetta sang with that sonority that bottoms the most basic African-American musical statement, "Sometimes I Feel Like a Motherless Child." Jimmy had been anything but motherless. As she sat surrounded by her children—Jimmy left eight sisters and brothers—and her children's children, their large eyes lighting their warm, open faces, the mystery of his gifts of spirit evaporated. The Baldwins looked like a clan from another planet where love is the guiding principle, their embracing vision shaded by the knowledge that that principle was fugitive here.

So one had to understand the metaphor in the old spiritual to hold onto clarity, that the equivalent of "Mother" was, again, "Africa"— as the song says, "a long way from home." The three songs Odetta irresistibly voiced shaped an historical parable beginning in the exile and bondage of "Motherless Child," marching beyond those limits with "Glory, Glory Hallelujah," and rounding off not in triumph but the healing of "Let Us Break Bread Together." These songs echoed the "love song" of Jimmy's voice described in the program note from the family: "Its constant refrain: 'love is a battle, love is war, love is growing up.' "

Mounting the spiral staircase to the peak of the high, elaborately carved altar, the speakers perched as though at the prow or quarterdeck of a three-master. We were all of us inside the vast, shadowy temple as though in a giant vessel, imperceptibly moving, against the tide to be sure, to carry its cargo, the coffin sitting detached, atop a black velvet drape, in the central space where the two wings of the cathedral crossed, to some safe and decent destination.

We needed somebody to say something. First Maya, then Toni, and finally Amiri in the eulogy evoked Jimmy as a person. I use first names, for our vulnerability drew us into family intimacy. As they spoke each occupied their space as Odetta had done, as black singers do, with a touch of trance, anointed, lifted by the message they bore to a theatrical presence that some scholars, thinking of preachers in their sermonizing, speak of as the self-investment of black people.

They spoke, Maya first, of him as a brother, a big brother, as he was not only to them but to a generation of still-young black people trying to find out what they were doing here. They made one remember his immediacy, he who after all had made racism in America *personal*.

They balmed anguish by making us see the reflexivity of our relation to him. His spirit, Baraka declared, "is part of our own." For Toni, he was "a two-way mirror" angering those who saw their human incapacities in his gaze and heartening those who were "always a bit better around you, smarter, more capable, wanting to be worth the love you lavished. . . ." Baldwin in death was becoming something possible to understand, to cope with. Toni's choice of direct address *to* him dissolved distance, implicated the present, suggested continuity and restitution. In life he had become more than a person, as legendary figures do. Now, with authority from the podium, words summed him as a spirit, as *the* ancestor.

These well-inhabited voices, invested by Baldwin, were evoking the essence of "Jimmy," the understanding that we *are* each other, and that by connecting with the divided parts of this Self we could find our best conditions. That had all along been the original African-American idea, its genius through such as Baldwin's to nurture and adorn.

The French ambassador, His Excellency Emmanuel de Margerie, in his brief, tasteful speech, aired out the in-house intensity. He recalled the mutual love between the people of France and Baldwin, reminding us at the same time of the breadth of Jimmy's compassion. The only speaker who was not African-American, his presence signified. The irony was inescapable that Jimmy, like so many black artists, had been more fully honored and respected abroad than by his own society. France had given him its highest tribute, the Legion of Honor. By contrast, what had American society done?

Something else wanted to be said. The character of the life could not be celebrated without honoring its combativeness, that the irreducible idea of selfhood seeking shared realization (which by this time I was convinced was a legacy from his family) had always had to fend off the weight of its mocking disbelievers. Baldwin's gift for prodding us to become more honestly ourselves showed up in Baraka's eulogy, being true to his unquenched rebel self. One felt a numbed surprise in the room as he spoke of the neglect and misunderstanding Baldwin the writer had encountered of late, even finding difficulty getting his work published. The house was roused when Baraka directed his words of challenge and contempt at those who scorned Baldwin's vision of life. He reminded us of Jimmy's rage, which had in fact seemed to become sharper in recent years, maybe because he had been steadfast to his vision while many had chilled out with the times.

After the speaking, "When the Saints Go Marching In" lit the huge hall with acoustical brilliance, played by Jimmy Owens, flugelhorn, Hugh Masekela, trumpet, and Danny Mixon, piano. The horns reached for the remotest corners of the chamber, echoing, somber but spirited. The sound of Hugh's unmistakable, poignant riff-commentaries, recalling South African pennywhistlers, made me, thinking still about "Africa," remember Willie Kgositsile's message on exile addressed to Hugh: "Home is where the music is," and how many times Jimmy's life and voice had been likened this day to a song.

It is no longer a surprise to me when black people gather for their most expressive and ritual occasions and some one most magnificent presentation is made, some production of human imagination and performance for which one is totally unprepared. Still, I was not ready. As the horns echoed quietly to a stillness, the hall was filled, without prior announcement (except baldly in the printed program), with the voice of James Baldwin, *singing*. "Precious Lord, take my hand. Lead me on . . ." I need not assure you that the cup of that church was filled at that unbelievable, culminating moment. It was that same voice (taped, of course) familiar to every literate person in America. But as a singer's it was, I felt, the equal of the great black singers, whose chops lay not in concert legitimacy, but in their own vocal authenticity, like Louis Armstrong or Ray Charles, or Billie. A husky baritone as certain and sensitive as he ever was, a cappella except for a muted trombone lick or two: it was a final revelation. He *was* a singer, could sing as well as he talked. It was Jimmy making his own final comment, as always finding the best word for the occasion. It was, most personal moment of all, Jimmy singing his "song" in his most complete self, a moment of purest truth.

What was being not said but expressed, signified, by the assembled celebrants of such a life in all but so many words was astonishing, and yet fully trustable. Not that Baldwin had been a prophet—everyone knew that, although he modestly described himself as a witness. By speaking of him as brother, friend, spirit, ancestor, and as *the* ancestor, what was being affirmed to general consent was that he was something more central, a transcendental human being. Not exactly a Christ; that carried too many questionable pledges to redeem. More like an avatar, a seed person, distillation of a cultural and human idea refined to the highest consciousness that could be attained and still shared with one's fellow internees of this century. And yet it would be a mistake to speak of this achieved vision of Jimmy Baldwin on this occasion as if it could be comprehended in worldly terms alone.

The feeling gathered in me, filing out, that one need no longer carry the weight of black burial in exile. The celebration of Jimmy's life made me see that the resting place of "Africa," where one is who one really is, can be no more nor less than a spiritually peopled homeland. And that this resting place was no more nor less whether one's bones were laid in Ferncliff Cemetery, Ardsley, New York, where Baldwin's soon would be taken, close to the graves of Paul and Eslanda Robeson, or in Gary, Tucson, Kumasi, or Benin. It was clear that our sensibility as a people had been inseparable from a sense of placelessness, or at least statelessness, "a long way from home." But was there not an ironic virtue of black people having furnished their peoplehood without benefit of proprietary investment in a national turf? That part of our salvation may have been to raise state-deprivation into a clarity where life, human life, all of it, is epiphany? And so I joined James Baldwin's nation on the broad steps of St. John the Divine, angling down into Amsterdam Avenue.

There, hundreds lingered. Writers, painters, journalists, activists, dancers, models, students, actors, publicists, filmmakers, lawyers, musicians, organizers, readers, dreadlocked, braided, balding, suited or jean-sneakered, the photographers among them snapping away at rare and unusual personality clusters. Some gathered into photos with Stokely Carmichael or other groupings, while Chinua Achebe greeted friends a few feet away. Eyes caressed Miriam Makeba. Minds wandered over the mosaic of faces, brains, hearts, and talents, perhaps struggling with the indigestion the assemblage of honorary pallbearers had given me, perhaps relieved to have disembarked from a momentous journey. Max Roach said, "You writers sure know how to put somebody away! When I go, I want the writers to put *me* away."

We lingered, reuniting with faces some of them not seen since the sixties. Chandra, Verta's daughter, who had been raised among this clan, said, "All my life I've been knowing these folks as Uncle this and Aunt that. Now I know who you *are*." Which is why we lingered. For Jimmy had given us this one last, most powerful reflection of ourselves in the glass of his wise eyes, our best selves, and we were not anxious to leave that image behind.

But we did, finally, scatter, some to visit "the house," eat the soulful food Verta and others had brought in, spend time with the family. For some the day had become its own holy day and we eased through it, a bit blissed out, consecrated, delicately carrying a new image of truth with us.

One crew of poets, novelists, editors, critics, painters, and lovers clustered in Mikell's, again closed for the day. Jimmy's brother David, who had been with him those final days in Southern France, officiated at the bar, and we talked and laughed and lived in the thought of Jimmy, our host. Stories passed in gentled voices. How many had been put back on track by him at some hopeless point in their lives? (How worthy a book might be made of these oral histories.) The grasp he brought to the job of being Jimmy Baldwin became freshly impressive. Toni Cade recalled how she would bump into Jimmy on the avenue and he would say, *"Girl*, what are you *doing?"* Not "What are you doing?" but "What are you *doing?"* giving his words that signifying intonation that came so naturally to him. And as the stories mounted I understood that it was not just busybodies he had to run away from, to France, in order to write, so heavy the responsibility of mentoring a whole generation of courageous black creators.

"It's the end of an era," literary agent Marie Brown summed up, meaning that Baldwin had been the last survivor, not of the powerful spokesmen of the 1960s, but of those few most powerful moral articulators who could effectively lecture the society, among the very few whom we could quote almost daily as scripture of social consciousness. But she was also voicing a requiem for ourselves, citizens of Baldwin country, a generation convinced still that we carried a sanity this society would refuse or become further incapable of accepting; written off as crazy idealists even by our children, thrashing, as Baldwin would say, as in a bubble, against a disordered tide. If Jimmy was gone, we would be, too. And where would our idea be then?

Drinks were swizzled and drunk as dusk turned to dark. More stories were told, more laughs recalled. Outside, on Columbus Avenue, vainly named for a sailor who didn't know where he was going, in the darkening mist and showered twilight, the Upper West Side flowed, bobbing and eddying, in some unfathomable direction. Marie Brown was right, as usual. It was the end of an era. But looking back on the day, the life we mourned and celebrated, the era it had witnessed had seen us a good bit closer to home.

· II ·

FRIEND AND BROTHER

The voice of James Baldwin has continually come through to sing the epic grandeur of a people: sorrowful, triumphant, biblical. But the voice has also come through to expose all monstrous pretension, all hideous hypocrisy, and all attempts to organize human society which violate the society of the human heart. In all this, that voice has found its resonance in the sacred and secular experience and expressions of African-American people. "More like the blues than a hymn," that voice has raised a love song, its constant refrain: "Love is a battle, love is war, love is growing up."

That true and faithful voice remains. What also remains is that smile, those eyes, that strong hand of our son, our brother, our uncle, our father—our Jimmy—now ancestral. As he has said, "the irreducible miracle is that we have sustained each other a very long time, and come a long, long way. . . ."

—THE FAMILY

A BROTHER'S LOVE

• by Maya Angelou •

Maya Angelou, poet, actress, activist, is no less complex a spirit than the one she celebrates in Now Sheba Sings the Song. *Her five acclaimed volumes of autobiography include* I Know Why the Caged Bird Sings *and, most recently,* All God's Children Need Traveling Shoes. *Her four collections of poetry include* Just Give Me a Cool Drink of Water 'for I Diiie, And Still I Rise, *and* Shaker Why Don't You Sing? *When not on lecture tours she lives in Winston-Salem, North Carolina, where she has a lifetime appointment as Reynolds Professor of American Studies at Wake Forest University.*

SPEECHES will be given, essays written, and hefty books will be published on the various lives of James Baldwin. Some fantasies will be broadcast and even some truths will be told. Someone will speak of the essayist James Baldwin in his role as the biblical prophet Isaiah admonishing his country to repent from wickedness and create within itself a clean spirit and a clean heart. Others will examine Baldwin the playwright and novelist who burned with a righteous indignation over the paucity of kindness, the absence of love and the crippling hypocrisy he saw in the streets of the United States and sensed in the hearts of his fellow citizens.

I will speak of James Baldwin, my friend and brother.

"A short brown man came to the door and looked at me. He had the most extraordinary eyes I'd ever seen. When he completed his instant X-ray of my brain, lungs, liver, heart, bowels, and spinal column, he smiled and said, 'Come in,' and opened the door. He opened the door all right. Lord! I was to hear Beauford sing later for many years 'Open the Unusual Door.' "

Thus James Baldwin describes meeting and being met by Beauford Delaney, the provocative black American painter who was to enlarge and enrich Baldwin's life. Baldwin's description of Delaney fitted Baldwin as well, for he, too, was small and brown and had the most extraordinary eyes.

I first met Jim fleetingly in the *boîtes* of Paris when he and I and the world were young enough to believe ourselves independently salvageable. But we became friends in the late fifties, just as the United States was poised to make its quantum leap into the future, as Martin Luther King, Rosa Parks, and other Southerners were girding themselves for the second Civil War in 100 years and while Malcolm X was giving voice to the anger in the streets and in the minds of Northern black city folks.

In that riotous pulse of political fervor, James Baldwin and I met again and liked each other. We discussed courage, human rights, God, and justice. We talked about black folks and love, about white folks and fear.

Although Jimmy was known as an accomplished playwright, few people knew that he was a frustrated actor as well. I had a role in Jean Genet's play *The Blacks*, and since Jimmy knew Genet personally and the play in the original French, nothing could keep him from advising me on my performance. He furnished me with my first limousine ride, set the stage for me to write *I Know Why the Caged Bird Sings*, encouraged me to take a course in cinematography in Sweden, and told me that I was intelligent and very brave. I knew Jim loved me when he gave me to Gloria and Paula, Wilmer and David Baldwin, and all the rest of his siblings and when he took me to Mother Baldwin and said, "Just what you don't need, another daughter, but here she is." I knew that he knew black women may find lovers on street corners or even in church pews, but brothers are hard to come by and are as necessary as air and as precious as love. James Baldwin knew that black women in this desolate world, black women in this cruel time which has no soundness in it, have a crying need for brothers. He knew that brother's love redeems a sister's pain. His love opened the unusual door for me and I am blessed that James Baldwin was my brother.

JIMMY IN THE HOUSE

• by William Styron •

A *native of the Tidewater region of Virginia, Wil-
liam Styron is the author of numerous books,
articles, and essays. He is the recipient of the
Pulitzer Prize for his novel* The Confessions of
Nat Turner, *and the American Book Award for*
Sophie's Choice. *A former editor of* The Paris
Review, *his works include* Lie Down in Darkness,
The Long March, Set This House on Fire, This
Quiet Dust, *and other writings.*

JAMES Baldwin was the grand-
son of a slave. I was the grandson of a slave owner. We were virtually
the same age and both bemused by our close link to slavery, since
most Americans of our vintage—if connected at all to the Old South—
have had to trace that connection back several generations. But Jimmy
had vivid images of slave times, passed down from his grandfather to
his father, a Harlem preacher of fanatical bent who left a terrifying
imprint on his son's life. Jimmy once told me that he often thought
the degradation of his grandfather's life was the animating force behind
his father's apocalyptic, often incoherent rage.

By contrast my impression of slavery was quaint and rather benign;
in the late 1930s, at the bedside of my grandmother who was then
close to ninety, I heard tales of the two little slave girls she had owned.
Not much older than the girls themselves at the outset of the Civil

War, she knitted stockings for them, tried to take care of them through the privations of the conflict, and, at the war's end, was as wrenched with sorrow as they were by the enforced leave-taking. When I told this classic story to Jimmy he didn't flinch. We both were writing about the tangled relations of blacks and whites in America and because he was wise Jimmy understood the necessity of dealing with the preposterous paradoxes that had dwelled at the heart of the racial tragedy—the unrequited loves as well as the murderous furies. The dichotomy amounted to an obsession in much of his work; it was certainly a part of my own, and I think our common preoccupation helped make us good friends.

Jimmy moved into my studio in Connecticut in the late fall of 1960 and stayed there more or less continuously until the beginning of the following summer. A mutual friend had asked my wife and me to give Jimmy a place to stay and since he was having financial problems it seemed a splendid idea. Baldwin was not very well known then—except perhaps in literary circles where his first novel, *Go Tell It on the Mountain,* was greatly admired—but his fame was gradually gaining momentum and he divided his time between writing in the cottage and trips out to the nearby lecture circuit, where he made some money for himself and where, with his ferocious oratory, he began to scare his predominately well-to-do, well-meaning audiences out of their pants.

Without being in the slightest comforted as a southerner, or let off the hook, I understood through him that black people regarded *all* Americans as irredeemably racist, the most sinful of them being not the Georgia redneck (who was in part the victim of his heritage) but any citizen whatever whose *de jure* equality was a façade for *de facto* enmity and injustice.

Jimmy was writing his novel *Another Country* and making notes for the essay "The Fire Next Time." I was consolidating material, gathered over more than a decade, for a novel I was planning to write on the slave revolutionary Nat Turner. It was a frightfully cold winter, a good time for the southern writer, who had never known a black man on intimate terms, and the Harlem-born writer, who had known few southerners (black or white), to learn something about each other. I was by far the greater beneficiary. Struggling still to loosen myself from the prejudices and suspicions that a southern upbringing engenders, I still possessed a residual skepticism: could a Negro *really* own a mind as subtle, as richly informed, as broadly inquiring and embracing as that of a white man?

My God, what appalling arrogance and vanity! Night after night Jimmy and I talked, drinking whisky through the hours until the chill dawn, and I understood that I was in the company of as marvelous an intelligence as I was ever likely to encounter. His voice, lilting and silky, became husky as he chain-smoked Marlboros. He was spellbinding, and he told me more about the frustrations and anguish of being a black man in America than I had known until then, or perhaps wanted to know. He told me exactly what it was like to be denied service, to be spat at, to be called "nigger" and "boy."

What he explained gained immediacy because it was all so new to me. This chronicle of an urban life, his own life, unself-pityingly but with quiet rage spun out to me like a secret divulged, as if he were disgorging in private all the pent-up fury and gorgeous passion that a few years later, in "The Fire Next Time," would shake the conscience of the nation as few literary documents have ever done. We may have had occasional disputes, but they were usually culinary rather than literary; a common conviction dominated our attitude toward the writing of fiction, and this was that in the creation of novels and stories the writer should be free to demolish the barrier of color, to cross the forbidden line and write from the point of view of someone with a different skin. Jimmy had made this leap already and he had done it with considerable success. I was reluctant to try to enter the mind of a slave in my book on Nat Turner but I felt the necessity and I told Jimmy this. I am certain that it was his encouragement—so strong that it was as if he were daring me not to—that caused me finally to impersonate a black man.

Sometimes friends would join us. The conversation would turn more abstract and political. I am surprised when I recall how certain of these people—well-intentioned, tolerant, "liberal," all the postures Jimmy so intuitively mistrusted—would listen patiently while Jimmy spoke, visibly fretting, then growing indignant at some pronouncement of his, some scathing *aperçu* they considered too ludicrous for words, too extreme, and launch a polite counterattack. "You can't mean anything like that!" I can hear the words now. "You mean—*burn* . . ." And in the troubled silence, Jimmy's face would become a mask of imperturbable certitude. "Baby," he would say softly and glare back with vast glowering eyes, "yes, baby. I mean *burn*. We will *burn your cities down.*"

Lest I give the impression that that winter was all grim, let me say that this was not so. Jimmy was a social animal of nearly manic gusto and there were some loud and festive times. When summer came and he departed for good, heading for his apotheosis—the flamboyant celebrity that the 1960s brought him—he left a silence that to this day somehow resonates through the house.

In 1967, when *The Confessions of Nat Turner* was published, I began to learn with great discomfort the consequences of my audacity in acquiring the persona of a black man. With a few distinguished exceptions (the historian John Hope Franklin for one), black intellectuals and writers expressed their outrage at both the historical imposture I had created and my presumption. But Jimmy Baldwin remained steadfast to those convictions we had expressed to each other during our nighttime sessions six years before. In the turmoil of such a controversy I am sure that it was impossible for him not to have experienced conflicting loyalties, but when one day I read a public statement he made about the book—"He has begun the common history—*ours*"— I felt great personal support but, more important, the reaffirmation of some essential integrity. After those days in Connecticut I never saw him as often as I would have liked but our paths crossed many times and we always fell on each other with an uncomplicated sense of joyous reunion.

Much has been written about Baldwin's effect on the consciousness of the world. Let me speak for myself. Even if I had not valued much of this work—which was flawed, like all writing, but which at its best had a burnished eloquence and devastating impact—I would have deemed his friendship inestimable. At his peak he had the beautiful fervor of Camus or Kafka. Like them he revealed to me the core of his soul's savage distress and thus helped me shape and define my own work and its moral contours. This would be the most appropriate gift imaginable to the grandson of a slave owner from a slave's grandson.

BALDWIN

• by Mary McCarthy •

Mary McCarthy was awarded the National Medal for Literature. She is also the recipient of the Edward MacDowell Medal and two Guggenheim fellowships, and has long been a member of the National Institute of Arts and Letters. Holder of the Stevenson Chair for Literature at Bard College, she is the author of The Group, The Stones of Florence, *and* Memories of a Catholic Girlhood, *among other notable books.*

"ELEGANT" is a word that keeps coming to me in connection with Jimmy Baldwin. That was how he struck me the first time I met him, back in the late forties in a midtown west-side restaurant—The Blue Ribbon, I think it was— and it is the word that came to the lips of a black girl student in a class I'm now teaching when I asked her how she would characterize Baldwin—we were talking of black writers. His voice, I suppose, was part of it—soft, light, slightly breathy, hesitant as if from fastidiousness. But my student cannot have known his voice; elegance (described by Webster as "refined grace") must have been conveyed to her by his writing. Unless as a child she heard him on radio or saw him on television.

The day I met Baldwin in The Blue Ribbon, William Phillips, one of the editors of *Partisan Review*, had asked me to come along to lunch. William must have attached some importance to the occasion, as he had dressed up for it and seemed nervous. Baldwin was at ease, so that I at once felt rather gay with him. He was not the first black writer I ever knew, nor the first black intellectual, but he was the first *literary* intellectual. As I remember, we talked about Henry James that day but also about figures on the current literary scene: Baldwin had read *everything*. Nor was his reading colored by his color—this was an unusual trait. He had what is called taste—quick, Olympian recognitions that were free of prejudice.

Trying to think now of what or of whom he reminded me, I light on Delmore Schwartz. Yes. That would have been the early Delmore Schwartz, when he, too, had a soft, breathy voice, careful diction, fancifulness, and an immense delight in books—the Delmore who likened himself to a Hershey bar and was writing at about that time of the red shoes of the Duchesse de Guermantes, not the crazed Delmore of the later years.

Anyway, it was a literary sort of lunch. I had never read anything Baldwin had written. *Go Tell It on the Mountain* was published later, in 1953, when I was no longer in New York. I liked it, both the manner and the matter. After that, I read *The Fire Next Time* and was moved, maybe shaken a little by it. And, after that, I'm sorry to say, I read no more of Jimmy. The reason was simple: I was afraid to. From what I heard, I did not think I would like *Giovanni's Room* or the books that followed and I preferred to keep my sense of Jimmy's gift pure and intact in my mind. (When we stop reading an author we like, that is usually why, I imagine: we do not want to change the idea we have of him.) Perhaps in this case I was overcautious. I might have liked *Giovanni's Room*, contrary to expectations, and despite the slight distaste I have for homosexual novels, not counting Proust.

Yet I did not lose touch with Jimmy as a person. Now and then I saw him in Paris, mostly with friends we had in common. He came to our apartment once or twice. But he was extremely erratic about keeping dates and he was drinking a lot. Finally we met, over several days, at the Book Festival at Nice in the early seventies. We were both on a jury to give a literary award. There we joined forces in a fight to get the Nice prize for Edmund Wilson. It was not easy. The French on our jury were hardly aware of Wilson; he had been published in France spottily and poorly and he was not the kind of writer the French liked to class as "American"—too civilized.

The French, if I'm not mistaken, wanted to give it to some third-world figure, shadowy in my memory, or perhaps they were divided as to which third-world figure they favored—it was at one of those jury sessions that I heard that García Márquez in *Cent Ans de Solitude* had plagiarized Balzac. . . . At the start of the proceedings, the only juror besides myself who was for Wilson was Stephen Spender. But Jimmy was not there; typically, Jimmy was late—he had to come over from St. Jean Cap Ferrat, where he lived. When he finally arrived and took his place among us at the table—Roger Caillois, Spender, Hans Junger, a third-world Nobel Prize winner, Calvino (I *think*)— he stunned us all by coolly coming out for Wilson. The French were the most taken aback; they listened with a kind of startled attention to the arguments Baldwin was advancing in a tone almost of self-evidence, still in that soft voice. The arguments were lucid but not so different from what Stephen and I had been contending to those all-but-deaf ears. What surprised them now was the *source*. And that was all it took; once Jimmy had spoken, the day was carried. Wilson had won.

Thinking back, I ask myself whether Jimmy's vote would have carried just as well for *any* candidate. I doubt it. What he had pulled off was a surprise attack on French and French-conditioned *idées reçues*. Our jury could not have expected an American black writer to champion an American white writer who was sometimes likened to Sainte-Beuve. And Jimmy, who had his full share of black mischief, must have been fully aware of that. He had counted on precisely the reaction he provoked, doing a good deed (Wilson was old, deserved an award, and needed the money) in a naughty way. In other words, he was very intelligent and possibly a bit willful. And his arriving late was a good stroke, too.

That's the end of the story. After those days, I did not see him again. In Maine a couple of years later, my husband got a long-distance call from Jimmy to ask if he knew somebody in the Embassy in Paris who could stop his furniture from being sold at auction for nonpayment of French taxes. Jim, unfortunately, contrary to Jimmy's hope, didn't know anybody at the Embassy. Yet somehow or other, I imagine, providence intervened, for we never heard any more about it.

Returning to Wilson, I was happy to be able to write to him that Jimmy had swung the Nice jury to give him the prize. And now I see what an act of generosity it was: he had laid himself on the line for Wilson in return for bookish pleasure Wilson had given him, perhaps many years before. A debt of gratitude. And now I see a small return I can make, also in literary coin: in Jimmy's memory, I will now read *Giovanni's Room*.

"VOUS ÊTES SWING"

• by Verta Mae Grosvenor •

Verta Mae Grosvenor is a writer, poet, actress, culinary anthropologist, commentator on National Public Radio's "All Things Considered." First recognized for her autobiographical cookbook, Vibration Cooking: or, The Travel Notes of a Geechee Girl, *she is a former contributing editor to* Essence *and has written for* The New York Times, The Village Voice, The Washington Post, Life, Ms, *and other magazines and newspapers. Grosvenor is at work on a novel about black expatriates in Europe.*

W*AITING for Godot* is theater of the absurd. Waiting for Jimmy was like being on hurricane watch. You knew a whirling storm was coming, but you didn't know what direction it would take. The winds might blow over an area of many thousands of miles or they might blow in one place for several hours. And anyway it was out of your control, so you took vitamin B–complex tablets and waited for the storm.

In the summer of 1984, I wanted to interview Jimmy for a National Public Radio special. He was in New York staying at his brother David's.

I called and was told, "He is expected any hour." The hour was a few days, but I got him! He said he would *"love"* to do the interview and he would be at his mother's later, so I should wait for him there. I waited. Mama Baldwin fixed me some tea. I waited. I visited her

51

sister Paula on the first floor. And waited. I went back down to Mama Baldwin's. We talked about her son.

"He was seven years old when he told me, 'I'm gonna be a great writer someday, Mama.' . . . I was worried because, you know, of financial circumstances. I knew he'd have a hard time, you know, it wouldn't be easy, but he said, 'Mama, it's the only thing I want to do.' And so he was willing to pay the price and so . . . I just let him alone. He was always reading. He'd sit at the table holding one of his younger brothers or sisters and reading . . . reading and writing were his passions. . . . I remember a verse he wrote in elementary school:

> *Once there was a careless boy*
> *Who did not obey the law*
> *He regretted very deeply*
> *When his mistake he saw.*
>
> *He did not obey the monitor*
> *Who seldom took a name*
> *The result was very tragic*
> *It really was a shame."*

"A law and order kid, huh?"

She laughed that warm rich Baldwin laugh and said, "He will be here soon." "Uuh-uhm," I said to myself, "I know about your son, *tout de suite* Jimmy."

I found him out in the spring of 1975. I was in Europe riding the Orient Express on assignment for the late *Tuesday Magazine*. I talked to Jimmy from Milan and we planned to rendezvous in Paris. He said he'd call me at my hotel.

I arrived in Paris on April 15. The city of light was in mourning. Josephine Baker, the St. Louis bombshell who shook her banana hips and brought the city to its feet in adoration a half a century ago, was dead. A teary-eyed taxi driver, detouring around the funeral procession and throngs of mourners at the Place de la Madeleine, kept repeating, *"La Baker est morte! . . . La Baker est morte!"* Only a few days ago I had seen her show at the Bobino Theatre . . . fantastic! And now *"La Baker est morte!"* All over the city they played La Baker's signature song, *"J'ai deux amours"* . . . I have two loves . . . my country and Paris.

If I was a singer I would have sung that song. I too loved Paris. I went to Paris when I was eighteen years old and fell in love with her. I was very excited about seeing Jimmy there. We had become friends in New York in 1970 and had been together *beaucoup* times, but never in Paris.

I was staying in a small, funky but clean Montparnasse hotel where you could receive calls, messages, but couldn't call out. The concierges were very strict. "Use the telephones in the café next door. No exceptions!" I waited around the hotel for Jimmy's call but I was too excited about being in Paris to stay inside. So I hit the streets. Paris is a supremely walkable city.

When I got back to the hotel the concierges had lost their Gallic cool. *"Madame, madame!"* they yelled before I was inside the door. *"Monsieur James Baldwin a vous téléphoné. Il faut que vous lui téléphoniez . . . tout de suite!"* I headed for the café next door. *"Ooh, non, madame, à votre service.* Please use this phone to call Monsieur Baldwin."

I dialed the number. "Jimmy is not here."

"What time do you expect him?"

"He is expected to arrive at any hour."

"Well, I just got a message to call him at this number *tout de suite.*"

"Of course, madame. He is expected to arrive *tout de suite,* at any hour."

"This afternoon?"

"Or this evening or tomorrow . . . but he is expected at any hour."

Jimmy called that evening. We made plans to meet the following day on the Boulevard Saint-Germain-des-Prés at the Café Flore. Jimmy chose the café. A small gesture that I interpreted as highly significant.

I had never been to the Flore. The Flore was the well-known meeting place for intellectuals and writers like Simone de Beauvoir and Jean-Paul Sartre. Jimmy had often heard me tell the story of how when I first came to Paris I walked past the Café Flore to "look" at the intellectuals. I thought I could tell by looking who they were because somewhere I'd read that all intellectuals in Paris wear black. Once I think I spotted Jean-Paul Sartre. Back in the States I carried his book *No Exit* around, title side up, as a badge of my budding intellectualism: but I was too self-conscious to go inside the café. Besides, I didn't speak French.

The Café Tournon, a few blocks from the Flore, was the hangout for black American intellectuals and writers. I walked by there, too. I knew who they were. I had seen their pictures in *Ebony*. They were heroes to me. The myth and legend of their triumphs and successes were such an inspiration I decided to seek my future in Paris. I was not as clearly focused on what I wanted as Jimmy and I didn't sing like Jo Baker, but Paris seemed a city of possibilities and adventure. I wanted both.

I caught a glimpse of Richard Wright several times. Once I saw beautiful Marpessa Dawn and she "confirmed" one of the myths about black women in Europe. She crossed the boulevard and the traffic stopped.

I had seen Jimmy many times. In cafés and on the street. He was intense and so damned interesting looking. He looked like somebody I needed to know. I could tell he knew where the possibilities and adventure were. I wanted to go up and talk to him, but I never did. Years later, when I told him that, he said very seriously, "You should have . . . you should have . . . you spoke English, didn't you?"

I interpreted the choosing of the Café Flore as a coming of age. Seventeen years later here I was, a writer, going there with one of the heroes of my youth. A small moment, but special to me.

I woke up very early on the morning of the Café Flore day. Went downstairs to the café. Some workers were having cognac and coffee. I laughed, remembering how shocking that seemed when I first came to Paris. I took my café and croissant and called Nancy Holloway.

Nancy is a singer from Ohio who has lived in Paris since the fifties. She had a place called the Mars Club that was very popular. I didn't know her in those years but we are friends now. We had a lunch date and I called to tell her that we had to do it on time, not *CP* ("colored people's") time, because of my four o'clock rendezvous at the Café Flore with Jimmy.

"Who is this . . . what time is it . . . you calling me about some café . . ."

Nancy lived in Montmartre. In the twenties, when Josephine was queen, Montmartre was "Harlem on the Seine." Sidney Bechet, Buddy Gilmore, and other black musicians who had brought jazz to town lived and worked there. During the jazz age one of the most renowned nightclubs in Paris, Le Grand Duc, was on Nancy's block. Black flying ace Eugene Ballard was the manager, Bricktop was the singer, a one-eyed cook whose specialty was fried chicken and cornbread was the chef, and a poet named Langston Hughes was the dishwasher.

Nancy lives a few blocks from Haynes' restaurant. At the end of World War II, Leroy Haynes, from Alabama, stayed in Paris and opened a soul-food restaurant. His dishes were sho' nuf down home. He made his own barbecue sauce and grew okra, collard greens, and other Southern vegetables at his place in the country. He was a great success. To thousands of Americans, white and black, a taste of Haynes was, if not *the* cure, the best treatment for homesickness.

I got to Nancy's on time and she was on time. She fixed a fabulous lunch and had such delicious gossip that it was three-thirty before I left. I ran to the boulevard and grabbed a cab. The traffic was worse than Josephine's funeral. At four o'clock I was still on the Right Bank. I told the cab to stop so I could make a phone call.

"No, no, madame. *Jamais.* If you get out of the cab you are out . . ."

"But I have to call James Baldwin at the Café Flore."

He looked at me and shrugged as only *ze French* can . . . "Okay."

(Joke: Why do the French spend so much time talking in cafés? 'Cause they can't get the phones to work.)

After about fifteen minutes I finally made a connection to the Café Flore.

"Is Monsieur James Baldwin there?"

"No, madame."

"Well, he should be, he will be arriving *tout de suite* so please tell him that Verta Mae is arriving *tout de suite.*"

"Oui, madame."

Now it was rush hour and rush hour is rush hour all over the Western world. Finally, we reached Saint-Germain-des-Prés and the Café Flore. Jimmy was not there. I took a seat on the outside. I'm not just talking about the outside terrace, I mean the outside section. I never learned to gracefully maneuver my six-foot body frame around those café tables. I may speak French with my mouth, but my body language is still American. My feet won't fit under the tables . . . I raise my arm in a gesture and hit three people.

I asked the waiter if Monsieur Baldwin had been in. No, but he has called, he is expected *"tout de suite."* I don't know if he is talking about my call to Jimmy or if Jimmy called; in any case I sit and wait. I order a glass of Pernod and wait for Jimmy. I didn't really like Pernod but it goes well with sitting in a Paris café, an art form in itself.

So here I am. Café Flore. They are dressed in black. I understand what they are saying. If that's what they were talking about in the fifties, I could've come in. Still I am not disappointed. I'm waiting for Jimmy. I don't really like Pernod, so I order some wine . . . and silently toast La Baker, a skinny girl from St. Louis so poor she wore secondhand shoes to school and came to Paris; brought the city to its feet in adoration of her talent and beauty; had hairstyles, makeup, and dolls named for her; and owned 150 pairs of shoes. I toast James Baldwin, a small, frail young man who wanted to be a writer and left Harlem with forty dollars, a Bessie Smith record, and a typewriter.

I have a laugh on myself remembering when I first came to Paris and walked up to the first black woman I saw and asked where she got her hair done. I was astonished she didn't speak English. It had never occurred to me that she could have been from anywhere else but the U.S.A.

The waiter comes over. "Madame Grosvenor?"

"Yes."

"You are waiting for Monsieur James Baldwin? . . . He will arrive *tout de suite.*"

I just fall out laughing, order another wine and wait . . . a beautiful brown-skinned woman crosses the street and the cars honk. She is jaywalking.

Et voilà! I see him coming toward the café, grinning that incredible gap-tooth smile and his splendid voice allows, "Hey baby, *vous êtes swing.*"

I first heard *"vous êtes swing"* on the Lower East Side in the sixties from a musician named Ron. Ron spent a lot of time in Europe. Whenever I ran into him he'd say, "*Vous êtes swing*, baby, *vous êtes swing.*"

I thought it was a powerful expression and I used it all the time, especially when talking about Europe . . . for me those three words captured all the ambiguities and nuances of the black American in Europe. Jimmy loved it, too. And so when we greeted each other, the first thing we'd holler was, *"Vous êtes swing*, baby, *vous êtes swing!"*

He had an entourage that included a filmmaker from the Cameroons, a young woman photographer from Pittsburgh, a writer from New Mexico, and an Algerian painter. They seemed to be his close friends. We talked and laughed an hour or so and then Jimmy announced that we had to move on to meet some people he was supposed to meet at six o'clock. Jimmy and I walked together. I know we must have looked the odd couple, li'l Jimmy and big Mae. I told him I wanted to write a novel but I was scared of doing it and couldn't get started. He said, "You'll do it when you're scared of not doing it."

As we walked people, young and old, acknowledged Jimmy. They would ever-so-slightly nod their heads and say, "Monsieur Baldwin." A few said, "*Allô*, Jimmy." He was very gracious to them. Royal.

The six o'clock people had gone to another café. They left a person there to give Jimmy the message. Now, that person joined the party. We went to another café where the tables were bigger. Around eight o'clock, Jimmy announced that he had a dinner engagement. Six of us went with him. We were to rejoin the rest of the party later that evening at a club. We were right on time for dinner.

Around eleven we went to the club. When we walked in I was surprised to see Miriam Makeba on stage. And then Diana Ross came in . . . and Sarah Vaughan, and then I understood that they were female impersonators. After the show, we went dancing and then to early breakfast. I went back to my hotel in the Paris dawn.

So all that to say, yeah, I know about *"tout de suite"* Jimmy. Still, I waited with Mama Baldwin. You know, you can get hooked on hurricanes. They can call for evacuation and there are some people who will not go. They got to stay and see what the storm will do, this time.

And then the storm arrived. With his handsome, elegant self, ready to talk. Berdis Baldwin, his mother, is a practical woman. She told him to sit down and eat first. She set up two folding tables and fed both of us fresh string beans, rice, and baked chicken.

And then we talked about everything from reading and rereading *Uncle Tom's Cabin* and *A Tale of Two Cities* as a child, to being a Pentecostal preacher at fourteen, to being intimidated by his high school French teacher, Countee Cullen. "I showed him one of my poems once," Jimmy told me, "and he said it was too much like Langston Hughes."

"Is this the poet Countee Cullen?" I asked.

"Yeah," laughed Jimmy. "I never showed him anything again."

Knowing that spoiled my appreciation of a line in one of Cullen's poems . . . "Yet do I marvel at this curious thing, to make a poet black and bid him sing."

We talked about Europe. And exile. Then Jimmy said, "Exile is another way of being in limbo. . . . Now, I imagine in my own case, I will spend the rest of my life, however long that will be, as a kinda transatlantic commuter."

We talked about myths and legends that sent me and thousands of blacks to Europe in search of greener pastures. We talked about the tall skinny girl from St. Louis who finally owned 150 pairs of shoes and the young man who left Harlem with forty dollars, a Bessie Smith record, and a typewriter, and went to Paris seeking a future.

"Were you scared?" I asked him. "I mean a Bessie Smith record and forty dollars? What were you doing?"

"Getting outta here!" he said. "Getting outta here!"

The interview with Jimmy was aired on National Public Radio, August 3, 1984, his sixtieth birthday. It was well-received, not only for Jimmy's candid remarks about his life but for Berdis Baldwin's sterling recitation of Jimmy's first verse. Everyone asked me, "How did you get it?"

"Nothing to it," I told them. . . . "I just waited around."

DINNER AT JIMMY'S
• by Caryl Phillips •

Caryl Phillips was born in Saint Kitts in 1958, and is the author of many dramatic pieces for stage, television, and radio. His first novel, The Final Passage, *was published in 1985; his second,* A State of Independence, *in 1986. The following essay is excerpted from his latest book,* The European Tribe.

WHENEVER I arrive at the tall iron gates separating James Baldwin from the outside world, my mind begins to wander. The gates remind me of prison bars. I wonder if Baldwin has been in prison, or whether this exile, his homosexuality, or his very spacious home are the different forms of imprisonment. My mind becomes supple, it feels strong and daring, and although the questions and thoughts Baldwin provokes are not always logical, I have always found that there is something positive and uplifting about his presence. Baldwin, unlike anybody else I have ever met, has this ability to kindle the imagination.

He is a much-photographed man so there is little I can add to the familiar image. Yes, he is small, but by no means diminutively so. His eyes bulge, but not as much as one might imagine. And, as the pictures often suggest, it is true that he is seldom without a cigarette.

His face is highly distinctive, and he is recognized everywhere he goes. I have been in restaurants and bars with him in Britain, America, and France, and in all three countries he has had to perform the task of shaking the quickly proffered hand or signing the book that has magically appeared as though from nowhere. No matter how full a restaurant might appear to be, Baldwin is always seated. His house is on the Provence "Tourist Coach" itinerary, and much Kodak is burned by those who have heard of him but probably never read any of his books. Baldwin is a star; he knows and loves it.

That evening we stayed at home, ate dinner, drank an excessive amount of Johnnie Walker Black Label, and watched a bad disaster movie called *Airport 77*. The film had been dubbed into French. I laughed at the physical humor, Jimmy at the verbal. After thirty years on and off, though mostly on, as a resident, Baldwin's French is perfect. When the movie was over Jimmy switched off the television and began to talk about integrity, and the greatest crime an artist can commit, which is to abandon that gift in order to pursue money or honors or both. He was beginning a "rap" I had heard from him before but this evening, Bernard Hassell, his personal assistant, was away in his gatehouse, and there were no other house guests. His tongue loosened by drink, his forehead streaked with tramlines of worry, Jimmy seemed to be finding words difficult to pin down. For such an eloquent talker, this suggested that I was now witnessing a Jimmy "confession" rather than a Jimmy "performance."

He moved on with his chosen theme, saying that to give up the artistic gift for a woman seemed a preposterous act. Take Mailer, for instance, or Styron. Their problem was that while women, their various wives included, admired them, what they desperately craved was respect. As I knew neither Norman Mailer nor William Styron, their wives, nor their "women," I was in no position to comment but Jimmy did not require any response. I was not an audience; as far as he was concerned I was merely present. He spoke on, and I tried to think of his own situation in relation to the other writers and artists on whose lives, misspent or otherwise, he passed judgment. I wondered how often he saw them, if he might be feeling just a little isolated, and worried about becoming a forgotten star.

Jimmy lives in St.-Paul-de-Vence, a hill village ten miles north of Nice. It is a colony which has attracted many of this century's foremost artists. Today its main residents are famous actors, Yves Montand, Donald Pleasence, and Hardy Kruger among their number. The old walled city excludes cars. It is riddled with picturesque narrow, cobbled streets, so tightly squeezed that in places two pedestrians must come to some arrangement as to who shall pass first. The stone is sandblasted clean so there is little evidence of soot or grime. St.-Paul-de-Vence has all the dramatic charm and aged glory of a Bavarian castle seen from the Rhine. The supposedly high-class art galleries, the "chic" card and gift shops are of the expensive and exclusive variety. It is a discreet and civilized ripoff. In stark contrast to the cramped splendor of the walled St.-Paul-de-Vence, larger houses with sprawling estates fan out down the hillsides. Living outside the village walls means not only having a garden in which to roam, but also that you could easily afford to live inside the village walls if you wished—it is a voluntary exile. These are the two faces of a very expensive kingdom.

In the late 1960s St.-Paul-de-Vence accepted a new visitor. He was ill and had reached a low ebb in his life. The proprietress of a local restaurant-hotel looked after him. Having broken off from his first French sojourn to return to America and participate in the civil rights struggle, Baldwin had returned to France. He was an older and wiser man, but exceedingly distraught, having endured the pain of living through the deaths of both Malcolm X and Martin Luther King, Jr. The civil rights movement as he knew it had come to an end. In St.-Paul-de-Vence he found a house and an environment in which he could, in a sense, begin again. It would be the same struggle, but waged from a different standpoint.

His home is a child's paradise of ten acres. It is graced by three eighteenth-century properties: an outhouse, a gatehouse, and the main villa itself. Jimmy lives and works in the basement of the main villa, in a two-roomed apartment he calls the torture chamber. The principal thoroughfare across his land is fringed with high rambling grass and a chain of different-coloured bulbs strung out between the trees. In the orchard there are lemons, olives, figs, bananas, pineapples, and pears. The land and property are enveloped by a high stone wall to ward off would-be trespassers. Bernard apart, there are no other black people resident in St.-Paul-de-Vence.

As I sat with Jimmy he continued to talk about respect and integrity, and about the old days in Paris when he, Richard Wright, and Chester Himes used to sit out on the Left Bank at the Café Tournan, or the Café Monaco. There was a tinge of nostalgia in his voice. I knew that he was currently involved in legal wranglings over his new book, *The Evidence of Things Not Seen*. It had started life as an award-winning essay for *Playboy* magazine, about the murder of twenty-eight young black males in Atlanta between 1979 and 1981. On delivery the book commissioned from the article had been rejected. For a writer of Baldwin's stature this was a terrible blow and had created a crisis of confidence, not so much in Jimmy himself, but in the way in which he felt others now perceived him. During his fifty-ninth year he had suffered a minor heart attack, and now had bronchial and tracheal problems. Every half-dozen sentences were punctuated by a high nasal whine, then a sharp, messy blowing of his nose into a large white handkerchief. The biblical, incantatory patter of his speech was peppered with the rhythms of age and illness. What was his legacy to be? Would his works be suddenly taken out of print on his death? He was sixty and not getting any younger. And there was yet more work to be done on *The Evidence of Things Not Seen*.

The following evening Jimmy pressed me to dine with him and his guest, Miles Davis, who was playing at the Nice jazz festival. Only a few months before I had seen Davis at the Royal Festival Hall in London. His audiences now are often indistinguishable from those who would attend a performance of a Beethoven symphony or a Brahms concerto. They listened attentively with looks of rapturous homage etched across their faces. I had always wondered what Davis made of this, and whether, as Le Roi Jones had once suggested, he really was blowing "fuck you" down his trumpet, and also whether the Miles Davis of today was the same man who had played with Charlie Parker at Birdland. My head was swimming with questions to field to him, but I decided not to attend the dinner. I made some lame excuse, walked up the hill into the walled village, and felt miserable.

I sat alone and drank beer in the first bar that I came to, pretending to read a book. When the manager of the bar switched on the television I began to watch the news intently. Then I felt embarrassed that somebody might ask me to comment on a particular item. As I understood only about twenty percent of the chatter, I left the bar rather than risk appearing foolish. A little way up the hill I found a small terrace café where I sat discontentedly and ordered some food. I idly held the fork, and failed to notice as the food fell from it and splashed olive oil onto my new trousers. To compound my clumsiness, I accidentally knocked over my bottle of beer, and the Frenchman at the next table began to shout. I shrugged my shoulders. People were looking at me. I should have stayed at Jimmy's, I thought, but it was too late now.

I had left Jimmy's before Miles Davis arrived. The reasons for my departure may seem a trifle feeble now, but I felt them intensely at the time. Part of me desired, however naïvely, access to whatever conversation they might have on more equitable terms than my age and status would allow, but the more important reason lay in the heart of Jimmy's talk the previous evening.

I had never before noticed how lonely Jimmy was. His garrulity could always overwhelm any occasion, company, or atmosphere; he is a larger-than-life character. But that night his quiet conversation was so saturated with references to his past, to what other writers should have done, and to people that he knew I had never heard of, but whom he still felt compelled to talk about, that I realized that he needed to be alone with someone who could relate fully to all the nuances of his predicament, past, present, and future. "When Sidney Poitier goes to the Cannes Film Festival he always calls by." "When Miles Davis comes to Nice, he stops by, too." A spiritual fix is a serious business, especially when they come as irregularly for Jimmy as they do these days. I would only have been in the way.

I overtipped the waitress. It was my way of apologizing for the chaos I had unwittingly caused on such a busy night for her. August 15 is a big holiday in France. As I began to stagger back down the hill, I passed hordes of people walking up it to witness the midnight fireworks display. The hill played havoc with the muscles on the back of my legs, but some fifty yards before I reached Jimmy's garden, I smelled the flowers. It was a warm, clear summer night, and I stopped outside the huge iron gates. The lights were on, and in the distance I heard a laugh. A Renault roared past, its headlamps disappearing like two eyes closing in the darkness. Across the road four blue-suited gendarmes eyed me suspiciously. Two stood attentively, while the other two were perched on a Citroën hood. They all had guns on their hips, and all but one had a Gauloise cigarette in his mouth. They scowled in my direction—French policemen seldom smile. I heard another laugh from inside the house, then one of the perched policemen turned to the others and passed a comment. He twisted back round and stared again at me. *"Les nègres, ils sont très jolis, n'est-ce pas?"* Perhaps he did not say that, and I simply imagined he did. Either way I did not care. I ambled on past the gates and down the hill. Up above the fireworks display began. Later, much later, I would sneak in unobserved and unheard. Like a naughty schoolboy, I slipped quietly into bed and listened to the old men's laughter until dawn broke.

THE LAST DAYS

• by Pat Mikell •

Pat Mikell met David Baldwin many years ago at Count Basie's Club in Harlem. She recalls, "We shook hands and that was it; we were instant friends. We stayed up all night having coffee and talking." When she and her husband Mike opened up Mikell's, an Upper West Side New York City jazz club, David joined their staff. For James Baldwin, Mikell's became a home away from home and Pat Mikell became a valued friend.

PEOPLE would crowd around Jimmy at the club. Some were very respectful, in awe just to see him, just to say a word to him. Others would become complete fools who wanted to challenge him and to get him into silly discussions. At those points, Jimmy would always ask me to sit next to him so it would balance out; in case they got to be outrageous, he had somebody there he could look at; he would just give me a look and it would be hard for me to keep from laughing.

The first time I met him, I turned to David and said, "One thing is for sure, you cannot lie to Jimmy Baldwin." He had that spiritual thing: he knew who a person was just like that. I mean his eyes would just go right through you. It used to be funny at the club because as soon as people would approach him, he'd know exactly where they were at and he'd give me a look that said, "Okay, they're out of their minds, or they're really negative, or they've really got a problem." That almost psychic special ability to see through things showed up in everything he did. He could cut right through all the bullshit and get exactly to the truth.

Once we went to someone's house to see a video. They wanted him to write a text for it. He sat there with a pen and pencil, with me next to him, and he just kept looking at me and at this video. There was nothing he could write. It was getting funnier by the minute, and the people were really getting upset because he wasn't reacting to the video. When they finished playing it, he said, "Well, what do you want me to write about it? Tits and asses?" The video was all about dancing, and they didn't focus on the artist at all, they just focused on these women dancers. So he said, "There is nothing more that can be said about tits and asses. It's all been said." They got very uptight trying to defend it and trying to talk him into writing about it. So in the lobby when we were leaving he looked at me with this deadpan face and he said, "There's something wrong with the wife, too." Jimmy was pretty clever.

Before Jimmy left New York for the last time, he sat me down and yelled at me. I don't mean he actually yelled, but he was giving me advice on what I should do—I wasn't taking care of myself, so he was getting on my case. David walked by and started to laugh at me sitting there crying. He said, "Well, Jimmy loves you; he only yells at the people he cares about."

I think Jimmy knew then that he wasn't coming back. I think he was trying to get people he cared about focused on what they should be doing, and where they were—not where they were messing up. And I think one of the reasons he insisted that David leave New York and move to France was that David needed to get some things together. This was in November 1986.

A year later, I went to meet a friend of David's for brunch and took along the August issue of *Architectural Digest* because Jimmy had a piece in there on his house in St. Paul. I had just looked at the pictures, and I wanted to show this friend where David was, to tell him that he went there with Jimmy and that they were happy. On the way back from brunch, I started reading Jimmy's text, and suddenly it struck me—"He knows he's gonna die." And as soon as I opened the door my daughter said a phone call had come and that David was trying to get in touch with me. I was already crying a few minutes later when the phone rang. It was David, and I said—before he even said anything—"I know, Jimmy's gonna die." And he said, "Yeah, the doctor just said that he doesn't have much longer. There's nothing that they can do at this point." That's when I said to myself, "Oh, Pat, you should go over there."

Jimmy and David had been trying to get me to France for years, but I'd always have an excuse. Work. This or that or whatever. But I knew what Jimmy's illness was doing to David because they were so close. Jimmy had always said that the one thing he worried about was that David would leave this earth before him and he didn't know how he could stay on earth without David. So I just spontaneously decided to go. A friend got me the plane ticket on a credit card.

I had no passport, and there I was down in the line at the passport place. You know how crazy it is right before Thanksgiving. But I saw one black man behind an official desk. So I scooted in front of everybody and went directly up to him and said, "Jimmy Baldwin is very sick and I have to get an emergency passport." So he took my passport application directly to the supervisor, who still gave me a very difficult time. They—the United States—only gave me six months. Then I went to the French consulate, which was only giving out three months or three years. But the minute they saw who I was going to visit, they said, "Do you want five years?" I said, "Okay, give me five years."

After the flight into Nice, I got a cab. But the cab driver was not that familiar with St.-Paul-de-Vence. And I didn't have a specific house address. So we rode around and rode around and the cab driver stopped at different places. Finally we came around a plaza where people were playing bocci and saw a restaurant bar that looked just like Mikell's; it was the same color green; had the same curtains and everything. "I bet Jimmy goes in there," I thought—it just had the vibe. So I told the driver, "Check in there." The driver came back and said, "The house is right down the road."

When I rang the bell on the gate, nobody knew that I was coming.

Bernard—Jimmy's longtime friend—came out, and I could hear—in the house—David yelling out, "Well, who is it—who is it?" Bernard stood there looking at me in shock. It was raining, pouring rain. David came down, and when he saw me, he screamed, yelling into the house, "Jimmy, you would not believe who's here!" As soon as I stepped into the room, there was Jimmy looking at me and he just cracked up laughing. He said, "Look at this, the orphan in the storm."

The house was cold and damp, and it was rough. David was exhausted, he had been crying—almost everything was on his shoulders. But some help had just come. One of the people used to be Jimmy's secretary, a wonderful man named David Lemming. And Lucien was there.

Before Jimmy left New York we had a long talk about the love of his life, but he never mentioned the name. So the whole time I was in St. Paul I had no idea that Lucien was the one he was talking about. I didn't know. But Jimmy had told me the whole story of how he had gotten sick and Lucien had taken him up to the mountains and that's how he wrote Go Tell It on the Mountain. Afterwards, he told me that "one has to learn to let go" and that one of the most difficult things in his life was to let go of Lucien. But he told me he had to let go of that, told me that "unless you let go, you know, you'll just never be free." He also said I should read the book Juno and the Paycock, which I haven't read yet. But I will. I don't know what's in there, but he never steered me wrong about anything.

So all I tried to do was just cheer up everyone. It was raining constantly. That first night, I went downstairs and wandered around and found wood and lit fires everywhere. I think I got on everybody's nerves lighting fires, but it did warm up the house. There is something very peaceful about fire. I lit one in Jimmy's room, which has a huge ceiling. I'd go in through the night and turn the fire up. When I tiptoed in, he would open his eyes and smile at me and then close them and curl up so he would be facing the fire.

On Thanksgiving Day, he did get up. We came into the dining room and all had the Thanksgiving dinner. It was a mishmash, you know. Somehow they managed to find a few traditional American things, actually southern—things like orange cup and sweet potatoes.

Valerie was the cook. She was everything, she did everything. Valerie, Bernard, David, Lucien, David Lemming, a lawyer named Bill, an opera singer named Sophia, others were there, too, I think—I lost track; one day just went into another after a while. After dinner, we went into Jimmy's room. David got a bottle of champagne; everybody had a drink in front of the fire and talked. Jimmy had a drink, too.

The day before I was scheduled to leave, I decided to put my feet on my homeland, Italy. It was very close and I had never been there. So I went into the room to speak to Jimmy. (Because he was getting so weak, I just didn't want to bother him. So I asked David if I could go in.) Jimmy always liked to see me dressed up. He would really get on my case if I was raggedy: "Get a haircut, Pat," you know? So I had made sure I was all dressed up. I said, "Jimmy, do I look okay to go to Italy?" He said, "You look fine, Pat, you're gorgeous." Then I said, "Would you like me to bring you something back?" He said, "Something frivolous." Then he took my hand and my arm and was just holding my arm. And he said, "I hear you're leaving tomorrow; will you stay three or four more days?" And I said, "Well, I'll speak to David." But he kept insisting. (I was so happy he asked me.) "I just want to thank you for having me here," I said. "It has been beautiful, it was just what I needed." And he replied, "No; I thank *you*. But please, promise me you'll stay three or four more days." And then the thought passed through my mind, "Oh, my God, don't tell me he knows that he's going to die."

A few of us went to Italy and had lunch that day. I think it was Sunday, and in a Catholic country like Italy, forget about it. Everybody wanted to get back, but I was trying to find something frivolous and insisted upon it. So while they were taking tourist pictures, I scooted and found a bakery shop. I couldn't speak a word of Italian. But somehow the woman understood, and gave me an espresso cup with the word "Italia" on it. And then I bought a bunch of gooey pastries.

When we got back, the doctors were there and said that this was it, that Jimmy's liver had gone. As soon as we walked into the house, the doctors told us that he wouldn't last more than a couple of days. I think he died on the third or fourth day.

People are into this New Age thing now—spiritualism and crystals; but Jimmy was into all of that way back. He was one of the most spiritual human beings I ever met. And I think that really there is no way he would be afraid of death—I think he dealt with that: life and death were one. Lots of people are afraid of dying; but then again, that's how *they* are and how they live their lives and what kind of spirit they are. I don't think he was afraid of death at all. There was no fear there at all. No complaint. He was courageous.

During those final days, people were calling from all over the world. Guests were coming from all over. At that point, my leaving would have just caused more confusion. And Valerie was not there at night. So at least I could help with serving people and cooking dinner and just basically being someone that everybody knew. One night I slept on the floor next to the phone so everybody else could get some rest.

The night that Jimmy died, three or four doctors were there. David said that Jimmy was lucid right up to the end. He knew he was passing, and he had seen his past positions on the wall, and he talked till the end. Then he just smiled and closed his eyes. Lucien ran into the room. David put on "Amazing Grace," and it resounded throughout the house. Everyone then knew that he had passed. They went into their own little corner and cried, went up individually, into the room, and then came back and sat down at the table.

David said I could stay in the room with Jimmy. His face had an unbelievably beautiful smile—absolutely peaceful. It was almost like he was still there; his spirit was still there. So I knelt down next to him and held his hand. His arm stayed warm for the longest period as if he were alive, just sleeping. I wasn't watching time, I don't really remember how long I knelt there. But Lucien came in at one point—and I took his hand and put it on Jimmy's still-warm arm. It was actually pulsating. Then I noticed that Jimmy's face seemed different. I said, "Look, Lucien—his expression," and he said, "Yes, his expression has changed." It was actually more of a smile. Later David came back in and sat with Jimmy through the night, in a chair.

It was after midnight and continually raining when Jimmy died, cold and raining. The next day the rain stopped. I don't know what that means but it must mean something heavy because he was a beautiful, spiritual man. I'm very grateful that I got to meet and know him. Jimmy was one of the greatest gifts that I have gotten in life. It means a lot to me to remember that he really did like me, you know, because he really could see through people.

The next day they came with the casket. It was made in France and beautiful, unlike any ever made in this country. Police officers, all in uniform, performed the ceremony of sealing the casket with such formality, dignity, drama, and respect. The head gendarme, a sergeant, stood there, very formally. Then they all surrounded the casket and put their hands on it, or their fingertips. Then they tightened the screws and carried it out in a procession. Later we all went to the airport and gathered in one room to say the last good-byes.

As it turned out, I think I left France on the same plane with Jimmy's casket. At the security check, I was so hysterical I could not say a word. I couldn't stop crying, didn't know where I was. David had given me a beautiful ashtray—all hand-painted—picturing a particular white bird that was very prevalent in St. Paul. And on it was written "Happy Birthday, Jimmy." I had put it in my bag. So I pulled it out. All I did was show the ashtray. That's all I had to do. The next thing I knew, I had people escorting me on the plane. I only showed the ashtray because I couldn't stop crying. And all of a sudden guards were there. They took me on the plane and didn't check anything. They didn't bother to ask. The guards also must have told the stewardesses, because they really looked out for me the whole ride back.

In St. Paul, they loved him too. They were so sad. The village people had besieged the stores for newspapers, to read about Jimmy's death. They don't sell a lot of newspapers there. But when Jimmy died, you could barely find one. Knowing the family would want a paper, I had to snatch one from a little old lady. She stared at me until someone else said, "Oh, she's with Jimmy. She's staying there." And the old lady said, "Take the paper, take the paper."

The people of the town had seen me going back and forth to get coffee and cigarettes and whatever was needed at the house. Even when I was in the kitchen preparing trays of food, they would come in and cry and hold me. Everyone, even the village bocci players, came to the house, to Jimmy's house, to pay their last respects. They loved Jimmy over there. The president of France, the French diplomats were calling, were all sending flowers and telegrams. Now I think of all those people who said, "Who does he think he is, living in France, he doesn't like America?" But once you've been there, you understand completely why he was there.

· III ·

WRITER

For, while the tale of how we suffer, and how we are
delighted, and how we may triumph is never new, it
always must be heard. There isn't any other tale to tell,
it's the only light we've got in all this darkness. . . . And
this tale, according to that face, that body, those strong
hands on those strings, has another aspect in every country, and a new depth in every generation.

—JAMES BALDWIN

LIFE IN HIS LANGUAGE

• by Toni Morrison •

Toni Morrison was born in Lorain, Ohio, and now lives in Rockland County, New York. She is the author of five novels: The Bluest Eye, Sula, Song of Solomon, *which won the 1978 National Book Critics Circle Award for fiction,* Tar Baby, *and* Beloved, *winner of the 1988 Pulitzer Prize for fiction. She is also the author of* Dreaming Emmett, *a play produced in 1986.*

J IMMY, there is too much to think about you, and too much to feel. The difficulty is your life refuses summation—it always did—and invites contemplation instead. Like many of us left here I thought I knew you. Now I discover that in your company it is myself I know. That is the astonishing gift of your art and your friendship: You gave us ourselves to think about, to cherish. We are like Hall Montana* watching "with new wonder" his brother saints, knowing the song he sang is us. "He *is* us."

I never heard a single command from you, yet the demands you made on me, the challenges you issued to me, were nevertheless unmistakable, even if unenforced: that I work and think at the top of my form, that I stand on moral ground but know that ground must

---

*A character in Baldwin's *Just Above My Head.*

be shored up by mercy, that "the world is before [me] and [I] need not take it or leave it as it was when [I] came in."

Well, the season was always Christmas with you there and, like one aspect of that scenario, you did not neglect to bring at least three gifts. You gave me a language to dwell in, a gift so perfect it seems my own invention. I have been thinking your spoken and written thoughts for so long I believed they were mine. I have been seeing the world through your eyes for so long, I believed that clear, clear view was my own. Even now, even here, I need you to tell me what I am feeling and how to articulate it. So I have pored again through the 6,895 pages of your published work to acknowledge the debt and thank you for the credit. No one possessed or inhabited language for me the way you did. You made American English honest—genuinely international. You exposed its secrets and reshaped it until it was truly modern dialogic, representative, humane. You stripped it of ease and false comfort and fake innocence and evasion and hypocrisy. And in place of deviousness was clarity. In place of soft plump lies was a lean, targeted power. In place of intellectual disingenuousness and what you called "exasperating egocentricity," you gave us undecorated truth. You replaced lumbering platitudes with an upright elegance. You went into that forbidden territory and decolonized it, "robbed it of the jewel of its naïveté," and un-gated it for black people so that in your wake we could enter it, occupy it, restructure it in order to accommodate our complicated passion—not our vanities but our intricate, difficult, demanding beauty, our tragic, insistent knowledge, our lived reality, our sleek classical imagination—all the while refusing "to be defined by a language that has never been able to recognize [us]." In your hands language was handsome again. In your hands we saw how it was meant to be: neither bloodless nor bloody, and yet alive.

It infuriated some people. Those who saw the paucity of their own imagination in the two-way mirror you held up to them attacked the mirror, tried to reduce it to fragments which they could then rank and grade, tried to dismiss the shards where your image and theirs remained—locked but ready to soar. You are an artist after all and an artist is forbidden a career in this place; an artist is permitted only a commercial hit. But for thousands and thousands of those who embraced your text and who gave themselves permission to hear your language, by that very gesture they ennobled themselves, became un-shrouded, civilized.

The second gift was your courage, which you let us share: the courage of one who could go as a stranger in the village and transform the distances between people into intimacy with the whole world; courage to understand that experience in ways that made it a personal revelation for each of us. It was you who gave us the courage to appropriate an alien, hostile, all-white geography because you had discovered that "this world [meaning history] is white no longer and it will never be white again." Yours was the courage to live life in and from its belly as well as beyond its edges, to see and say what it was, to recognize and identify evil but never fear or stand in awe of it. It is a courage that came from a ruthless intelligence married to a pity so profound it could convince anyone who cared to know that those who despised us "need the moral authority of their former slaves, who are the only people in the world who know anything about them and who may be, indeed, the only people in the world who really care anything about them." When that unassailable combination of mind and heart, of intellect and passion was on display it guided us through treacherous landscape as it did when you wrote these words—words every rebel, every dissident, revolutionary, every practicing artist from Capetown to Poland from Waycross to Dublin memorized: "A person does not lightly elect to oppose his society. One would much rather be at home among one's compatriots than be mocked and detested by them. And there is a level on which the mockery of the people, even their hatred, is moving, because it is so blind: it is terrible to watch people cling to their captivity and insist on their own destruction."

The third gift was hard to fathom and even harder to accept. It was your tenderness—a tenderness so delicate I thought it could not last, but last it did and envelop me it did. In the midst of anger it tapped me lightly like the child in Tish's* womb: "Something almost

*A character in Baldwin's *If Beale Street Could Talk.*

77

as hard to catch as a whisper in a crowded place, as light and as definite as a spider's web, strikes below my ribs, stunning and astonishing my heart . . . the baby, turning for the first time in its incredible veil of water, announces its presence and claims me; tells me, in that instant, that what can get worse can get better . . . in the meantime—forever—it is entirely up to me." Yours was a tenderness, of vulnerability, that asked everything, expected everything and, like the world's own Merlin, provided us with the ways and means to deliver. I suppose that is why I was always a bit better behaved around you, smarter, more capable, wanting to be worth the love you lavished, and wanting to be steady enough to witness the pain you had witnessed and were tough enough to bear while it broke your heart, wanting to be generous enough to join your smile with one of my own, and reckless enough to jump on in that laugh you laughed. Because our joy and our laughter were not only all right, they were necessary.

You knew, didn't you, how I needed your language and the mind that formed it? How I relied on your fierce courage to tame wildernesses for me? How strengthened I was by the certainty that came from knowing you would never hurt me? You knew, didn't you, how I loved your love? You knew. This then is no calamity. No. This is jubilee. "Our crown," you said, "has already been bought and paid for. All we have to do," you said, "is wear it."

And we do, Jimmy. You crowned us.

"THE WAY LOVE
NEVER DIES"
▪ by Eugene B. Redmond ▪

*Eugene B. Redmond, Poet Laureate of East St.
Louis (Illinois), has written or edited fifteen
books, including five by the late Henry Dumas.
His edition of* Goodbye, Sweetwater, *stories by
Dumas, came out from Thunder's Mouth Press
in 1988. And Dumas' collected poems,* Knees of
a Natural Man, *will be published under Redmond's editorship in 1989. During the 1960s,
Redmond helped found several weekly newspapers
(including the* East St. Louis Monitor), *taught
at Southern Illinois University and Oberlin College, and served as senior consultant to Katherine
Dunham at SIU's Performing Arts Training Center. The author of* Songs from an Afro/Phone *and*
Drumvoices, *Redmond spent fifteen years as a
professor of English and poet-in-residence at California State University–Sacramento.*

I am sitting on a mourning bench, in *The Amen Corner*, with other witnesses from Civil Rights and Black Arts Campaigns. Some, like Henry Dumas, Larry Neal, Fred Hampton, Medgar Evers, Sarah Webster Fabio, Taylor Jones III, Sister Zubena, Malcolm X, and Marvin Gaye, have long since departed the material plane. Others, *live* and in color, include a burgeoning list of literary-activist offspring: Amiri Baraka, Sonia Sanchez, David Henderson, Mari Evans, Quincy Troupe, Joe Scoggins, Donald Stone, Toni Cade Bambara, Raymond Patterson, Audre Lorde, William Keorapetse Kgositsile, Clyde Taylor, Ishmael Reed, Toni Morrison, Stephen Henderson, Val Gray Ward, Calvin Hernton, Jayne Cortez, Angela Davis . . . the beat goes on and the diasporan continuum lengthens. Bambara and Lorde, to my mind, are most intense-direct heirs to the particular legacy we emulate in this *Amen Corner*. There is rock. There is roll. We swim and swoon in circles, like Morrison's concentric multi-rings of sadnesses. Avalanche upon avalanche of griefs are layering up into stone-quiet unknown blue yonders. Blues intervenes. Adding tonality, rhyme, and ritual to the blizzardlike pain we savor, lamenting, as it were, the late, *Beloved* James Arthur Baldwin. Associations and correspondences begin their free-throws. I am inundated by rises. Now I am doing a swirl-dance of re-memory. *Jimmy Jimmy Jimmy.*

No need to rewind in order to replay this one. Love is for keeps. Love is forever. It comes with the territory. Co-joined, our dance is the consummate and eons-length grief that can never go public; that can never go private: eternal intimate discourse. How the *hole* of hurt gets iced by a bassy blues-balm-of-a-*whole*. But this is *the way love never dies. Immersion.* Because you could never read, 'rite or run with James Baldwin unless you were immersed. Intensity, commitment, call-and-response, involvement, funkencense, edge-percher, illustrative, intimate, fish-eye, visceral, hip. White women come to him, Richard says (in *Blues for Mr. Charlie*) "when they want some *loving*, funky, down-home, bring-it-on-here-and-put-it-on-the-table-style—" But in Bloodville, where there is call there is response. And the proud, black, and beautiful Juanita comes back at him: "I'm studying abnormal psychology."

. . . *All heaven had broken loose*: August, an August day, 1963— *the* March on Washington (D.C.) for jobs and freedom. Bless yo' golden slippers, everybody was there. Including James Arthur Baldwin, thirty-nine years old and pint-sized: literary priest, freedom fighter, expatriate, racial mood interpreter, and social harbinger. I had seen innumerable seas upon seas of faces—melding to a kaleidoscopic blur—youngish journalist *cum* college student turned black weekly newspaper editor that I was. Fleet, caravan, cotillion, or crusade, we had left East St. Louis with hopes humming: Elmo Bush, Clyde C. Jordan, Taylor Jones III, Homer Randolph, Joseph E. Harrison, Welbon Phillips, Ethel Scott, Roland and Ike Austin. Fathers, sons, pillars, entrepreneurs, publishers, politicos, N.A.A.C.P.ers, C.O.R.E.-catalysts, mothers, educators, poets, students, integrationists, essentially, integrationists. "Young Jimmy B.," the late Clyde Jordan was fond of calling me. I dressed like Jimmy, tried to look like Jimmy, talked like Jimmy, walked like Jimmy, gave a Baldwinesque tone and structure to my weekly editorials in the *Beacon*, the *Voice*, and the *Monitor*. In his shadow, like scores of others across the transurban black belt, I walked. East St. Louis doomsayer; harbinger; vicarious denizen of *Another Country*. Here. Hoping to glimpse the warbler, the proselytizer, the prophet, the atoner who had died, and would die over and over and over again, for America's—i.e., the white man's—sins. Meanwhile I saw Luminaries! Warriors! Leaders! Martin Luther King, Jr., Whitney Young, Medgar Evers, John Lewis, Marlon Brando. All around there was pride. Resoluteness. Wherewithal. Resourcefulness. Upturned faces, now silent, now audible, recollecting Charles White imagoes—and Charlie Parker. And yes, some were even blowing in the wind. Grounds. There were grounds. And occupation forces. *All heaven had broken loose.*

This was, I thought, GOOD NEWS. And then, without warning aforethought, I stepped into His presence. There, as I rounded a corner in my rather listless meander across the grounds, was James Baldwin. Sitting on some marble steps. "Jimmy," I thought, but did not speak; it was the name he was called by intimates. (This I knew from having read the *complete* James Baldwin, *ad* rote!) One never, ever forgets that kind of portrait, pause or impending pandemonium. There I was facing the GREAT James Baldwin, whose terrifying novel, *Another Country*, I had only recently recovered from. We surprised each other (Jimmy loved the story upon hearing it a decade later), he sitting, initially, striking a kind of Rodin pose, but more of a boy-lost-toy look, slightly mannish, irreverent, half-cocked smile. Far, far from the physical giantree my mind's eye insisted on *seeing* and *seeing*. Continental mohair suit, double-breasted, with high-water pants. Clean, clean, undeniably, unutterably clean. And *challenging*. He was challenging me! But what was I supposed to do? What was this duel of eyes all about? (Later I would learn about the "duel"—the Jimmy-look into souls, his own special/spatial, depth-charged kin-gaze.) *Are you in*, I mean unceasingly committed to, the struggle to breathe free, to be liberated, *or are you out?*

This was *serious*. I knew, from my reading and the grapevine, that James Baldwin had been "serious" at ages fourteen, sixteen, nineteen, and twenty-one. Knew that he had been "called." Had ministered in his teens. Had been surrogate father-confessor to younger siblings. Had worked to provide the bacon. Had gone to the thrashing floor, like Elisha (in *Go Tell It on the Mountain*), in the early hours, in the wee, wee times, in the early years. And I knew, by looking at him now, that he was still quite serious; *very, very* serious. Few things were funny to Baldwin. Laughing matters, yes—funny . . . infrequently . . . Now he was rising, rising oh-so-slowly, questioningly, as if demanding—gently, though—what I wanted with him. Why I had invaded his space. Was this communion, that is, intimate discourse, as in *Amen Corner*, or war? Somehow, at the time, I perceived the episode as a Robin Hood/Little John face-off, but stood my own ground, albeit terrified, which shook—as dungeons have been known to shake—under me.

All heaven had broken loose! Finally, I would—was about to— experience the EXPERIENCE! About to get the soul-literary transfusion. About to undergo the conversion, the catharsis; all my trials, all my tribulations, all my wildernesses, all my wastelands gathering at the confluence of superliteration: *James Baldwin!* Our eyes, which had widened progressively, suddenly started narrowing. What would it be? Which weapons? Baldwin gave no quarter, sought no quarter. Sought no homage. Only the gaze of the ages, that weathery stare. A plethora of clichés stampeded down my tongue, prancing in place at its tip. But nothing would come forth. No word would sing . . . Suddenly, footsteps. First one, two, three . . . and then dozens . . . accompanied by clicking of cameras, unsnapping of tape recorders, flapping of notebooks, and a tidal wave of inquisitions. Disbelief mingled with terror in me: a sizable portion of the more than 2,900 journalists covering the "March" had seen what I had seen—or had they?—and were now moving almost singularly, like a human blizzard, to get the latest lode from the shepherd of Harlem's flock. Here, live and in color, was Jimmy's "Amen Corner."

Baldwin, brilliant and unabashed, with his irreverent glow, wrote himself into posterity—into immortality, if that's the word I seek. Try this epitaph for starters: "Here Lies James Arthur Baldwin—*live!*" He had so much *life*—during his life—that he could seemingly resuscitate the lifelike. The "walking dead," in fact, was one of his favorite themes. Across the long reach of his writings, he decried the semi-conscious, the sleepwalker. The minister preaching Rufus Scott's funeral in *Another Country* warns the congregation about rushing to judge Scott's death by suicide. Hordes of folks strolling the avenues have "taken their own lives," he moans, and some are even "wearing the cloth," i.e., preaching. And who would know this better than James Baldwin? Who had sat in *The Amen Corner* any earlier? Any more intently? Any more devoutly? But the price of "getting into consciousness" (as the West Indian cab drivers in New York put it) is "madness," according to Baldwin's analysis. The responsibilities required of those who "come to" are too grave and too great. Hence many elect to remain in a blind spiritual hell so horrible that "no one can describe it," he tells us in his "Notes for Blues." The application is for whomever the shoe fits— black or white, man or woman. All of the players in the cruel hoax of color. All of the *dramatis personae* in the skin game, the coon show, the invisible-man opera, the white right.

Up front, *game* (in the sense of being "ready for Freddie"), giving, gay (and *gay*), fragile, formidably literate, painstakingly stored, cannily conscious, culturally astute, empowerer, intrepid, affably belligerent, life-gazer, storm-riser, statistician, self-taught, James Baldwin suffered the good fortune of not being educated beyond natural wit, natural creativity, natural law, and natural love. Funk, fire, passion, raw carnality, and precious need are part of his baggage. (Sister Margaret, in *Amen*, tells her husband, Luke: "You ain't changed, have you? You still got the same carnal grin, that same carnal mind—you ain't changed a bit.") And he carried "all of his equipment" with him at all times. Unchanging love. The beautiful Juanita—though she is not described, we know she is beautiful—tells Lorenzo in *Blues for Mr. Charlie*: "I am not worried about my hair [in the rain]. I'm thinking of wearing it the way God arranged it in the first place." *Au naturel*. In 1963, mind you. When only sporadically—Margaret Burroughs in Chicago; Beau Richards in Los Angeles; Malcolm X in Harlem—was there prominent display of God-given hair and features among the Afro-American flock.

Like Miles Davis in another, but yet related, sphere, James Baldwin set a pace for his generation of writers and thinkers. Especially those wanting to wrestle "consciously," "seriously" with the race/sex pogrom. Especially those seeking a way to build bridges. Those wanting to be hip, *black* and *literate* at the same time. For Jimmy was the preeminent *hip, black* intellectual of his time. Before, and to some extent after him, to be black and intellectual was to suffer a mental paralysis brought on by cultural schizophrenia. Blacks who were intellectuals— or so-called; and there were some exceptions—addressed issues and exigencies that made them brightly acceptable to the white *literati*. What Don Lee was to call "thinking black" in the late 1960s had been achieved in a very funky, dap, hip, thorough, and provocative way by Baldwin in his essays, plays, and novels—and especially in his lectures and conversations. The reconceptualization of local, regional, national, and global priorities—*vis-à-vis* race—had been the task (and *achievement*) of James Baldwin. Of course, legions of brilliant scholars, cultural scientists, activists, writers, teachers, institution-builders, and "race" men had laid hearty foundations for his work. His amazing, indelible contribution was to define and relax the arena in which we did mental battle with the cancerous demons of racism, deceit, oppression, hatred, violence, poverty, crime, dope, suicide, and loneliness. Baldwin brought us to the common plane of *The Amen Corner*, sermonizing us with *Another Country, Nobody Knows My Name* (or *yours!*), *Blues for Mr. Charlie, No Name in the Street, Just Above My Head*, and other natural cadences.

A severe and oxymoronic juxtapositioner, he created the hip cultural/racial matrix that, if one chose to dig it, allowed a reader to curl up with his own catharses. Using love as his balm in the Gilead of America, Jimmy sparred with, and jarred, the public and private (and sometimes the pubic) consciences. There was no apologia; no footnotes. This was *it*—sparse, eloquent, controlled, luscious, liquidy, illuminating: a weave here, a bob there, a prance, a dance, a jab, a sudden spinning turret of Armageddon-like harangue, the words *fuck* or *nigger* or *ass* or *shit* or *slave* interpolated into the most exalted sermon. The natural. The funk. The Park Avenue champagne shuffle. The Left Bank boogie. The wine time. The eloquent critical sense and tinge. Of Norman Mailer (*The White Negro*) Baldwin noted that even though that writer saw himself as *in*, bloods did not consider him "even remotely hip, if that is the word I want." (And, of course that *was* the word he wanted.) Trans-urban language met at the confluence of James Baldwin. The hippest of two, three, four—and the nether—worlds met at the point of Jimmy.

A lot was happening. A lot had happened. Bombardments. Beatniks. Le Roi Jones. Dick Gregory. Between the publication and production of *The Amen Corner* and *Blues for Mr. Charlie*, I had finished Lincoln Senior High School, which is Miles Davis's *alma mater*, where I had seen Barbara Ann Teer act and heard Amos Leon Thomas sing, and completed a stint in the Marine Corps. Through *Ebony*, *Jet*, the *Chicago Defender* and the colored weeklies, we stayed abreast of the civil rights movement and Negro belles lettres. These, along with a very reliable Afro-American cultural grapevine and the "current events" bulletin boards at Lincoln High, kept us hip and aware. We were listening to *Bird* and newly arriving Byrd (Donald), Ella, Nancy (just happening), Billie, Roosevelt Sykes, Howling Wolf, Bo Didley, Jimmy Reed, Grace Bumbry (just out of high school in St. Louis), and Langston Hughes. Through the black college grapevine, we heard about Owen Dodson's production of James Baldwin's *The Amen Corner*. Around the same time, 1955, an incident that was destined to be the allegorical impetus for *Blues for Mr. Charlie* rocked our rhythm 'n' blues lifestyles. While jogging back to Lincoln High School from nearby Lincoln Park, Leon Thomas, other track team members, and I were told by passersby that a "young cat from Chi-town named Emmett Till had just been lynched by crackers in Mississippi. I think they cut the stud's dick off," one of our classmates said. We arrived at our locker rooms nervous, angry, and bewildered. It was nothing new—bodies of black men were being pulled from the delta waters all the time. We read about it in *Jet*. But Emmett Till was only fourteen years old! *Close.* Inside the locker room, we peeled off sweaty clothes for showers. I was a star hurdler. Leon was a high-jumper. Suddenly we all started to chant. Nervous merriment abounded. Then a steady rhythm came from one corner. It was Leon, tapping on a wall locker:

Who did they kill?
  ba-ka ba-ka ba-kop!
Emmett Bobo Till
  ba-ka ba-ka ba-kop!
Who did they kill?
  ba-ka ba-ka ba-kop!
Emmett Bobo Till

Ritual. Rites of passage. Communion. Intimate travel. Salvation. These are the stuffs of righteous drama. "I was armed, I knew, in attempting to write the play [*The Amen Corner*], by the fact that I was born in the Church. I know that out of the ritual of church, historically speaking, comes the theater, the *communion* which is theater." Thus Baldwin hands us the conceptual baton, the *donnée*, for his play, performed for the first time in 1954 at Howard University. The *dramatis personae* comprise saints, much like the ones that "go marching in"—under the gravelly African throatings of Satchmo. Like all of us, Harlem Minister/Sister Margaret has her secrets, her skeletons, raising her teenage son, as it were, amidst the physical and spiritual rubble of urban mania. Her "secret" is that she has left her husband, Luke, ten years before, instead of his having left her, an assumption that Sister Margaret has allowed to perpetuate itself. Luke returns from the "world" of sin to claim a deathbed (consumption has overtaken him) in the house of his minister-wife and eighteen-year-old son, David. Women's internecine combat, running a subsurface parallel to the main action, consorts with Sister Margaret's own weaknesses and "needs" to create the "fall."

Minister, or minister figure, and musician, or artist-activist figure, were indelible creations in Baldwin's literary/inconographic constellation. Sister Margaret is a vessel through which a moral note is sounded. And Luke, the musician, who like all of Baldwin's creative artists is misunderstood, misused, and abused, is a link in the continuum of Afro-American resistance, defiance and rebellion. In some contexts, the text is rearranged, like Larry Neal's "charts," to meld minister and musician, harbinger and artist, as in Meridian Henry's crossover/change in *Blues for Mr. Charlie*. A minister of mild language and manners, Reverend Henry turns almost Malcolm-like after the murder of his son Richard in Plaguetown, Mississippi. He tells Parnell James, a local newspaper editor who is obliquely reminiscent of William Bradford Huie, "You know, for us, it all began with the Bible and the gun. Maybe it will end with the Bible and the gun."

Immersion. Because you have to *experience* it to get to Baldwin. One cannot be an outsider, an impostor or an unimpassioned, distanced observer. *You've got to bring some to get some,* we used to say, growing up in the South End of East St. Louis. Never knowing that there was a Native Son aborning to show us how to assert ourselves, via hip and via eloquence, through the use of our own rap. ("You know how we talk, *callings* and all.")

A Powerful Long Ladder, Owen Dodson, dexterous and innovative forger of Afro-Americana, was also one who knew "how we talked," how and why we did the things we did. Speaking of his 1954 production of *The Amen Corner,* Dodson exclaimed:

> Here is a wonderful voice that doesn't need to scream to make itself heard . . . so many depths, so many eddies and plumbings into human relations. The depth of this play goes beyond the relations of man and woman who just spit at each other, who just love and hate at the same time. All throughout the play there is a flexible sense of humanity amid the terror of the heart: a son that loses his father, and a mother who loses her lover, people who love each other but find each other's company impossible.

So stingingly real and earth-down were the characters Baldwin created in *Amen* that, as Dodson noted, Howard University audiences instantly recognized them, embracing them as their own. Earthbound, but with astral or bidimensional qualities, Baldwin's people are, like the man himself, *far out* and *far in* (this latter phrase courtesy of Miles Davis). *Texto y contexto* are at work both intradramatically and intercommunally. Communion occurs initially and throughout the play. So much so, Dodson declared, that on opening night the audience entered the commune with such sanctified lust that its wild clapping drove Dodson and others to push Jimmy to the stage. Tasteful and testimonial, sacred and sexual, street and citadel, all are the dusky domain of Baldwin and his congregation *cum* community in *Amen*.

"Amen! Let the church say Amen."

To this challenge/call from Sister Margaret, the church responds with:

"Amen! Hallelujah! Amen!"

And the ritual is on. Sisters outdoing and redoing sisters. Flow-shows. On the streets and in the sheets, as they say. Every other verbal jab (i.e., signifying/slash) is forgiven in a ritual-prayer of makepiece. It's a party, second floor above the storefront, but it's called church. During one of her prayers, Sister Margaret asks the Lord to "drive out them tormenting demons." A statement of pure ecstasy. In another breath, close behind, however, Sister Odessa verbally punches inside at two cousin-saints: "I hope the Lord will forgive me, but, declare, I just can't help wondering who's on top in that holy marriage bed." Few emotions or psychological nuances escaped the sweep of those beacon-eyes in Baldwin's observatory. His spectrum was broad; but he mined deep for the gold of the soul. Sister Moore reveals, for example, that it "*was* under Elder King that I come into church"; however, she becomes a vehicle for Baldwin's nascent feminism when she utters (also regarding Elder King) this statement: "All that talk about not wanting women to preach. He didn't want women to do nothing but just sit quiet."

Love. Love was another of Jimmy's common denominators. After having carried on, borne the cross, without her man Luke for ten years, Margaret tells one of her confidant-saints: "It's an awful thing to think about, the way love never dies." Love, Baldwin posited, in all of its ways, shapes and forms, is the constant. The abiding *one*. But love—or lack of it, or the perceived lack of it—can also be a tormentor. Check out Margaret. Check out the average edgy brother or sister on the stroll. Perhaps, Baldwin suggested, love is even a kind of God—especially when we're unable to trust—or scorn—anything else. For as sure as Margaret is, via faith and experience, that "love never dies," the immensely sageful Juanita, in *Blues for Mr. Charlie*, is just as certain that "the world is a loveless place." *Lord, Love, Struggle* and *Faith*. Mean dilemma. A fusion, as in *Amen*, of expiations. "Where," asks the song, turning back unto itself, "can I go but to the

Lord?" Enigmatically, the late Reverend Honorable Adam Clayton Powell used to salute his and Jimmy's fellow Harlemites with "Keep the faith, Baby."

Blues for Mr. Charlie followed *Amen* by ten years. During the interregnum, Jimmy finished *Another Country* and *The Fire Next Time*. According to William Styron (*The Paris Review*, 106, Spring 1988), Baldwin "really needed . . . a place to get away and live for the winter [1960–61]. So he came up and lived in the little house which I use off and on as a studio. . . . He spent a lot of time horsing around on the lecture circuit. . . . These were the really innocent days before the sixties really got started. They [women] didn't know Jimmy was gay, but they were smitten by him because he represented some kind of beginning of the revolution." That stay ended up being a costly one for both Styron and Baldwin. Styron says he "learned a lot from Jimmy that winter," during which he was "collecting notes and making outlines" for *The Confessions of Nat Turner*. Hell cut loose, later, upon publication of *Nat Turner*, with black writers generally condemning both book (which won the Pulitzer Prize) and Baldwin. According to Styron, Baldwin was "a little worried because he had mixed allegiances. When the book came out, I don't think he necessarily wanted to be on my side, but he was." (See *William Styron's Nat Turner: Ten Black Writers Respond*.) A lot happens.

Amen and *Blues* are set at opposite ends of the then-known American racial caldron. *Amen* was drawn in the Promised Land of the North, "Upsouth," a potent, ritualistic drama of expiation. A staple of Afro-American community theatre, it has been performed in the thrashing Afro-cities and in small, active hamlets like Cairo, Illinois. I have had the good fortune to direct both plays in various venues and to see them on several other occasions. A peak point had been reached in the civil rights movement when *Blues* appeared, broadening Baldwin's base of literary notoriety and giving him a renewed celebrity status in league with other luminaries in the "movement." *Blues* spoke of many issues on sundry levels. Baldwin was always on the cutting edge of linguistic and social changes, "black-based and other" (to borrow a Gwendolyn Brooks phrase). So that *Blues* was at once a play in blues form, a blues-tragedy; a provocative meditation on civil rights (i.e., racial strife); and a chronicle/barometer of life, love, death, and sex in an interracial Mississippi town.

Approached by Elia Kazan, who asked if he'd be "interested in working in the theatre," Baldwin says he "did not react with great enthusiasm because I did not then, and don't now, have much respect for what goes on in the American theatre. I am not convinced that it *is* theatre; it seems to me a series, merely, of commercial speculations, stale, repetitious, and timid. I certainly didn't see much future for me in that framework, and I was profoundly unwilling to risk my morale and my talent—my life—in endeavors which could only increase a level of frustration already dangerously high. Nevertheless, the "germ of the play persisted." It is based, "very distantly indeed, on the case of Emmett Till—the Negro youth who was murdered in Mississippi in 1955."

In the writing of *Blues*, Baldwin waded into the Deep South/salt of America's racial and sexual wounds. The "beauty" that pairs with "truth" and relentlessly brilliant creative expression galvanized legions of loyal lovers/supporters of what was good in art and good in human— i.e., Jimmy—albeit via exposure of the kinky racial underpants of the nation's attire. Lacing the American dilemma with humor—flip-sided in blues ironies—Baldwin painfully lifted, through love, those who in turn loved and lifted him—higher. "Once in a while," one group of such admirers wrote upon the completion of Jimmy's durable *Blues for Mr. Charlie*, "a play transcends its form and becomes an experience—as real, as imposing, as true as experience itself. . . . This play's value is beyond entertainment, and beyond the cause with which it is connected. It is a gift of great value to the American heart. . . ." *Signatories*: Tennessee Williams, John Oliver Killens, James Farmer, Sidney Poitier, Lillian Hellman, Richard Avedon, Ossie Davis, Katherine Dunham, Terry Southern, William Warfield, A. Philip Randolph, Peter Mathiessen, Shelley Winters, Geraldine Page, Marlon Brando, Sammy Davis, Jr., George Plimpton, Ruby Dee, Lena Horne, Whitney Young, Leontyne Price, Diahann Carroll, Lorraine Hansberry, Miles Davis, Charles Wright, Brock Peters, Harry Belafonte,

The Reverend Sidney Lanier, Mr. and Mrs. William J. Strawbridge, Jr., The Reverend and Mrs. Robert L. Pierson.

In Baldwin's literary cosmos, as in our own reality tales, fathers and sons endure each other, never prevailing, just enduring and aiming to secure sanity and peace in the household. David clings to his father in *Amen* as Elisha clings to his in *Go Tell It on the Mountain*, as Richard clings to his in *Blues*, as Jimmy clung to his in the reality-morality tale. From the reality tale, however, Baldwin embarks upon the high and low roads of metaphor and allegory. The father may be the land or the country or the deed needing to be redone right or executed initially. Richard, like Rufus Scott, like Baldwin, wanders, physically or metaphysically, away, far away, from home—and eventually has to "return" and settle contingencies. (That was the message of the "kin-gaze" at the Washington March: "What do you have to say for yourself? Where are you headed? What is the nature of your mission? Have you been blessed by the church? By the clan? By the forces?") And the picture, enveloped and developed by the son, has to be *whole*. No race bashing. No gender bashing. No homophobia. That was the only way that Jimmy could fly. *That was Jimmy's blues.*

Indeed, had Jimmy not chosen to enter and inhabit the human realm wholly, he would have made Lorenzo's white killer (Lyle Britton in *Blues*) the slutty, guiltless glob of human feces that everyone assumed, or pondered, him to be. Instead, Baldwin drew a full portrait of this murderer, whose real-life fictional brother, Jimmy tells us, is "now a deputy sheriff in Rulesville, Mississippi." While "in one part of my mind," Jimmy states, "I hate them [lynchers/murderers like those who killed Emmett Till] and would be willing to kill them . . . yet in another part of my mind, I am aware that no man is a villain in his own eyes." Therefore, to commit and recommit such heinous crimes against themselves—that is, their own brothers and sisters—humans are required to enter a web-realm of blithering denial, "a spiritual darkness," Baldwin asserts, "which no one can describe."

Since we are responsible for each other, we create in mind, body, and deed the Lyle Brittons and Ku Klux Klans of the world. The Nazis of the world. The Nixons of the world. Baldwin could "cut loose," I mean cut irreverently, irreducibly loose, on such subjects. In 1976, I was visiting Quincy Troupe in New York City from my Sacramento, California, base, and hobnobbing with Mukhtarr Mustapha, Toni Morrison, Verta Mae Grosvenor, Hugh Masekela, Paule Marshall, Imamu Amiri Baraka, Toni Cade Bambara, David Baldwin, Louise Meriwether, Marie Brown, David Jackson, Audreen Ballard, Rosa Guy, Leon Thomas, and others. Baldwin was scheduled to receive a major award with ceremonies to be held at St. John the Divine Cathedral. Our clan joined hundreds of others—we'd all been hanging out at Mikell's and other oases with Jimmy over several days—for what was a jam-packed, breakdown of a session. Jimmy was in rare presence, hyperliterate, winding and winding through his complex and cathartic labyrinth of racial and sexual rhapsodies. When all of a sudden he made a reference to [former President] Richard Milhous Nixon. Everyone appeared to be distancing themselves from Nixon right now, Jimmy noted. "But what I want to know is, Who voted for the motherfucker anyway?" A hush of ages went over the church. One female writer turned to me and asked, "Did he say . . . ?" I nodded my head up and down. Others just sat, flabbergasted. Needless to say, when the berobed church hierarchy approached Baldwin for the final honors, which included the kissing of cheeks, there were, in spite of all the breath-holds, such contingencies, such fear and trembling, such shaking of dungeons.

Poetry flourishes across the Baldwin canon. Poetry of blues. Poetry of sermon. Sermonical essays. Sermonical assayer that he was. Poetry of tumult. Poetry of narrative. Poetry of rebellion. Great poetry gets uttered as motherwit and wisdom as when Margaret-admonisher tells Sister Boxer in *Amen*, "You sound like you done forgot your salvation." Poetry in the wasting, in the waiting: "loveless world." Poetry, technical mastery (of many forms and feelings), insight, love, tolerance, genuine concern, fundamental passion, longstanding care, succor, embrace— these are the ingredients of his righteous rock. Rock is where and how Jimmy stood. Like his fictional fathers and sons. They are standing, even if, as Luke complains, God is white and discriminates against colored folks. Even if, as Lorenzo and Richard cry out in *Blues*, that God hangs, beats, lynches, and generally abuses Afro-Americans because He is the Savior of white people. Richard comes home, from his New York City collapse via drugs and white women, comes home to retool and refocus. Arrogant, intelligent, black, banished, abused, but unbound—indeed boundless—he brings Blues for Mr. Charlie. And he brings Blues to himself. Sonny's Blues is Richard's Blues is Luke's Blues is Harlem's Blues is Rufus's Blues is Plaguetown's Blues. Poetry, murder, racism, sexual détente, squandered hopes, pontiffs in exile, royalties without portfolios, love that never dies, love on the run, loveless worlds. One helluva jaded concoction. But Baldwin churns it up, pulls us all out and away from the shields of fear behind which we hide. His is the terrible swift sword of literature, high poetry, sermonical persuasion. You hear but you don't hear.

"I love men but I'm not a homosexual," Jimmy told *Black Scholar* editor-publisher Robert Chrisman and me during a dinner at Maya Angelou's home in Sonoma, California, in the mid-1970s. "Bullshit," came a retort from a third listener, who clearly was out of Jimmy's earshot by that time. I think I knew what he meant. I, too, love men, especially my big brother, John Henry Redmond, Jr., and, I am, it goes without saying, not homosexual. But I think Jimmy meant something else, something having to do with labels and dismissals and categories and what he once referred to as wrongful familiarity, i.e., "tampering with the insides of a stranger." But there was poetry in that enigma. In another breath, always another breath hovers right around the corner, came the compliment: "I love what you're doing with Henry Dumas," he said, referring to my posthumous editing of the late writer's works. "He's brilliant. We must preserve him. We must preserve him." Indeed, Baldwin did much to preserve Dumas—and other black writers—for before I had spoken to him in person about the Dumas project, he had sent a word of thanks to me through Maya Angelou and Paul DeFeu. As a judge for *The Black Scholar* magazine's creative writing competition in 1976, Jimmy selected Dumas's story "Thalia" for first prize. Gayl Jones was among the other contestants.

In 1978 I was serving as a visiting professor at the University of Wisconsin–Madison when Dr. Charles Means, a childhood friend, invited me to Bowling Green State University in Ohio to be on a panel with Jimmy. Other panelists included activist Harry Edwards, Jr., and educator Roosevelt Johnson, both East St. Louis natives. During dinner, someone asked Jimmy how many books he had written, a question to which he gave an equally quizzical look. Whereupon another turned to me: "You're the literary historian here, you tell us." Without a blink, I said, "Eighteen!" Jimmy, his face broad with grin and surprise, seemed to be tabulating quickly. "That's right," he said, stuttering, "the nineteenth'll be coming out soon."

Later, on the subject of a title for the panel, the party was again stumped. This time Jimmy cooed, "Hey, baby, why not call it *Poets and Rebels!*"

I HEAR MUSIC IN THE AIR: JAMES BALDWIN'S *JUST ABOVE MY HEAD*

▪ by Eleanor W. Traylor ▪

Eleanor W. Traylor is currently Professor of English at Montgomery College. A specialist in Afro-American Literature, she has produced docudramas for the Smithsonian Institution and since 1984 has directed the Larry Neal Cultural Series at the Afro-American Historical and Cultural Museum in Philadelphia to bring Afro-American Literature into the curriculum of the public schools. Her essays have been published in The Dictionary of Negro Biography, Callaloo, Black American Literature Forum, Twentieth Century Views, *and several collections of critical essays on Afro-American literature.*

They began playing something very slow and more like the blues than a hymn.

—*Another Country*

*J*UST *Above My Head* is a gospel tale told in the blues mode. Its beauty is achieved by an opposition of contraries arranged not merely by an eloquence of words, but of moods, of scenes, of chords, and of mighty beats. The tale begins with a death but celebrates a life. It laments a loss, yet it sings a love song. It is both a dirge and a hymn. It is simultaneously a blues moan and a gospel shout. Its scheme of ironies evokes the sublimity of the songs of the elders, lines of which begin each of the five sections of *Just Above My Head:*

> *I hope my wings gonna fit me well*
> *I tried them on at the gates of Hell.*

The heights and depths of Arthur Montana, a gospel singer, as his life is seen by his older brother, Hall, is the story told in *Just Above My Head*. The story is both dreadful and beautiful, but it is not new. It summons, once again, a tale told consistently for twenty-six years by a narrator whose features are clearly etched among the splendid in twentieth-century global literature. Both in his folly and in his greatness that narrator, the Baldwin Witness, in works as formally different as *Go Tell It on the Mountain* (a novel), "Sonny's Blues" (a story), *The Amen Corner* (a play), *The Fire Next Time* (two epistles), *Notes of a Native Son* (a history of thought), *Nobody Knows My Name* (literary and cultural criticism), *Little Man, Little Man* (a children's book), *One Day When I Was Lost* (a documentary scenario), *The Devil Finds Work* (an anatomy), essentially sketches one tale or one theme. That Witness has, himself, told us as much:

> *For while the tale of how we suffer*
> *and how we are delighted, and*
> *how we may triumph is never*
> *new, it always must be heard.*
> *There isn't any other tale to tell,*
> *it's the only light we've got in*
> *all this darkness. . . . And this tale,*
> *according to that face, that body,*
> *those strong hands on those strings,*
> *has another aspect in every country,*
> *and a new depth in every generation.*
> —"Sonny's Blues"

The Baldwin narrator-witness has dramatized that tale in now six novels and one collection of stories, and has staged it in two plays. Its theme of the perilous journey of love which, if not risked, denies all possibility of the glorious in human life, which, if risked, ensures the depths of sorrow but the ecstasy of joy; which, if betrayed, leads to madness and death; and which, if ignored or avoided, is directly responsible for the misery that afflicts the human world, is once again and powerfully the theme of *Just Above My Head*. The tale of the terrifying journey of the possibilities and failures of love is the dramatic center of the blues-gospel narrative mode of James Baldwin.

The older brother of Arthur Montana, gospel singer-star, like the older brother of Sonny, the blues-jazz pianist of "Sonny's Blues," tells the story of his younger brother as Arthur attempts the discovery of his song, his love, and himself. This story forms the base-line, the unparaphrasable drama of the novel. We have met Arthur before if we know the John of *Go Tell It on the Mountain*, the David of *The Amen Corner*, Rufus Scott of *Another Country*, Fonny of *If Beale Street Could Talk*, and, of course, Sonny of "Sonny's Blues." These young men in the world of Baldwin's fiction are all of like sensibility— they share the possibilities of a distinct heroic mode. They are blues boys: they must become blues men. The struggle to achieve blues manhood engages the union of the sacred and the secular, of mind and feeling, of lore and fact, of the technical and the spiritual, of boogie and strut, of street and manor, of bed and bread. The struggle demands the abyss: the achievement commands the mountain.

Arthur's tale spans thirty-nine years of his life. That is the longest history of the blues life that the Baldwin narrator-witness has attempted. The events of the life of the John of *Go Tell It on the Mountain*, as seen in retrospective glimpses, occur on the day of his fourteenth birthday. He is "on his way," "coming through." We know that he is, for he has experienced a blues epiphany. On "the threshing floor" of a ritual in his passage, he has a vision, the sacred and secular vitality of which begin to shape his consciousness. The details of the life of the David of *The Amen Corner* are seen in the span of a church service and in a glance into the kitchen and bedroom of his estranged but finally spiritually reunited parents' flat just before the death of his father, Luke. As David leaves his dying father's bedside, discerning where the music of a man really comes from, we know that he is on his way to the marriage within himself of the poles of his preacher-mama/blues-pappa's experience of the world. When Rufus Scott poises his arched body on the George Washington Bridge, "giving himself to the air," we have clearly seen one year of his life while glimpsing and understanding the years which have brought him to the water— and not to be baptized. Rufus, possessing so much in him that we love, has nevertheless cooperated with hideous external circumstance and, finally, betrayed his song. The death of a budding but unachieved blues-manhood is one of the most anguished human experiences (and perhaps one of the most sublime) that modern literature has achieved. On the other hand, Fonny of *If Beale Street Could Talk* is the young stuff of blues heroism. And Tish, his young love, is a portrait of girl/ blues-womanhood. Fonny will "keep his appointment with his baby," for he has already done it in his will. Sonny of "Sonny's Blues" is glimpsed by his brother and us on a set in a nightclub. We have seen, as in a capsule, the formative years of his life. We have read a letter that he has written from jail. We have heard him answer his brother's question: "Sonny, what have you been?" We have heard his answer, "more than I thought possible." Then we see Sonny offer the performance for which his life has prepared him. What we see is the portrait of a young blues hero. But Arthur's rite of passage in *Just Above My Head* is the longest journey that we have taken with the Baldwin gospel-blues man. Its junctures are the compelling experience of the book.

The story of Arthur's life is told us by his older brother, Hall, whose memory arranges its details two years after Arthur dies at thirty-nine in a London pub where "the damn'd blood burst, first through his nostrils, then pounded through the veins in his neck, the scarlet torrent exploded through his mouth, it reached his eyes and blinded him, and brought Arthur down, down, down, down, down." The death of Arthur has triggered his brother's memory of those years when Arthur, who had become a gospel star, had first sung in public:

> *Beams of heaven as I go*
> *through this wilderness below.*

In those years, Julia, the child evangelist, whose life story parallels and comments upon Arthur's, is eleven, her brother Jimmy, whose life mirrors Arthur's, is nine. In those years, the Trumpets of Zion gospel quartet is soon to form, and the lives of each member—Peanut, Red, Crunch, and Arthur—in relation and in opposition to each other are to map Arthur's journey from church to pub where "the steps rise up, striking him in the chest . . . pounding between his shoulder blades, throwing him down on his back, staring down at him from the ceiling, just above his head."

Hall's need to tell the story of his brother's life arises at a moment, two years after Arthur's death, when he realizes that "I was so busy getting my brother into the ground right that I've hardly had time to cry, much less talk." The death of Arthur has caused Hall to confront transition. He has been Arthur's manager, producer, and protector, and despite both his illustration and statement that his wife Ruth "makes me happy, simply" and despite even his fascination with his children, it is Arthur who has occupied center stage in Hall's life. Arthur's death has left a void the nature of which surfaces to consciousness in Hall's dreams:

> A *thunder rolled inside my head,*
> *a stunning thunder, and I woke up.*
> *My white-washed ceiling, with the*
> *heavy, exposed, unpainted beams,*
> *had dropped to crush me—was*
> *not more than two inches,*
> *just above my head. This weight*
> *crushed, stifled, the howl in my*
> *chest. I closed my eyes: a*
> *reflex. Then I opened my eyes.*
> *The ceiling had lifted itself, and*
> *was where it had always been. I*
> *blinked. The ceiling did not move,*
> *neither up nor down. It looked*
> *like it was fixed there, forever . . .*
> *fixed, forever, just above my head.*

Moreover, he dreams of trying to rescue a five-year-old Arthur on a landscape which conspires against him in the attempt; he dreams of a descent underground: running through subway cars in search of Arthur; he dreams of kicking open a door to a subway car and "all of a sudden the door just flew open, on the sky. I couldn't catch my balance. I arched myself back but my feet began slipping off the edge, into space." Hall Montana dreams of the abyss. But he not only dreams. He consciously realizes himself as a dweller therein:

> *By and by, I sat sipping coffee*
> *in the kitchen windows at the*
> *exiled trees which lined the*
> *sad streets of a despairing*
> *void. It's better than the*
> *City—that's what we say: it's*
> *good for the children—my royal*
> *black ass. It's one of the blood-*
> *soaked outposts of hell. The*
> *day is coming, swiftly, when*
> *we will be forced to pack*
> *our things, and go. Nothing*
> *can live here, life has abandoned*
> *this place. The immensely calculated*
> *existence of this place reveals a*
> *total betrayal of life.*

Hall, now a suburban dweller, has grown up in Harlem on "streets where life itself—life itself—depends on timing more infinitesimal than the split second where apprehension must be swifter than the speed of light." He is a man of many parts whose ability to see one thing and understand two or more offers us the drama of oppositions on which his story turns. Through his eyes we see the personal histories of the people of *Just Above My Head* whose lives adumbrate Arthur's and his own. We see how the attitudes and values of Paul and Florence Montana, blues-parents of Arthur and Hall, counter those of Amy and Joel Miller-tainted-gospel parents of Julia and Jimmy. Paul Montana is a blues-jazz pianist whose wife and sons thrive upon his music; Joel Miller is parent-pimp-assaulter of the child-evangelist, Julia, whose younger brother, Jimmy, suffers his father's neglect and contempt. While Florence Montana is the vital center of her home, serene but competent, Amy Miller, ailing and agitated, is peripheral in her house.

Through Hall's eyes, we see the disintegration of the child-preacher Julia and her slow re-creation of herself. First, with the aid of her Southern grandmother's tutelage, then from the succor of a love affair with Hall himself, and then by a perception she receives from her journey to Abidjan, Julia "had begun to create herself." By contrast, we see through the eyes of Hall the slow dissolution of Arthur, "his heart," his younger brother whose attempt to harmonize his sacred song with the cacophony of his secular life finally breaks his willing but unequal heart. With Hall's ears, we hear Arthur say,

> *When you sing . . . you can't*
> *sing outside the song. You've*
> *got to be the song you sing.*
> *You've got to make a confession.*

And it is with Hall's sensibility that we come to understand the song and the relationship of the man to the song:

> *Time attacked my brother's face . . .*
> *Time could not attack the song.*
> *Time was allied with the song,*
> *amen'd in the amen corner*
> *with the song. The song inconceivably filled*
> *Arthur as Arthur sang, bringing*
> *Arthur and many thousands, over.*
> *Time was proud of Arthur, so I*
> *dared whisper to myself, in the*
> *deepest and deadliest of the midnight*
> *hours: a mighty work was*
> *being worked, in time through the*
> *vessel of my brother, who, then,*
> *was no longer my brother,*
> *belonging to me no longer, and*
> *who was yet, and more than*
> *ever, forever, my brother, my brother still.*

Hall understands that

> [N]o one knows very much about
> the life of another. This ignorance
> becomes vivid, if you love another.
> Love sets the imagination on fire,
> and also, eventually, chars the
> imagination into a harder
> element: imagination cannot
> match love, cannot plunge so
> deep, or range so wide.

Yet only an imagination fired by love and charred into "a harder element" could envision the portraits and hear the inner music of a Peanut who meets hooded death cloaked hideously in a monstrous robe called Klan; of a Red who brings death home from a Korean battlefield whose mud has splattered "America the Beautiful"; of a Crunch who does not know his incredible beauty, who betrays "his heart," becomes a profligate, and wastes himself. Hall's imagination, despite a certain myopia which blinds him to manifest ambiguities within himself, is embracive. It is epic in its scope and lyric in its formulations. But most of all, it is musical in its presentation of the reality which it perceives. Therefore, as memory takes over the shape and rhythms of his brother's life, he is not only able to envision fragments of that life and shape them as an act of re-creation, but he is able also to *hear* Arthur's life as well; for he has heard the music of which Arthur has been vessel. He hears his brother's life as one melodic theme off which he riffs the personal history of those whose rhythms lend that theme both assonance and dissonance. Off the melody of Arthur's life, he also riffs the history of an era as the details of that history affect the interiority of a cultural community so splendid as the people who arise from within it, so dreadful as the abyss. That community is Harlem: the central physical and spiritual location of the traveling, and, therefore, global people of *Just Above My Head*. It is that community where

[E]verything is happening and nothing is happening,
and everything is still, like thunder . . .
And always, the echo of music, the
presence of voices, as constant
and compelling as the movement of the sea.
  —Tell Me How Long the Train's Been Gone

Hall's ability to see *out* blurs, sometimes, his ability to see *within*. For really, it is Hall's story, via Arthur, that we witness. He thinks that he has "come out of the wilderness," that Ruth (so obviously, *"whither thou goest, I will go"*), his wife, "makes me happy, simply." But it is not Ruth who has fired his imagination to a mighty act of poetry. It is the sublime—the terrifying and the glorious—life of Arthur at one pole and Julia at the other which has inspired the music of *Just Above My Head*. And because the vital presence of Arthur has fallen "down, down, down, down, down," in a London toilet and because the streets between his house and Julia's are "terrifying," Hall is able to hear that music which translates the moans of anguish and the shouts of triumph—the blues/gospel mode—of Afro-American experience of the world. The absence of Arthur and the defused position of Julia in the physical center of Hall's life (for he has persuaded us that love finds it power not only in spiritual but in physical assertion—action) has led him to "a stage of transition . . ."

The metaphysical abyss both of god
and man . . . nothing rescues man
(ancestral, living, or unborn)
from loss of self within this abyss
but a titanic resolution of the will
whose ritual summons, response,
and expression is the strong alien
sound to which we give the name
of music. On the arena of the living,
when man is stripped of excrescences,
when disaster and conflicts (the
material of drama) have crushed

and robbed him of self-consciousness
and pretensions, he stands in
present reality at the spiritual
edge of the gulf, he has nothing
left in physical existence which
successfully impresses upon his
spiritual or psychic perception. It
is at such moments that transitional
memory takes over and intimations
rack him of that intense parallel of
his progress through the gulf of transition,
of the dissolution of his self and his
struggle and triumph over
subsumation through the agency of will.
—Wole Soyinka, *Myth, Literature, and*
    the African World

This will of the Baldwin narrator-witness to report the abyss, to marry the sublime music to sublime word, and, therefore, to attempt the mythopoeic rendering of a great people in their and his disintegration in the abyss and by "a titanic resolution" reassume the shape of things beautiful, is his mighty strength. He "re-creates through the medium of physical contemporary action, reflecting emotions of the first active battle of the will through the abyss of dissolution" (ibid.) He who is able to report the abyss while, at the same time, encouraging us in celebration of our possibilities is a blues hero.

And yet, it is not only the *will* of the narrator-witness, Hall, which propels his story. It is also his *need* to answer the question put by his son, Tony: "What was my uncle—Arthur—like?" that provides him final urgency to tell his tale:

> *Nobody can really talk about it*
> *until I can talk about it.*

Arthur's life, as seen by Hall, is a blues life. Arthur, a vessel of music, has invested his sacred gospel song with the secular nuances of his experience of life. That life has known anguish, but it has also created joy. In telling the story of that life, Hall Montana, the narrator, has offered his children, Tony and Odessa, a gift. The importance of that gift has been stated by the creating author, James Baldwin:

> *I am using them [the blues] as metaphor . . .*
> *they contain the toughness that manages*
> *to make . . . this experience of life or the*
> *state of being . . . out of which the blues*
> *come articulate. . . . I want to suggest*
> *that the acceptance of this anguish one*
> *finds in the blues, and the expression*
> *of it, create also, however odd this may*
> *sound, a kind of joy.*
> —*Playboy* magazine, 1963

Perhaps a kind of joy, realized even in our struggle through the abyss of dread reality, is the best that an art form can offer us.

Just Above My Head inspires a vision: in a mighty city, just beyond its borders, fields of cotton, corn, and cabins, stands a tabernacle called the House of Tales. Inside the tabernacle, down the middle aisle, stands a great welcome table. On the right aisle of the table, there are many pews in which a host of elders sit—singing. On the left aisle of the table, there are many pews in which sit a host of their children's children. From the right aisle comes a song. Its strains seem to root in the cotton fields, reverberate throughout the city, and fill the tabernacle. "The songs of my brethren in bonds," sings a voice. From the left aisle comes a chorus, its contrapuntal echoes resound from the fields: its chant, "Solomon done flew, Solomon done fly away, Solomon gone Home," fills the tabernacle. At the head of the welcome table stand three figures. One, on the left, is suffused in light; he stares fixedly as at the horns of a star which he has ridden. The other, on the right, stands solid, visibly beautiful, stating a silent affirmation: "I am what I am." The one in the middle, gesturing first to left and then to right, steps slightly forward; looks straight ahead, cries out in a soft but resonant voice as to a congregation waiting at the door:

> *Come on in the Lord's house*
> *it's gonna rain.*

The vision fades: its meaning clear. The tabernacle is a structure built by tale tellers since the real and mythical sea voyage of Equiano. The tale is the welcome table. On its right sit the ancient tellers of the tale: on the left, the new. The three figures at the head stand like three hosts: Richard Wright on one end; Ralph Ellison on the other; James Baldwin stands in the center between the two. We are in the congregation invited to the feast. This member

> *bows on my knees*
> *crying Holy!*

AN APPRECIATION

• by Mel Watkins •

Mel Watkins is currently working on a novel and a history of black American humor. Recipient of an Alicia Patterson Foundation journalistic grant, he is a former editor at The New York Times Book Review, *former editor of the book page for* American Visions *magazine, and the editor of* Black Review. *His essays and reviews have appeared in* The New York Times *and in numerous other periodicals and magazines, among them* The New Leader, Penthouse, Channels, Amistad, *and* The Southern Review.

MY last meeting with James Baldwin took place in 1985 on one of those sweltering Manhattan summer days that typically bring New Yorkers' temperatures and tempers to the boiling point. After a conference at *The New York Times Book Review* offices, where we discussed an interview that Julius Lester had done with him and the possibility of his writing a front-page essay for the *Book Review*, we ducked into the first decent air-conditioned restaurant that we saw. It was one of those Midtown eateries that supplement ordinary menus with glittering Art Deco furnishings and giant-screen music videos. As strange as it may seem, despite the cacophony and outsized visual distractions, for Baldwin the restaurant was much more comfortable than the closeted, tradition-bound offices of the *Times*. Consequently our conversation switched from stiff professional chitchat to a more informal and meandering discussion of what he might write for the *Book Review* and what was on our minds personally.

After the meal, as we sipped cognac in the nearly empty dining room and mused over possible article ideas—occasionally looking up to view the frenetic gyrations of the pop musicians projected all about us—a Michael Jackson video appeared on the screen. Almost immediately, Baldwin's eyes widened and, after a few moments of thought, he suggested doing a piece on the distorted image of the black male in mainstream America.

As it happened, the interview eventually appeared in the *Times Book Review*. The essay did not. Transformed into a piece on the ascent of androgynous behavior in American society, it appeared in *Playboy* as "Freaks and the American Ideal of Manhood" and later in Baldwin's collected essays, *Price of the Ticket*, as "Here Be Dragons."

What is memorable about that meeting for me, however, is not the article that was ultimately published but a brief moment in our conversation when for the first time the opportunity arose to express to him what I, and probably a large part of an entire generation of blacks, would like to have said. For despite the invective heaped upon him near the end of his career by a few critics—among them, Eldridge Cleaver in "Notes on a Native Son," the misdirected, groin-pumping attack that appeared in *Soul on Ice*—many black Americans of my generation are at least partially indebted to Baldwin for, as even Cleaver admitted, unalterably changing and liberating them.

I had seen Baldwin on a number of occasions prior to that Midtown luncheon. Most often, however, those meetings were at literary cocktail parties or dinners where genuine sentiment was routinely eclipsed by fancy hors d'oeuvres, dry martinis, and practiced intellectual posturing. On other occasions heated political discussions created a tense, impersonal atmosphere that was equally impenetrable. One such meeting occurred in Oakland, California, where Jimmy was being honored by a contingent of West Coast writers and educators—among the guests were Huey Newton and Angela Davis. The tension surrounding that get-together is perhaps best reflected by an incident that occurred when, seeking to complete an interview with Jimmy, I stopped to ask an

Oakland police officer about the location of the address given me.

"Well, it's about four blocks up ahead," a young, belligerent officer informed me after disdainfully scrutinizing me and the rented car I was driving. "Just look for the street that's lined with patrol cars, you can't miss it."

Our discussion in the Midtown restaurant—despite the hectic surroundings and the omnipresent clamor of Bruce Springsteen, Madonna, Sting, and The Jacksons—was without either the pretentiousness of most literary cocktail parties or the tension of that California rendezvous. So, in that comparably relaxed and informal atmosphere, for the first time I was able to admit just how much of an impact his writings had on me—how much his work had influenced my life and career. More than the works of Richard Wright or W. E. B. DuBois, both of whom had touched on themes revisited by Baldwin, the essays that appeared in those first two collections, *Notes of a Native Son* (1955) and *Nobody Knows My Name* (1961), were beacons that illuminated aspects of myself that previously had been suppressed and stifled.

For growing up in the small, northern Ohio industrial town in which I was raised in the late 1950s was to experience a subtle, inexplicable, but no less eroding sense of outwardly imposed restriction and negation of self. The near absence of any tangibly aggressive imposition of that condition made it all the more confounding. It was, I discovered later, somewhat like one of Franz Kafka's nightmarish parables—external madness masquerading as sanity. And since nearly everyone with whom I came into contact accepted the situation as normal, defiance seemed imprudent lest one be self-designated as psychotic.

Of course, legal battles over voting rights and school desegregation were being waged in the South during that time. But these problems were not at issue in Ohio; thus the only observable resistance in my community outside the extreme claims of the upstart Black Muslims was curiously oblique, surfacing in harmless, ritualized humor or within the sanctity of the church. Knowing the perimeters of one's place and staying well within it were the keys to survival and social acceptance.

Therefore a sizable proportion of the black population of my hometown could live in the city's sprawling one-story projects and, like those whites who ignored or despised them, call their neighborhood "The Monkey's Nest." Cocaine and, most certainly, crack were not serious problems in those projects then. In fact, the only estimable substance abuse derived from a nearby steel mill's *coke* plant, which regularly spewed a sulphuric stench and fine spray of red dust that drifted the few hundred yards across the railroad tracks and chemically polluted river to settle on the projects like a scarlet cloak of inferiority. Not even Nathaniel Hawthorne's Hester Prynne was more dramatically stigmatized. But no one complained about the defilement or wondered, aloud, why the project site had been chosen in the first place. After all, it was their place, and they stayed in it.

The city swimming pools, supported in part by the considerable tax dollars paid by black workers (the then-booming steel industry assured that everyone could work), could be opened to blacks on only one day a week, Monday. On Tuesday the pools were drained, cleaned, and again restricted to whites. And, typical of the good old days of the halcyon Eisenhower era in America, most restaurants, motels, and hotels were off-limits to blacks. Unlike the condition in many Southern states, no signs were deployed. One simply knew—one knew his or her place.

Perhaps even more destructive, at least psychically, advisers in the integrated school system—when not suggesting the futility of any ambition or self-initiative—could with impunity and self-righteousness guide even the brightest and most productive black students into careers as typists, nurses, manual laborers, or, at best, teachers. "You sure you want to go to college?" I was asked. "You can make plenty of money around here working in the mills and you won't have to face all that prejudice and disappointment in the professional world." It was midwestern America in the late 1950s. As poet-musician Gil Scott-Heron has described the times: "Television and movies were in black and white, and so was everything else." We knew our place—or were quickly reminded.

But staying in one's place exacts an extremely high toll, not only in stunted aspirations and blighted talent but also in frustration and deeply submerged anxiety and anger. In his essays, Baldwin, like no other writer before him, touched those submerged feelings—the unuttered, personal torment buried beneath social compliance. His writing engaged the frustration underlying blacks' stoic resignation and passive acceptance of America's separate and unequal society. Writers such as Frederick Douglass, David Walker, W. E. B. DuBois, and Richard Wright—whose works, incidentally, were foreign to my hometown educational system—had passionately and eloquently spoken out against racism and segregation before Baldwin. But, even though they often wrote of personal experiences, their approach was usually polemical; their arguments were sociological, political, and, ultimately, objective.

DuBois, for instance, in a classic passage from *The Souls of Black Folk*, clearly describes black America's rendered psyche, its ambivalent relationship to mainstream America: "One ever feels his twoness—an American, a Negro; two souls, two thoughts, two unreconciled strivings; two warring ideals in one dark body, whose dogged strength alone keeps it from being torn asunder." Despite the eloquence and prophetic insight, however, DuBois remains a scholar; his remarks, objectively set forth, depict the condition of being black in America. In retrospect, one could conclude that he merely delineated a landscape that would be claimed and more thoroughly tilled and cultivated by Baldwin about a half century later.

One need only compare a passage from Baldwin's essay "Notes of a Native Son," which initially appeared in *Harper's Magazine* (November 1955), to observe the difference in approach. Describing the Harlem riot of 1943 and, more precisely, the relationship between black and white America, which, at the time, severely limited black aggression, Baldwin wrote:

This relation prohibits, simply, anything as uncomplicated and satisfactory as pure hatred. In order to hate white people, one has to blot so much out of the mind—and the heart—that this hatred becomes an exhausting and self-destructive pose. . . . One is absolutely forced to make perpetual qualifications and one's own reactions are always canceling each other out. One is always in the position of having to decide between amputation and gangrene. . . . going through life as a cripple is more than one can bear, but equally unbearable is the risk of swelling up slowly, in agony, with poison.

The same problem of split identity is engaged, but the soul of the problem is tapped and bared. Baldwin's point of focus was not the surface dilemma—fascinating enough in itself—but the festering ambivalency, the personal, moral quandary that lay beneath the surface.

Along with the timing of his emergence, as much as anything else, that focus distinguished Baldwin from the black writers who preceded him and partially accounts for his unprecedented influence on American society as well as generations of black and white readers. After his writing career began in the late 1940s with essays and reviews in magazines such as *The New Leader*, *Commentary*, *The Nation*, and *Partisan Review*, he became the most widely read and, arguably, the most influential Afro-American writer in the history of the United States. He was also among the most prolific. During his nearly forty-year career, he published plays, novels, and short stories, as well as articles, reviews, and essays.

Both of his plays, *Amen Corner* and *Blues for Mr. Charlie*, were greeted with mixed reviews. *Blues*, of course, was the more controversial. Based loosely on the murder of Emmett Till—a black youth from the North who was lynched in the South for allegedly peering too intently at a white woman—the play opened at the ANTA Theatre on April 23, 1964. The *New York Times* critic, James Taubman, wrote: "Baldwin has written a play with fires of fury in the belly, tears of anguish in its eyes, and a roar of protest in its throat." Most other critics were not as thoroughly impressed, however, and the play became the center of a furor rarely witnessed on Broadway. Baldwin's blunt portrayal of the hatred stirred in blacks because of white racism shocked critics and audiences alike and, after the initial uproar, the play floundered at the box office. Despite the efforts of luminaries such as Sydney Poitier, Lorraine Hansberry, Marlon Brando, Lena Horne, and members of the Rockefeller family to raise money for its continuance, *Blues* closed at the ANTA in August. Still, its structural faults aside, the searing realism of Baldwin's depiction of black-white confrontation brought a dose of street reality to New York's nearly comatose legitimate theatre. Few who saw it will ever forget the tension that spilled from the stage and onto the awkwardly integrated crowds who viewed it. Later, Baldwin was to say, simply, "I wanted to upset people—and I did."

Among his fictional works—although he never wrote the great book that critics predicted he would—Baldwin's first novel, *Go Tell It on the Mountain* (1953), remains his highest achievement. That superbly crafted work is still the most powerful novel written about the black church in America. Robert A. Bone, in *The Negro Novel in America* (1958), ranked it, along with Jean Toomer's *Cane*, Richard Wright's *Native Son*, and Ralph Ellison's *Invisible Man*, as one of the handful of novels by blacks that had made a "major contribution to America's literature." The rather stringent critical standards applied to black fiction by Bone notwithstanding, that assessment places Baldwin's first fictional offering in very exclusive company. And deservedly so, for Baldwin's complex, deeply textured tale of a black youth's salvation and religious conversion not only captures the frenzy and almost orgiastic passion of the black Baptist church but also vividly relates that experience to blacks' struggle for salvation and self-identity in a white America where blackness is itself the embodiment of evil.

The rich potential heralded by that first novel, however, was not to be actualized. Baldwin's next novel, *Giovanni's Room* (1955), was a sketchy, tentatively drawn tale of a triangular love affair set in Paris. The real surprise in this story was that the protagonists were all white and that Baldwin had ventured into the tangled web of homosexual love. Moreover, he had done so in a way that implicitly revealed his own homosexual leanings; this despite the fact that in a later essay ("The Male Prison," in *Nobody Knows My Name*) he would criticize the French writer André Gide: "His homosexuality, I felt, was his own affair which he ought to have kept hidden from us. . . . If he were going to talk about homosexuality at all, he ought, in a word, to have sounded a little less *disturbed*." Here again, though, the theme was redemption and self-identity, as David, an American visiting Europe, was faced with the dilemma of deciding between the traditional love of his fiancée and the more idyllically portrayed affection of Giovanni, the handsome Italian who becomes a priest after he is rejected by David.

Baldwin's next novel, *Another Country* (1962)—perhaps his most ambitious and controversial—and his last two, *If Beale Street Could Talk* (1974) and *Just Above My Head* (1979), like *Giovanni's Room*, were greeted with either mixed or less than enthusiastic critical response. Although these books seemed to strive for the large-scale social statement that his critics had demanded of him, they were not able to overcome blatant structural flaws and the Achilles' heel that plagued his fiction from the outset—a penchant for excessive rhetoric. Still, the opening section of *Another Country*, which is focused on jazz musician Rufus Scott, contains some of the most wrenchingly moving writing to be found anywhere about the plight of urban blacks during the late 1950s.

Baldwin's truly impressive fictional works, then, are limited. Although there are some extraordinary passages and set pieces strewn throughout his books, his first novel, the remarkable first section of *Another Country*, and "Sonny's Blues," the brilliant short story collected in *Going to Meet the Man* (1965), are probably his only undeniably masterful fictional accomplishments. Fiction, however, is only one form in the literary galaxy, and Baldwin was to find his ascending star in a distinctly different one.

The essay—a term that the Frenchman, Michel de Montaigne, first used in 1550 to describe his reflections on himself and mankind—can range effectively from journalistic accounts of current or past events to the brilliantly illuminating dissertations on the triumphs and follies of human beings seen in the works of Charles Lamb or, in America, Mark Twain. Despite the nearly four decades that have passed since the publication of Baldwin's first essays, few writers have equaled the passion, eloquence, and insight that he brought to his writing on black-white relationships in the United States. Even fewer have seen their essays attain the influence and impact that his have had upon the very structure of a society as well as on a generation of that society's offspring.

When Baldwin emerged as an essayist in the late 1940s the civil rights movement was barely ambulatory. Rosa Parks would not decide that the back of the bus was too far to walk to and defy the Montgomery,

Alabama, transit authority until December 1, 1955. Richard Wright's Bigger Thomas, whose pathological and decidedly unrevolutionary violence was so vividly portrayed in *Native Son*, was rare enough to be primarily a fictional phenomenon, and elsewhere in black literature Ralph Ellison's "Invisible Man" was still harmlessly ensconced in a cellar listening to Louis Armstrong wail "What did I do to be so black and blue?" (a theme echoed, incidentally, by Baldwin's Rufus Scott— "You took the best, so why not take the rest?"—as he plunged off the George Washington Bridge in *Another Country*). It was in that climate of superficial racial tranquillity that Baldwin published his first collection of essays, *Notes of a Native Son*, to instant acclaim.

Alfred Kazin called it "one of the one or two best books written about the Negro in America," and said that Baldwin operated "with as much power in the essay form as I've ever seen." Baldwin's next two volumes of essays—*Nobody Knows My Name* and *The Fire Next Time* (1963)—elicited even more enthusiastic praise. Perhaps more important, Baldwin became the most widely read black author in American history.

From the moment those first essays appeared, Baldwin's passion, honesty, and persuasiveness became crucial factors in freeing the impasse in racial discourse and in helping create what now seems the fleeting illusion that a majority of nonblack Americans could actually empathize with blacks and seriously confront the nation's immense racial problem. Along with Martin Luther King, Jr., and a few other leaders and activists, he was largely responsible for shaping the idealism that fueled the sixties' civil rights protest.

But Baldwin and King, while demonstrating that blacks were "the conscience of the nation," also exposed the depth of American intransigence regarding the racial issue. They were instrumental in exhausting the dream of an effective moral appeal to Americans and, in effect, set the stage for Malcolm X, and the emergence of Black Power activists such as Stokely Carmichael, H. "Rap" Brown, Huey Newton, Eldridge Cleaver, and George Jackson—figures who reacted in a purely pragmatic (and therefore quintessentially American) manner to the blighted expectations of the sixties' failed idealism. Baldwin and King, just as surely as they helped to obviate black America's passive, knee-jerk acceptance of the "in your place" doctrine, ultimately shaped the conditions that facilitated the "in your face" attitude which eventually supplanted it.

Since he was a political leader, King's influence on the events of the sixties is readily understandable. The source of Baldwin's impact on those events as a writer is less apparent, particularly since, as we've seen, the ideological content of his essays was rarely new. In this regard, besides the accident of timing and his gut-level focus, Baldwin's uniquely personal perspective and original style offer a clue to his ascendancy.

His essay style, in fact, set a literary precedent, and when a similar approach was employed by Norman Mailer, Tom Wolfe, and others, it was hailed as the "New Journalism." This despite the fact that *Notes of a Native Son* predated and probably influenced the style of *Advertisements for Myself* as well as Mailer's later forays into egocentric reportage. Alfred Kazin, again, was particularly revealing when he commented on the personal nature of Baldwin's essay style: "More than any other Negro writer whom I, at least, have ever read [Baldwin] wants to describe the exact place where private chaos and social outrage meet. . . . the 'I,' the 'James Baldwin' who is so sassy and despairing and bright, manages, without losing his authority as the central speaker, to show us all the different people hidden in him, all the voices for whom the 'I' alone can speak."

Moreover, as Kazin intimated, Baldwin did not write solely as a black advocate. In his essays, the multiple voices of the "I" spoke from the viewpoint of the American heritage as well as the Afro-American heritage. The following passages from "Stranger in the Village" (*Harper's Magazine*, October 1953) and "Many Thousands Gone" (*Partisan Review*, November-December 1951) are illustrative, first, of Baldwin's use of the omnipotent perspective and, second, of a white American viewpoint: "Thus it was impossible for Americans to accept the black man as one of themselves, for to do so was to jeopardize their status as white men. But not so to accept him was to deny his human reality, his human weight and complexity, and the strain of denying the overwhelmingly undeniable forced Americans into rationalizations so fantastic that they approached the pathological." Or,

"This is the dream of all liberal men, a dream not at all dishonorable, but, nevertheless, a dream. . . . It proceeds far from us in the heat and horror and pain of life itself where all men are betrayed by greed and guilt and blood lust and where no one's hands are clean. Our good will, from which we yet expect such power to transform us, is thin, passionless, strident: its roots, examined, lead us back to our forebears, whose assumption it was that the black man, to become truly human and acceptable, must first become like us."

As a writer, then, Baldwin is part of the tradition of black-American polemical essayists that include David Walker, Henry Highland Garnet, Frederick Douglass, Booker T. Washington, and W. E. B. DuBois. But he is just as much a part of the tradition of American Romantic moralists—a group that includes Ralph Waldo Emerson, Henry David Thoreau, and John Jay Chapman. This dual approach, the ability to assume the voice of black as well as white Americans, accounts, in great part, for his popularity and acceptance among Americans on both sides of the racial issue.

His appeal to America's mainstream society notwithstanding, he became, as Albert Murray pointed out in *The Omni-Americans* (1970), a hero of "the Negro revolution, a citizen spokesman, as eloquent . . . as was citizen polemicist Tom Paine in the Revolution of '76." But, most often, he did not, as Murray asserts, "write about the economic and social conditions of Harlem." Quite the contrary, Eldridge Cleaver was more accurate when, in the previously mentioned vitriolic essay on Baldwin, he wrote that Baldwin's work "is void of a political, economic, or even a social reference." For Baldwin's technique was to write through events, to penetrate the external veneer of sociological generality and probe the darker underside—"the real world" that Jesse Jackson alluded to at the 1988 Democratic convention—focusing finally on the enigmas that resided beneath the social and economic, enigmas that ultimately plagued his own psyche as well as our own. His influence and popularity, then, depended largely on the extent to which his psyche corresponded to the mass American psyche.

"Many Thousands Gone," one of Baldwin's earlier essays, suggests both the direction that his nonfictive writing would take and the technique that he would most frequently use. In this piece, ostensibly an analysis of Bigger Thomas, the protagonist of Richard Wright's *Native Son*, Baldwin probed the relationship between white society's mythical notions of the "nigger" and black Americans' real identity. What makes the essay so effective—what in fact distinguishes much of Baldwin's writing—is the grace and apparent ease with which he moves from the objective to the subjective; in this instance, from Wright's fiction and society's stereotypes to the underlying reality and complexity of flesh-and-blood black people.

Wright's Bigger Thomas—according to Baldwin, a symbol of the debased, vengeance-seeking "monstrosity" that is the essence of America's mythical "nigger"—is contrasted with ordinary blacks who, though they may have considered the course taken by Bigger, have instead resisted that temptation and affirmed their own humanity by living their lives within a complex social milieu that is virtually unknown to whites. The point being that, even as Wright indelibly reaffirmed the murderous outcome that might evolve if whites did not help improve the impoverished conditions in which America's Biggers live, by omission he suggested that black life in America was nothing more than the myth that whites had created. In this poignant, subtly constructed essay Baldwin argues that black humanity is finally dependent upon blacks' ability to resist capitulation to white myth and mold a positive, humane image of themselves.

"And there is, I should think, no Negro living in America who has not felt, briefly or for long periods, with anguish sharp or dull, in varying degrees and to varying effect, simple, naked unanswerable hatred," he wrote. "No Negro, finally, who has not had to make his own precarious adjustment to the 'nigger' who surrounds him and to the 'nigger' in himself." Then, speaking for white Americans: "This was the piquant flavoring to the national joke, it lay behind our uneasiness as it lay behind our benevolence: Aunt Jemima and Uncle Tom, our creations, at the last evaded us; they had a life—their own, perhaps a better life than ours—and they would never tell us what it was."

Similarly, in "The Harlem Ghetto" (*Commentary*, February 1948), Baldwin's analysis of Harlem's politics and institutions—primarily the press and church—is transformed into an examination of the uneasy co-existence of blacks and Jews in Harlem and of the reason for the continued antipathy between these two beleaguered groups. "The Negro's outlets are desperately constricted. In his dilemma he turns first upon himself and then upon whatever represents to him his own emasculation. Here the Jew is caught in the American crossfire. The Negro, facing a Jew, hates, at bottom, not his Jewishness but the color of his skin."

"Stranger in the Village," a portrait of a Swiss village whose inhabitants had never seen a black American before, through Baldwin's irresistible drive for the subterranean implications of the situation becomes an examination of the psychological connection between slave owners and slaves. "For this village brings home to me this fact," he wrote, "that there was a day, and not really a very distant day, when Americans were scarcely Americans at all but discontented Europeans, facing a great unconquered continent and strolling, say, into a marketplace and seeing black men for the first time. The shock this spectacle afforded is suggested, surely, by the promptness with which they decided that these black men were not really men but cattle . . . and it is also true that this idea expresses, with a truly American bluntness, the attitude which to varying extents all masters have had toward all slaves."

"Fifth Avenue, Uptown" (*Esquire*, July 1960), a meditation on the dehumanizing reality of Harlem's projects as contrasted with the wealth and abundance of lower Fifth Avenue, is transformed into a comparison of southern and northern racism. In it Baldwin concluded: "It is a terrible, an inexorable, law that one cannot deny the humanity of another without diminishing one's own. Walk through the streets of Harlem and see what we, this nation, have become."

Throughout his work, from the earliest essays to his last published book, *The Evidence of Things Not Seen* (1985), the same pattern prevails. Baldwin used external events, temporal situations, as a springboard to address the deeper, more lasting issue of the frailty of the human spirit. Consequently, *Evidence of Things Not Seen*—purportedly a journalistic overview of the Atlanta child murders in which during a period of almost two years between 1979 and 1981 twenty-eight blacks (all, save two, children) were killed—emerges as a continuation of Baldwin's energetic scrutiny of the American psyche and its dearth of morality.

Even *The Fire Next Time* (1963), perhaps Baldwin's most powerful essay, certainly his most controversial, is finally not the belligerent, uncompromising warning of an impending racial holocaust that some observers have insistently proclaimed it is. It is, rather, Baldwin's most passionate and affectionate testament to the enduring and transcendent spirit that allowed America's blacks to survive one hundred years of subjugation after Emancipation. ("I am proud of these people not because of their color but because of their intelligence and their spiritual force and their beauty. The country should be proud of them, too, but, alas, not many people in this country even know of their existence. And the reason for this ignorance is that a knowledge of the role these people played—and play—in American life would reveal more about America to Americans than Americans wish to know.") The cutting, or, to use Kazin's term, "sassy" dissection of American racial policy and final epigram (*"God gave Noah the rainbow sign, No more water, the fire next time!"*) aside, this terse, eloquent essay was ultimately, like much of his other writing, a plea for sanity, for the ending of America's Kafkaesque racial madness. It was a plea that went unheeded, and smoldering inner cities in Los Angeles, New York, Detroit, Cleveland, Chicago, and elsewhere only emphasized its urgency.

Pleas for moral rectitude, however, like warnings not to drink and drive or advisories to see one's dentist annually, have a way of becoming annoying, particularly when the group to whom those pleas are directed stands to lose so much if the plea is heeded. And for white Americans, as Baldwin wrote, "the danger . . . is the loss of their identity." Consequently, toward the end of his career, Baldwin found himself besieged by critics who challenged his message as well as his self-righteousness.

He himself, in *No Name in the Street* (1972), seemed to have lost faith in his commitment. "Since Martin's death," he wrote, "something has altered me, something has gone away. Perhaps even more than the death itself, the manner of his death has forced me into a judgment concerning human life and human beings which I have always been reluctant to make." And perhaps because, as he admitted, he and the civil rights movement had demanded from Americans "a generosity, a clarity, and a nobility which they did not dream of demanding from themselves," one was led to expect a more harsh judgment, perhaps even a condemnation of American intransigence on the racial issue in that essay. It was, however, not to be. The reader was left precisely where he was at the conclusion of *The Fire Next Time*. Instead of the threat of an apocalytic holocaust, we were told that "it is terrible to watch people cling to their captivity and insist on their own destruction" and warned of "the shape of the wrath to come." After examining the political and sociological forces that rendered the sixties' idealism unworkable and the tragedy that ensued, he concluded by taking a moral stance that was not significantly different from the position he had taken in previous essays. It is easy to see, now, why for black political activists such as Eldridge Cleaver his message had become simply an echo of bygone times when, like Rufus in *Another Country*, one could go down shouting, "You took the best, why not take the rest?"

But one may, with equal significance, observe that Baldwin represented the timeless voice of a unique Afro-American tradition. His essay style was the literary parallel of the black preacher's style and delivery. It is not simply that his essays were sermonic and that his books were filled with terms such as "redemption," "damnation," "sinner," "soul," and "redeemed." Baldwin's experience as a minister in a black storefront church was so vigorously applied to his prose style that it seems a demonstration of the "stylistic features" enumerated in Henry H. Mitchell's *Black Preaching*.

Aside from oral intonation and physical gesture, according to Mitchell, rhythm, repetition for intensity, role playing, folk storytelling techniques, personal involvement, and rhetorical flair are the chief features of the black preacher's stylistic approach. Admittedly these features are general enough so that the presence of one or another of them may be seen in the works of any writer. In Baldwin's prose, however, *all* of them are found in abundance.

Nearly every critic cites rhythm as a prominent feature of Baldwin's writing, and closely associated with this is the frequent use of repetition for emphasis—"much, much, much, has been blotted out" or "by a terrible law, a terrible paradox, these innocents who believed that your imprisonment made them safe are losing their grip on reality." Kazin's remarks concerning Baldwin's ability to "show all the different people hidden inside of him" affirm his use of multiple voices, and almost every page of a Baldwin essay provides elaborate and melodramatic anecdotes that demonstrate his use of folk storytelling techniques.

Since his prose style was such a consummate literary adaptation of the stylistic features of black preaching, it is reasonable to assume that his writing would share some of the attributes and limitations imposed by those features. The goal of black preachers (in fact, of most religious interpreters) is to adapt mythic scripture to the mimetic needs of their congregations—making the tenets of Christianity relevant to the reality of the black experience. The style and goal is contrary to rationalistic conception; instead, it seeks to communicate known religious doctrine through the emotions and senses. Baldwin used the same style for secular purposes. Instead of redemption in the eyes of God, however, he was concerned with redemption in the eyes of man. God was replaced by moral rectitude and love. His message was finally as basic as it was undeniable: If we do not love one another, we will destroy one another.

At the peak of his popularity and critical acclaim, both his approach and his message were wholeheartedly embraced. He was able, as perhaps no other writer has been, to evoke a passionate concern for the rights of America's oppressed. His essays unveiled horizons previously closed to countless Americans, black and white, and were crucial in creating the optimism and idealism of the sixties' civil rights movement. Most important, he was instrumental in setting the stage for the dialogue on race and racism that has survived even as the sixties' idealistic promise has faltered.

Still, when his essays are subjected to rigorous analysis, as by Marcus Klein in *After Alienation*, it is not surprising that the conclusion is that they are "evasive," lacking in "ideational development," and only accomplish a prophetic posture and an "indulgence of Edenic fantasies." Such conclusions are ultimately irrelevant, however, since Baldwin's intent was to effect change through dramatization and empathetic involvement, not to explicate. What was, and still is, important about Baldwin's essays is the style and eloquence with which he evoked the underlying torment and human devastation of American racism and his ability to make us feel, if only momentarily, that redemption and ascendancy were possible.

Near the end of his career, the few years just prior to his death on December 1, 1987, it was fashionable in some quarters to dismiss Baldwin's work as outdated and irrelevant. But, though his essays may not be as shocking or revelatory as they were when they first began appearing in the late 1940s, they remain as eloquent, compassionate, and insightful today as when they were initially published. That they may not seem as germane is not an indication of *his* failure. It may very well be a more serious indictment of ourselves, a palpable sign of the moral indifference of the Ronald Reagan era. Only if an eloquent appeal for probity and human dignity is irrelevant in our "me" generation is James Baldwin's work outdated.

For many Americans, myself included, the very suggestion is preposterous. Baldwin's lasting legacy is that he was able to penetrate and demolish the veneer of rectitude and implacability that concealed the insidious reality of America's oppression of its nonwhite minorities. Our institutionalized racism, which seemed a virtual *fait accompli* until the early 1950s, was weakened and opened to question; the hallowed myths, the protracted lies that buttressed our most cherished illusion were revealed, quite simply, as insubstantial, makeshift supports and thrust into the national consciousness. Through Baldwin's work, the sham was disclosed, and brought forth for discussion. Today, many of us take that disclosure for granted. But some of us remember when not staying in one's place was not an option and realize that we may not have come this far if not for the courage and vision of Baldwin and others. And none of us should forget that there are those among us who would attempt reestablishing the sham, exhuming and redressing the myths and lies. For that reason alone, James Baldwin's writing remains relevant—an essential part of our literature as well as our dreams of a better, more humane nation.

· IV ·

WITNESS AND ADVOCATE

It is power, not justice, which keeps rearranging the map. . . .
—JAMES BALDWIN

" J I M M Y ! "

• by Amiri Baraka •

Amiri Baraka (Le Roi Jones) is the author of over twenty plays, two jazz operas, seven nonfiction books, and thirteen volumes of poetry. He has received grants from the Rockefeller Foundation and the National Endowment for the Arts, has taught at Columbia and Yale universities, and for years has had a jazz program on public radio. Currently he is a professor of African-American studies at the State University of New York at Stony Brook. He and his wife, Amina, coauthored Confirmation: An Anthology of African-American Women.

WE know, or ought to know by now, that what we call "reality" exists independent of any of the multivisioned subjectivisms that nevertheless distort and actually peril all life here. For me, one clear example of the dichotomy between what actually is and what might be reflected in some smeared mirror of private need is the public characterization of the mighty being for whom we are gathered here to bid our tearful farewells.

You will notice, happily, or with whatever degree of predictable social confusion, that I have spoken of *Jimmy*. And it is he, this Jimmy, of whom I will continue to speak. It is this Jimmy, this glorious, elegant griot of our oppressed African-American nation who I am eulogizing. So let the butchering copy editors of our captivity stay for an eternal moment their dead eraser fingers from our celebration.

There will be, and should be, reams and reams of analysis, even praise, for our friend but also even larger measures of nonanalysis and certainly condemnation for James Baldwin, the Negro writer. Alas we have not yet the power to render completely sterile or make impossible the errors and lies which will merely be America being itself rather than its unconvincing promise.

But the wide gap, the world-spanning abyss, between the James Baldwin of yellow journalism and English departments (and here we thought this was America) and the Jimmy Baldwin of our real lives, is stunning! When he told us *Nobody Knows My* (he meant Our) *Name*, he was trying to get you ready for it even then!

For one thing, no matter the piles of deathly prose citing influences, relationships, metaphor, and criticism that will attempt to tell us about our older brother, most will miss the mark simply because for the most part they will be retelling old lies or making up new ones, or shaping yet another black life to fit the great white stomach which yet rules and tries to digest the world!

For first of all Jimmy Baldwin was not only a writer, an international literary figure; he was man, spirit, voice—old and black and terrible as that first ancestor.

As man, he came to us from the family, the human lives, names we can call David, Gloria, Lover, Robert . . . and this extension is one intimate identification that he wore so casually, in that way of his, eyes and self smiling, not much larger than that first ancestor, fragile as truth always is, big eyes popped out like righteous monitors of the soulful. The Africans say that big ol' eyes like that mean someone can make things happen! And didn't he?

Between Jimmy's smile and grace, his insistent elegance even as he damned you, even as he smote what evil was unfortunate, breathing or otherwise, to stumble his way—he was all the way live, all the way conscious, turned all the way up, receiving and broadcasting, sometimes so hard, what needed to, would back up from those two television tubes poking out of his head!

As man, he was my friend; my older brother, he would joke, not really joking. As man he was Our friend, Our older or younger brother, we listened to him like we would somebody in our family—whatever you might think of what he might say. We could hear it. He was close,

I n 1955.

B eauford Delaney's portrait of Baldwin, early 1950s.

3

4

W ith Lucien
Happersburger in
Switzerland.

W ith his brother, David
Baldwin.

In Puerto Rico.

In Paris in the 1950s.

In Harlem, 1963.

_____

At a reading in 1962.

_____

Italian press conference.

Addressing a CORE (Congress of Racial Equality) meeting in Los Angeles, California, June 1963.

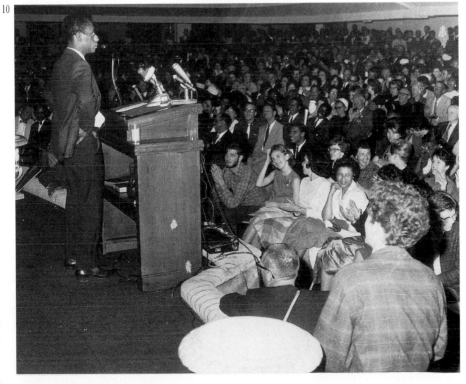

11

12

W ith Lee Strasberg.

W ith Bayard Rustin in
1963.

With Charlton Heston, Harry Belafonte, and Marlon Brando in front of the Lincoln Memorial during the March on Washington in August 1963.

At a christening in Paris in the 1960s.

15

Celebrating the opening of *Blues for Mr. Charlie* in April 1964 with stars Diana Sands and Burgess Meredith.

In Africa.

16

as man, as human relative; we could make it through some cold seasons merely warmed by his handshake, smile, or eyes. Warmed by his voice, jocular yet instantly cutting. Kind yet perfectly clear. We could make it sometimes, just remembering his arm waved in confirmation or indignation, the rapid-fire speech, pushing out at the world like urgent messages for those who would be real.

This man traveled the earth like its history and its biographer. He reported, criticized, made beautiful, analyzed, cajoled, lyricized, attacked, sang, made us think, made us better, made us consciously human or perhaps more acidly prehuman.

He was spirit because he was living. And even past this tragic hour when we weep he has gone away, and why, and why, we keep asking. There's mountains of evil creatures who we would willingly bid farewell to—Jimmy could have given you some of their names on demand. We curse our luck, our oppressors—our age, our weakness. Why? And why again? And "why" can drive you mad, or said enough times might even make you wise!

Yet this "why" in us is him as well. Jimmy was wise from asking "whys" giving us his wise and his "whys" to go with our own, to make them into a larger "why" and a deeper Wise.

Jimmy's spirit, which will be with us as long as we remember ourselves, is the only truth which keeps us sane and changes our whys to wiseness. It is his spirit, spirit of the little black first ancestor, which we feel, those of us who really felt it. We know this spirit will be with us for "as long as the sun shines and the water flows." For his is the spirit of life thrilling to its own consciousness.

His spirit is part of our own, it is our feelings completion. Our perceptions extension, the edge of our rationale, the paradigm for our best use of this world.

When we saw and heard him, he made us feel good. He made us feel, for one thing, that we could defend ourselves and define ourselves, that we were in the world not merely as animate slaves, but as terrifyingly sensitive measurers of what is good or evil, beautiful or ugly. This is the power of his spirit. This is the bond which created our love for him. This is the fire that terrifies our pitiful enemies. That not only are we alive but shatteringly precise in our songs and our scorn.

129

You could not possibly think yourself righteous Murderers, when you saw or were wrenched by our Jimmy's spirit! He was carrying it as *us*, as we carry him as *us*.

Jimmy will be remembered, even as James, for his *word*. Only the completely ignorant can doubt his mastery of it. Jimmy Baldwin was the creator of contemporary American speech even before Americans could dig that. He created it so we could speak to each other at unimaginable intensities of feeling, so we could make sense to each other at yet higher and higher tempos.

But that word, arranged as art, sparkling and gesturing from the page, was also man and spirit. Nothing was more inspiring than hearing that voice, seeing that face, and that whip of tongue, that signification that was his fingers, reveal and expose, raise and bring down, condemn or extoll.

I had met him years before at Howard, when Owen Dodson presented his *Amen Corner* there. But it was not until later confined by the armed forces that I got to feel that spirit from another, more desperate angle of need, and therefore understanding.

Jimmy's face, his eyes, the flush of his consciousness animating the breath of my mind, sprung from earlier reading of his early efforts in literary magazines, and the aura those created, stretched itself, awakened so to speak, when I stared newly arrived in New York from my imprisonment and internal confusion to see this black man staring from the cover of *Notes of a Native Son* at me unblinking. I looked at that face, and heard that voice, even before I read the book. Hey, it was me—for real! When I read those marvelous essays, that voice became part of my life forever. Those eyes were part of my instruments of judgment and determination. Those deliberations, that experience, the grimness and high art, became mine instantly. From the moment I saw his face, he was my deepest hero, the agent of consciousness in my young life. Jimmy was that for many of us.

What was said of him, the so called analysis, often reeking of the dead smell of white supremacy and its nonexistent humanity, made no difference. All of that did not really register, except as recall for dull conversations with fire plugs or chairs or stone steps when abroad in the practiced indifference called U.S. society.

What he gave me, what he gave us, we perceived instantly and grew enormous inside because of it. That black warm truth. That invincible gesture of sacred human concern, clearly projected—we absorbed with what gives life in this world, contrasted as it is against the dangerous powers of death.

Jimmy grew as we all did, but he was growing first and was the measure, even as we claimed understanding and transcendence. Just as he wanted to distance himself from a mentor like Richard Wright, better to understand more clearly where he himself, his own self and voice, began and Richard's left off.

Happily for some of us, when we distanced ourselves from Jimmy, it turned out that this not only let us understand ourselves more clearly, but it allowed us finally to come to grips with the actual truth, power, and beauty of this artist and hero.

It was Jimmy who led us from critical realism to an aesthetic furthering of it that made it more useful to the still living. He was like us so much, constantly growing, constantly measuring himself against himself, and thus against the world.

It was evident he loved beauty and art, but when the civil rights movement pitched to its height, no matter his early aestheticism and seeming hauteur; he was our truest definer, our educated conscience made irresistible by his high consciousness.

Jimmy was a "civil rights leader," too, *at the same time*, one of those thinkers of outmoded social outrage. He was in the truest tradition of the great artists of all times, those who understand it is beauty AND TRUTH we seek, and that indeed one cannot exist without and as an extension of the other.

At the hot peak of the movement Jimmy was one of its truest voices. His stance—that it is *our* judgment of the world, the majority of us who still struggle to survive the bestiality of so-called civilization (the slaves), that is true and not that of our torturers—was a dangerous profoundity and as such fuel for our getaway and liberation!

He was our consummate and complete man of letters, not as an unliving artifact, but as a black man we could touch and relate to even there in that space filled with black fire at the base and circumference of our souls. And what was supremely ironic is that for all his aestheticism and ultra-sophistication, there he was now demanding that we get in the world completely, that we comprehend the ultimate intelligence of our enforced commitment to finally bring humanity to the world!

Jimmy's voice, as much as Dr. King's or Malcolm X's, helped shepherd and guide us toward black liberation.

And for this, of course, the intellectual gunmen of the animal king tried to vanquish him. For ultimately, even the rare lyricism of his song, the sweeping aesthetic obsession with feeling, could not cover the social heaviness of his communication!

The celebrated James Baldwin of earlier times could not be used to cover the undaunted freedom chants of the Jimmy who walked with King and SNCC or the evil little nigger who wrote *Blues for Mr. Charlie*!

For as far as I'm concerned, it was *Blues for Mr. Charlie* that announced the black arts movement, even so far as describing down to minute fragments of breath the class struggle raging inside the black community—even as it is menaced by prehuman maniacs.

But attacked or not, repressed or not, suddenly unnewsworthy or not, Jimmy did what Jimmy was. He lived his life as witness. He wrote until the end. We hear of the writer's blocks of celebrated Americans, how great they are, so great indeed that their writing fingers have been turned to checks, but Jimmy wrote. He produced. He spoke. He sang, no matter the odds. He remained man, and spirit and voice. Ever expanding, ever more conscious!

Gratifying to me in the extreme was that each year we grew closer, grew to understand each other even more. Ultimately I did understand, as I feel I always did, but now consciously, that he *was* my older brother—a brother of the communal spirit!!

One day I took him to Newark's Scudder Homes, the toilet bowl of the world, with a film crew. Seemingly deserted at first, the streets, once the vine got to graping, filled quickly and Jimmy found himself surrounded by black people eager only to look at him, ask him questions, or tell him he was still their main man. At that nadir of social dislocation one young brother, his hat turned halfway around, said, "I just read *Just Above My Head*, Mr. Baldwin. It's great! How you doing?" Jimmy's smile of recognition alone would have lit up even the darker regions under the earth.

We hung out all night one time lurching out of Mikell's after talking to David, and the next morning, Jimmy still leading and gesturing, clear as a bell, was still telling me some things I really needed to know, and I was still giving him feedback that yes, there were a bunch of us who knew who he was, and loved him for it, since it was one of the only ways we could ever really love ourselves!

Jimmy was one of those people whose celebrity is recognized, whether by name or not, by the very aura that accompanies them, whose intelligence is revealed in the most casual gesture or turn of apparel and bearing. We were aware at once that such dignity was the basis and result of great achievement, of serious regard for the deep, the heavy, the profound.

Yet because of this deep and deeply-felt-by-us integrity Jimmy carried like his many hats, his film of Malcolm X was rejected; reviews of his later works began to appear on page two because he could not be permitted to tell the truth so forcefully. Finally, great minds even forbade him to publish his last work, *The Evidence of Things Not Seen*, exposing the duplicity of the legal machinations obscuring the real killers of the black Atlanta children. He had to sue the publisher in order to get the book out. When he told me this last outrage, I remember the word *Weimar* flashed through my head. Reading this formidable completely mature and awesome work I could understand the terror of white supremacy and its worshipers at its appearance. It is important that I include this quote from the work as his man/spirit voice, flesh of his soul, speaking to us with the clarity of revelation:

The Western world is located somewhere between the Statue of Liberty and the pillar of salt.

At the center of the European horror is their religion: a religion by which it is intended one be coerced, and in which no one believes, the proof being the Black/White conditions, or options, the horror into which the cowardly delusion of White supremacy seems to have transformed Africa, and the utterly intolerable nightmare of the American Dream. I speak with the authority of the grandson of a slave, issue of the bondswoman, Hagar's child. And, what the slave did—

despised and rejected, *'buked and scorned*—with the European's paranoid vision of human life was to alchemize it into a force that contained a human use. The Black preacher, since the church was the only Civilized institution that we were permitted—separately—to enter, was our first warrior, *terrorist*, or *guerrilla*. He said that freedom was real—that *we* were real. *He* told us that *trouble don't last always*. *He* told us that our children and our elders were sacred, when the Civilized were spitting on them and hacking them to pieces, in the name of God, and in order to keep on making money. And, furthermore, we were not so much permitted to *enter* the church as corraled into it, as a means of rendering us docile and as a means of forcing us to corroborate the inscrutable will of God, Who had decreed that we should be slaves forever.

But it was Jimmy's life that puts such demonic tragedy in ever-tightening jeopardy worldwide. He would not be still, he would not and never could be made to be just a mouthpiece for the prettily obscene. He sang of our lives and our needs and our will to triumph, even until his final hour.

Jimmy always made us feel good. He always made us know we were dangerously intelligent and as courageous as the will to be free!

Let us hold him in our hearts and minds. Let us make him part of our invincible black souls, the intelligence of our transcendence. Let our black hearts grow big, world-absorbing eyes like his, never closed. Let us one day be able to celebrate him like he must be celebrated if we are ever to be truly self-determining. For Jimmy was God's black revolutionary mouth. If there is a God, and revolution his righteous natural expression. And elegant song the deepest and most fundamental commonplace of being alive.

If we cannot understand our love of Jimmy Baldwin it is too late to speak of freedom or liberation, it has already been lost!

But it is his life that was confirmation of our love, and our love that is continuing proof that "Hey, did you see Jimmy last night, you hear what he told so-and-so?" What he said was part of our long slave narrative, as we speak to ourselves from within ourselves, and it is Jimmy's voice we hear, it has always been.

DIALOGUE IN BLACK
AND WHITE
(1964–1965)

• by James Baldwin
and
Budd Schulberg •

Widely acclaimed for his novels, screenplays, tele-
vision documentaries, and articles, Budd Schul-
berg is the recipient of numerous awards and
citations for his work, including the Academy
Award for On the Waterfront *(for best story and*
screenplay). Currently living in New York, he is
the former director of the Douglass House Watts
Writers Workshop in Los Angeles, California.

What follows is excerpted from an impas-
sioned and friendly dialogue that James Baldwin
and Schulberg continued between 1964 and
1965.

SCHULBERG: What is the real goal of the Negro revolution? Is it to
become part of the American body politic, something
not yet achieved despite all the good old laws and the
good new laws? If it is, then . . . you need all the genuine white allies you can find. I mean me, Saul Alinsky,
Nat Hentoff, Walter Reuther, Bobby Kennedy, the white
kids who die with the black kids in Mississippi; you need
anyone who actively despises the color line, trying to
save our country from what you call "the racial nightmare."

On the other hand there has begun to run through
the attitude of some Negro leaders and intellectuals a
feeling that it is too late for American whites—indeed,
for the entire Caucasian Western civilization—that we

had our chance and blew it, in Vietnam and Algeria, Harlem and Watts. Elijah Muhammad sees only a few short years until the new Armageddon in which the non-white races of the world—from the black ghettos to Red China—will regain their rightful place as dominant. . . .

It seems to me that you, as a celebrated Negro spokesman, have not quite decided—which side are *you* on, Elijah Muhammad's side or what you call my sloppy liberal-interracial side?

BALDWIN: Baby, don't lay that on me. It's not for *me* to decide, it's for *you* to decide. I don't mean you, personally, I mean you and all my well-meaning white friends. From where you sit, maybe you think we're making encouraging progress. But from where I sit, and from where my brothers are huddling tonight in their black ghettos from Boston to San Diego, we can't wait for laws that take so long to pass and then so much longer—it seems forever—to enforce. We're ready now. We've been ready for generations. And if white America isn't ready with us, then Elijah has a point—history will swallow you up as it has swallowed other arrogant civilizations that seemed invincible but that carried along in them some cancer, some fatal flaw. . . . It's the nature of the human race, isn't it, to categorize, to label? Using both of us as abstractions, you and me, Budd Schulberg and Jimmy Baldwin, one crucial difference between us is that you, Budd Schulberg, are one kind of abstraction, or legend, in the eyes and ears of people who don't know Budd Schulberg. And I'm another kind of abstraction, or menace, in the eyes and ears of the people who don't know me.

SCHULBERG: But, Jimmy, when you talk about abstract difference— I feel no difference, no abstract sense of superiority or inferiority between you, James Baldwin, and me, Budd Schulberg—

BALDWIN: As a matter of fact, there are a great many differences between you and me. I'm James Baldwin. That's a very essential difference.

SCHULBERG: I mean I feel no subjective superiority because my skin happens to be fair and yours dark. I know that doesn't make me smarter or more talented and I don't believe it should give me any special privileges. It does but it shouldn't, and I think I have a right to resent it as much as you do. There is, of course, that practical difference between us. You go out on the street, as you reminded me on Central Park West, and you can't get a cab. And you—not Jimmy Baldwin, but speaking for Negroes generally—can't get a job, or as good a job.

BALDWIN: Well, as far as that goes, sometimes neither can you.

SCHULBERG: If you're thinking of me not as a WASP but as a member of another minority, that's perfectly true. It's forgotten in the light of all that talk about Jewish success in America, just how many big American companies still have anti-Jewish policies, how many hotels, resorts, real estate developments discriminate against Jews. That's why I think it's tragic when Negroes and Jews start to stereotype each other. I agree with a lot of what you say, Jimmy. But what happens with racial suffering as it happened to the Jews and is happening to the Negroes is that they fight back with their own counterprejudice.

BALDWIN: Let me put a parenthesis here—a dangerous parenthesis, but one that may serve to illuminate something of the American Negro's resentment. And it's this: I was here first. I mean, historically.

SCHULBERG: Who?

BALDWIN: The Negro.

SCHULBERG: On what basis—

BALDWIN: I, the Negro, arrived before the Jew.

SCHULBERG: What are you talking about, Jimmy? I've read a lot about the Muslims—I'm not talking about the black nationalists or the followers of Malcolm X now—and I think that's Muhammad's pseudo-history. I don't dig anybody's racism—white, black, or yellow. That "I was here first" is Muslim bullshit.

BALDWIN: Now we're getting down to it.

SCHULBERG: I don't know what that means—you came first. It is the most absurd—

BALDWIN: Obviously, you know that. I don't mean that we came first on earth.

SCHULBERG: But it sounds so close to the Muslim oversimplification, what Elijah Muhammad said about the black man being the original man and the white man a pale, mongrel, "white-devil" bad imitation. It's just the blond-Aryan-supremacy myth in reverse; it has no real, no scientific basis. It's the crude theory of the white racist turned inside out. If you really want to go back to the origin of man, we'd have to go into all—but that's not what we're talking about. We're talking about today.

BALDWIN: Precisely. Let's take me, Jimmy Baldwin. Historically speaking, I've been here for four hundred years. Let's say that you just got off the boat on Friday and you can't speak English yet; but on the following Tuesday I'm working for you.

SCHULBERG: Jimmy, nobody could speak English! The Jews, the Italians, the Germans, the Poles—who could speak English when they arrived here except the first settlers who came from England? None of these people could speak English, but they brought with them their share of European culture and education that enabled them to pull themselves out of the ghetto—although it didn't happen overnight. First-generation Jews, Italians, Irish lived in slums, worked in sweatshops, they suffered; and if they painfully pulled themselves up, it is culturally explainable.

But the Negro was brought here forcibly in chains—the cultures of his homeland were crushed, wiped out. The slave was no longer allowed to identify with his past; he sang "Sometimes I Feel Like a Motherless Child"—he was a motherless child in a cruel new world. But the Jews had thousands of years of written culture and recorded oppression to relate to—it could not be stamped out, unless you gassed them by the millions, as Hitler did. You can't take the Negro "nightmare" and the fact that the Jewish culture was more intact, and then try to compare one kind of persecution with the other. I feel we're drifting into what could become a careless attack on the Jews. That's what some of the Muslims do. The positive things that Elijah Muhammad does for the dignity of his disciples, and what other black nationalist groups do for their followers—I can understand the appeal; I can understand why that attracts you. But at the same time you can't swallow the "all white men are white devils" theory, not quite.

BALDWIN: I'm not aware that I've ever been even vaguely tempted by the "white-devil" theory. I would certainly never teach it or allow it to be taught to any child of mine, or to anyone I cared about. But I'm trying to get to something else—

SCHULBERG: I think if there is any value in this conversation, this dialogue, in which we agree, I think, on immediate issues, it's to root out our differences. Are you, Jimmy Baldwin, disagreeing with me? Or are you the Negro saying good-bye, even to your white liberal or—since that has become a worn-out adjective—your white allies? It's an odd question—

BALDWIN: It's a very curious gamble.

SCHULBERG: —because there is so much that we agree on and yet there is this rankling difference. I am willing to say to you, to every citizen of this country—

BALDWIN: I am not a citizen of this country. Or I am not so considered by the people of this country.

SCHULBERG: Then we have to make them consider you a citizen, Jimmy. We have to make you one.

BALDWIN: But, baby—

SCHULBERG: I mean, either you go the Negro separatist route, like the Muslims, or you go the full-citizenship route. The former is more dramatic. It's an emotional answer to galling frustration. I really get the Elijah Muhammad message: The "full citizenship" thing is maddeningly slow, yes, and suspect—years and years overdue and still so damned far from genuine acceptance, the kind of acceptance where race prejudice is an archaic problem, like capital punishment for ten-year-old pickpockets. Not that we all have to be the same color; but that we finally accept each other's humanity—what's *inside* of us, not the superficial coloring of the epidermis. I'm ready for that *now*. I don't see any other way. But all this talk about the past—"I was here first"—frankly, Jimmy, I don't see how that helps to—

BALDWIN: Budd, what I am trying to get at when I talk about the past is not meant principally to refer to the past, but to the present. When I said, "I was here first," I wasn't trying to pass myself off as some kind of aristocrat. I was trying to suggest the depth and tenacity of the *antihuman* attitudes which have ruled in this country for so long and which have effectively prevented the Negro, for the most part, from acquiring or from using those modern skills which you say Europeans brought here with them.

It's these attitudes which have created so dangerous a depth of Negro bitterness, resentment and despair. My image of you getting off a boat on Friday and my working for you on Tuesday wasn't pulled out of the air. A Negro in this country is endlessly confronted with the spectacle of somebody getting off a boat, from Hungary, from France, from England or Switzerland, from Germany, from anywhere in Europe, who can't speak English when he arrives, who has certainly not, this time, brought from Europe skills more modern than those which should be at the disposal of the Negro here; and, yes, on Friday, he *does* get off a boat and on Tuesday, you, the Negro, are working for him and he tells you what to do. It takes him that long to become an American. Only that long. You, the Negro, have been here for four hundred years and you haven't made it yet—you're still expected to "wait"—but he's made it in a matter of hours. And he treats you like all other Americans do.

What more can any society do to make vivid how profoundly you are despised? And how is one supposed to react to this? I must say that I think the Negro patience or resilience or whatever—I don't know what the word would be—has been incredible, is a fantastic achievement. But, of course, there are Negroes who feel that this patience has been abject, is ignoble, and, frankly, I'm unwilling to dismiss their point of view. It's a point of view which would simply be taken for granted if we were talking about white men. Which throws a very curious light on that Judaeo-Christian ethic we have argued about from time to time. I'm forced to realize, after all, that the creators, the heirs, of this ethic have, very deliberately, with a ruthless single-mindedness, attempted to reduce me to something less than a man. And where you get confused, Budd, I think, and talk about my throwing in the towel with Elijah—although you know very well that that could never happen—is that, of course, out of motives of self-respect and self-preservation, I'm bound to question an ethic, or a way of life, or a system of reality which has nearly destroyed me and which obviously intends to destroy my children. How long am I expected passively to acquiesce in the mouthing of an ethic in which no one—at least no society, and certainly not this one—believes? One begins to feel despairing, one begins to feel foolish; and one begins to dig beneath the bequeathed realities in the hope of arriving at a new coherence and a new strength, in the hope, in fact, of being released from an incipient schizophrenia. But at that moment, the moment one begins to pull away in order to see, one is accused of thinking "black." But I don't really know what thinking "black" means—except that it seems to pose a threat to people who think, I suppose, "white."

SCHULBERG: Okay. You put it well. I agree with you that the Negro has been fantastically patient, resilient. I know it's heresy to what they call the "white power structure," but in Watts, from my firsthand experience, the young people are mentally healthier, have more pride, a stronger sense of identity since the revolt. Mayor Yorty and even the *McCone Report* called it "a riot of criminals and hoodlums," and refused to dignify it as rebellion. But the overwhelming majority in Watts called it The Revolt. It cost thirty-one Negro lives and three white lives—thirty-four human lives: a terrible price; but they broke through a wall; apathy turned inside out became hostility.

I have members of my writing group, talented writers, who are antiwhite. I think I understand them. As long as we have the Birchers and the Reagans and the Murphys who "think white" with a vengeance, some of my young poets in Malcolm X sweatshirts will draw their energy and inspiration from being antiwhite. If I can understand that, maybe I am able to "think black," too.

It all depends on what we mean by "thinking black." Maybe I don't think as black as Malcolm X, but I have a hunch I think a hell of a lot blacker than the Urban League or the brass of the NAACP. "Thinking black" sounds like an absolute, but it's a relative term—there are so many shades of black, so many shades of white. I agree I shouldn't try to put you in the same bag with Elijah, if you won't put me in another kind of bag—the ofay bag. Only the truth can set us both free, not over-simplifications like black *this* and white *that*. As a writer, you would have a hard time describing that—

BALDWIN: Well, perhaps. Of course, I'm a writer. But I must say this: This is the first time I've ever tried to talk about Jews at all; because I really *did* grow up in the Old Testament, because my father was a preacher. But when I was very young, in high school, my best friend was a Jew. And this was very strange. Because all Jews were in the Bible. And I had never seen a Jew my age, and I had been taught to hate them by my father, who considered himself a Jew. Now this is probably very interesting: who considered himself a Jew in terms of the children of Israel coming out of Egypt. We have that song, you know, "I Wish I Had Died in Egypt Land." That's all Old Testament.

SCHULBERG: So, you see, we're very close.

BALDWIN: That's why I'm here today, because we can talk together. But as a writer, I didn't dare try to create a Jew. I didn't dare. I never have; because I was at once too close and too far. I did not know what it meant—what it meant to the Jew to be a Jew. And since so much of my life had been involved with Jews, and so much of my life had been saved by people technically called Jewish whom I loved very much, I didn't dare malign, by my own inadequacy, a people who meant so much to me.

There is an irreducible fact, I think, which contributes to the Negro resentment of the Jew. I don't think it's rational—it's rooted, perhaps, in the expectations one victim has of another victim, and maybe it has something to do with the Old Testament and old songs; but, you know, whatever Jews came here, came here to get away from something. You know—in the main, not entirely; and in the spirit, perhaps, not at all. On the contrary, I suppose the journey here was an attempt to hold onto, to keep alive the Jewish heritage. But here they came, and in the main they prospered and did not appear to have any difficulty in adopting the racial mores of the country. And I suspect that the Negro resents this from the Jew far more than he resents it from anybody else. And, of course, I think it's likely that anyone whose history has been destroyed envies and resents those whose history remains intact. And the Jew is the only American, in any meaningful sense, to have brought his history across the ocean. Everybody else really left their history behind them, happy, I think, to be rid of it; though perhaps they have begun to miss it now. Anyway, I think that part of the resentment, or let us simply say the tension, comes from the fact that the Jew managed to survive the European pogroms and came here, to another country, and made no effort at all to understand that what had been happening to the Jew in Russia is happening to the Negro here; and that, furthermore, the Negro has no place to go.

SCHULBERG: I don't think that's true—that the Jews don't understand. I think a hell of a lot of them—a hell of a lot of us— do understand.

BALDWIN: Where can the Negro go? The Russian Jew came here. An American Negro cannot go back to Africa. He's an American. Not according to the Americans, perhaps, but according to him, and according to me!

SCHULBERG: According to me, too. I'm an American, and I say—

BALDWIN: But you are not. Neither of us is. We're both very American, but we do seem to be, as far as most of the country is concerned, marginal Americans, suspect, perhaps expendable—

SCHULBERG: Jimmy, look—you ask where can a Negro go—I feel there is a significant difference between the Jew caught in the Polish and Russian and German pogroms, who escaped to America, and the Negroes caught in the pogroms in the South or trapped in the black ghettos in the North. You might call those big-city riots in the North pogroms in reverse. The Jews of Europe had total state power against them; not just a hostile population, stupid peasants, narrow-minded burghers, but the full power of the national government of those countries against them. The Negroes here in the middle sixties, no matter how wronged, no matter how desperate their lives are now, how bleak their future may be—still have a lot of federal power on their side. They have civil rights laws and voting laws. Yes, we have white state juries automatically acquitting white murderers of Negro freedom fighters. But we also have federal courts finding white Southern officials guilty of contempt for not protecting civil rights marchers. You may laugh, but we even have Lyndon Johnson singing "We Shall Overcome" on national television. Of course the Negroes are still far, shamefully far, from "Freedom Now." But they are not as alone as the Jews were in Russia and Poland and Germany. I mean, the czar and Marshal Pilsudski and Hitler never sang the "Kol Nidre," at least in public. Here the Negroes have allies—if they want them. I know how hard it is for the hostile Negro in Watts to realize that, and maybe there aren't enough allies to satisfy alienated Negroes in the neglected ghettos. But I still think there is a difference between the Jew driven out of Russia or Poland and the Negro fighting for his life, his identity, in Watts, Cleveland, and Chicago.

Those Jewish victims of hate in northern Europe had no organizations they could turn to as the Negro has— a whole spectrum, from S.N.C.C. and C.O.R.E. to King's S.C.L.C., the N.A.A.C.P., not to mention all the contesting black nationalist groups. As the Jews went from Poland to America, the Negro can go from hopelessly white America to an America he is fighting to change and where a hell of a struggle is going on North and South.

A good example is Fannie Lou Hamer, the Mississippi sharecropper's wife who's been in the middle of the voter registration fight. I think the Fannie Lou Hamers are your answer to, Where can the Negro go? From no freedom to some freedom to, hopefully, full freedom is where the Negro can go in America.

I know he's not there yet—we're not there yet, not by several city blocks, like the blocks in Watts and the ghettos of Chicago—we're at the *some*-freedom second stage. I realize, if you have to qualify freedom, it's like saying, we've got a pretty good race horse—if only he had a fourth leg! I realize time is running out. Hope, for millions of young Negroes, for acceptance from the white man as fellow *men*, is running out fast. And I'm not saying, Be patient. I think the only way to galvanize what hope is left is to be impatient. But some hope is there. I know it's hard for the unemployed in Watts to see it, or the voteless in Mississippi and Alabama. You can't eat hope. You can't pay your rent with hope. But it's there. Maybe that's what our argument is about—is there any hope for the Negro in a white-majority society? Or, to put it another way, is there no place for the white who genuinely despises the color line, in the so-called Negro revolution?

BALDWIN: You're very persuasive. And very moving, too. Perhaps I've talked too much about "Where can the Negro go?"

It wasn't I who was planning to go anywhere. I wasn't thinking about my generation at all, in fact. Our children are being murdered. This has been very much on my mind, I didn't realize how much. And some of us have been trying—despairingly—to figure out what to do to save at least a remnant on that day when we are forced to realize that there is no hope for us here, no hope at all. As far as I am concerned, when my countrymen can set dogs on children and blow children up in Sunday school, the holocaust is not far off. And, more than that—if I'm to be honest—one can't but feel, no matter how deeply one distrusts the feeling, that the holocaust, the total leveling, salvation by fire, "no remission of sins save by the shedding of blood," may be the only hope.

Well. Let me quarrel, provisionally, anyway, with your principal assumption. You say that the Jews in Russia, Poland, etc., had the power of the state against them—a power which was often, if not always, reinforced by the Christian Church. Which raises the by-no-means-trivial question of the precise relation of this church to the Judaeo-Christian ethic you spoke of earlier. But the American Negro, here, you say, has the power of the state behind him, at least the federal power. This is a very attractive formulation and it would make me very happy to be able to accept it. But I am forced to question it. I am not sure that the implied contrast between the European states and America can be made so quickly; and it seems very clear to me that what we must here call the American state is of a ferocious complexity and is at war with itself. If the real power of the state is behind the Negro, then it is impossible to explain why the people feel free to victimize the Negro as they do. Power, after all, is power; and the very definition of power is that it controls action. It may indeed be true, and this is our hope, that the aspirations of the state are sympathetic to the Negro's claims; and it may again be true that the highest intelligence operative in the state recognizes their urgency. But I think it is also true that the structure of the state, and the habits and presumed self-interest of the citizens, constitute the mightiest of bulwarks against social change, particularly a social change so radical and so deep. This is why I am less impressed than you are by the Civil Rights Act and the Voting Rights Act—it is my impression that these rights were guaranteed me by the Constitution over a hundred years ago.

Fannie Lou Hamer impresses me very much, indeed. I know her a little, and I don't think anyone can possibly admire her more than I. But she doesn't own General Motors or General Electric, nor does she yet have any relevant existence for them. Her power is entirely moral. But this is not a power which her countrymen, in the main or at this moment, feel themselves free to respect. They consider that they have, materially, too much to lose. We have not discussed the economic structure of the American state in relation to the American Negro, but it is very clear that the problem of his presence can scarcely begin to be resolved without a radical alteration of that structure. Of course, these present days, to suggest that social problems can have economic ramifications, or that the Negro's present and continuing plight is due, to an incalculable degree, to the fact that he began his life in the West as a source of cheap labor, is to leave oneself open to the charge of communism (which has become, simply, a know-nothing term). But facts are facts, and they outlast labels.

Finally, however, I certainly agree with you and Mrs. Hamer—I must. The question, for me, isn't whether or not there's any hope for a Negro in a white-majority society; the question is whether or not the society is able to free itself of these obsolete terms and become, in effect, and joyously, color-blind. If the society can't do this, then there's no hope for anybody in it—which answers, it seems to me, your last question concerning the role of white liberals. I've had very hard things to say about liberals, but I'm bound to say that I was never thinking of you or people like you. I was thinking of that vast army of people whose convictions are mere quotations and whose goodwill costs them nothing, who are always presuming to lecture the Negro on his table manners and who are hurt, to the point of vindictiveness, whenever their utterly useless goodwill is questioned. I think you owe it to me, as my friend, to fight me, to let me get away with nothing, to force me to be clear, to force me to be honest, to allow me to take no refuge in rage or in despair, or in the peculiar form of complacency sometimes known as Negro militancy. And, of course, I owe you the same. This means that we're certainly going to hurt each other's feelings from time to time. But that's one of the ways in which people learn from each other. And we're tough.

SCHULBERG: Okay, Jimmy, I've been listening to you, carefully; and since I agree with so much of what you say, it may be that to make my point about the difference between the predicament of the Jew in czarist Russia and the predicament of the Negro in late–twentieth-century America I have overstated or oversimplified my argument. "A ferocious complexity" is a phrase I accept for the conditions of our present-day society. That is a much more accurate description of our common dilemma than to say that federal power is on the side of the Negro or that the Negro has no place to go and that all hope is gone. I don't want to be trapped into saying that because Johnson shrewdly adopts the slogan "We Shall Overcome" or pushes new voting laws through Congress, all is sweetness and light and the American dream has at last come true. Every hour I spend in Watts—and I have logged hundreds of hours there with my writers' class; I know—

149

I see with my own eyes that the American dream is an ugly nightmare along what we call Charcoal Alley Number One. I still don't know whether we have the guts, the imagination, the generosity, the empathy—yes, and the sense of self-preservation—to break through and cure that nightmare.

But I wonder if we can cure it by pitting black against white as the Muslims have been preaching and the white segregationists keep trying to do. And I'm not talking only of the Ku Kluxers but the real estate boards who draw a color line across our cities. I'm talking about the people who voted for Proposition 14, a know-nothing prejudiced proposition to repeal a law favoring racial justice in the real estate field. I am against white nationalists and black nationalists, but I think I have more sympathy for the latter, because they are the inevitable outgrowth of the former. They are the children of despair and neglect and centuries of racial hatred. I think the Negro revolution needs as its ally the white democratic revolution. I think I understand the call for black power, but I don't think ten percent of the population—make that five percent, because the other five percent are probably Uncle Toms—can ever win its battle without the enlightened whites who are just as much against the *status quo*, the power structure, as are the militant Negroes.

I think the militant Negro movement is a welcome test of our sincerity—it cuts through our hypocrisy and it may even save us from our most dangerous enemy within, complacency. I think our society could eventually fall apart from smugness and complacency and that it's toughened by criticism. I think we should stop kidding ourselves. Look at our affluent Los Angeles, with Watts festering in unemployment and frustration—hell, it's one city, *divisible*, with liberty and justice for *some*. As long as we have a mayor and a police department whose attitude toward the ghetto is almost identical to the attitude of the Nazis toward the Warsaw ghetto, what looks like lawlessness—criminality—to the outside is more like self-defense and self-determination to the inside. That may be dangerous talk, but societies can be strengthened and even saved by dangerous talk and tough criticism. Sure, it makes a lot of people mad, but that's good.

I was talking publicly against Proposition 14. I took along your book *The Fire Next Time*, and I read aloud from it. I closed my talk with it. I passed on to public audiences in southern California the warning that if they didn't bestir themselves in behalf of Negro *social* rights—not just civil rights but what I call *soul* rights, full acceptance of Negroes into all the streams of our national life—they would face the fire next time. To the shame of California, Proposition 14 passed, about two to one, even with Governor Brown and the state administration trying to defeat it. And, sure enough, the fires lit up the skies in Los Angeles in August 1965. And next time, unless much more is done than is being done, the Negroes may sweep into the white communities that deny them jobs and transportation and decent schools and hospitals and pride.

So I agree with ninety percent or maybe ninety-five percent of what you say. But where I disagree, where I want to pull you over to my side and away from what seems to me a tendency to the Negro-isolationist side, is to urge you, beg you, to keep on thinking in terms of your own happy phrase, "joyously color-blind"—against falling into the danger of looking at the world as if it is inevitably, hopelessly, bloodedly divided between black and white. I know it may seem more realistic to think that way, to think negatively and pessimistically that the white man had his chance and goofed—irretrievably goofed. But that leaves out the millions of whites who keep fighting against job discrimination, housing and school discrimination, *facto* and *de facto*, and the whites who have been dying and hurting with their Negro friends in Selma, in Mississipppi, in Chicago. If those are what the Klan and the hoodlums of Cicero call "white niggers," then I hope the "white niggers" have the "white bastards" outnumbered in America.

BALDWIN: No, Budd—

SCHULBERG: I am appealing as man to man, writer to writer, not for anybody to say to me—as Dick Gregory said when I said, "I agree with you"—"We don't need you white liberals to agree with us." I notice he's a little more careful when he gets on TV and plays coy, but that's what he said to me: "We don't need you white liberals to agree with us." Maybe that is what this dialogue is finally about. There are millions, scores of millions of bigoted whites. Does Dick Gregory really want to join us in fighting them? Or does he want to lump us all together as "white devils" à la Elijah Muhammad? That's what I'm calling on you for, as an influential American writer—to make the choice.

BALDWIN: Yes, I see. I don't know what happened between you and Dick, so I won't talk about that. Dick's a friend of mine. But I must say, if I'm to be honest, that I have no difficulty at all in understanding how even an almost totally, or even absolutely totally, unchauvinistic Negro can yet be driven, in a given hour, on a given day, to saying, and saying with venom, "You whites!" He may, at the next moment, embrace you and apologize—I've been there, and I know. But Budd, we live with pain and rage—with pain and rage. And it's got to come out— for your health as a white man, for my health as a black man. That's the only way we'll ever be free. We *are* attempting, after all, to break a very, very long silence.

And we've always known that what lived in this silence was hideous and full of danger; we have to grow—

SCHULBERG: Grow from there. I am not "you white" and you and Gregory are not "you blacks." Are we to be a society of people—all kinds of people—or not? Not a "Great Society" the way LBJ keeps cheerleading us on. That's the post-postgraduate course. Have we matriculated as a *society*?

BALDWIN: That's the dilemma, the American problem. At the moment we have no society at all. Look at what happened with Proposition 14, for example. You mentioned it earlier. I was in California at the time, you remember. Well, of course, out there in that American El Dorado, that unmitigated horror of a place, of course, good, clean, empty American clowns like Reagan and Murphy would be very popular. Ain't a damn thing paid for out there; they're all living in terror of the poorhouse. American backbone! If your Cadillac and your swimming pool aren't paid for and you know you can't go any farther West—the next stop is Tokyo, God help us, which is East—then, of course, any black boy or Mexican coming anywhere *near* your monstrously mortgaged joint, which is *all you have*, is an intolerable threat. And it's on this level the country lives, *that's* our society. Then, when the riots come, they tremble for their unpaid-for swimming pools and ask, "What does the Negro want?" and all *that* bullshit, and ask the Negro to respect the law. *What* law? The law which has just robbed him of any possibility of moving out of the ghetto and beats him and brutalizes him, in order to protect their swimming pools? Those riots are always blamed on Negroes, but they're not the Negro's fault. Negro "looters"—who's looting whom, I'd like to know—

SCHULBERG: Wait a minute, Jimmy, this is something I feel I can talk about firsthand. I mean I swim in those swimming pools and I also have sweated out a lot of time on East 103rd Street in the heart of Watts, on murderously hot days when the older unemployed wander through the vacant lots and the restless, unemployed kids cluster on street corners and dream of the momentary manhood they enjoyed—it's crazy, but maybe enjoyed *is* the word—under the guns of the National Guard. In a piece I wrote about it for the *Los Angeles Times*—a piece that provoked a hundred love letters and a score of hate letters—I wrote that there are candles flickering in the darkness of Watts but that the funk is deep; and I said that it was not Negro funk but white funk, white know-nothingism; and I said that, to crib from *Marat*, unless we pick ourselves up by the hair, turn ourselves inside out and reexamine our sick city—our sick society—with new eyes, we will be inviting riots which are actually deeply rooted rebellions. That piece I wrote was put up on the bulletin board of the Westminster Neighborhood Center and the Watts Happening Coffee House. In fact, they're still up there; and I honestly believe if we can't live up to what I wrote—and Jimmy, I know how big an *if* that is—if we can't match our performance to our promises, if we can't live up to our noble words from the Declaration of Independence to the Emancipation Proclamation to the new voting laws, this could be the beginning of our decline and fall, even deserves to be. And I'll help you write the epitaph!

Our society will die on the rack of injustice to Negroes if we don't solve it. We're only arguing now about whether we're going to have a Negro explosion against the "white devils" or a common effort of Negroes and whites to solve it. I don't want to sound melodramatic, but we just may be facing the democratic last stand. And I can only pray—not to God but to Sandburg's *The People, Yes*—that somehow we emerge from this battle in better shape than either Custer or the Sioux.

BALDWIN: In this society, more than any other I can think of, with the exception of the Third Reich, one needs precisely an affirmation of the possibility of human life. And what I am trying to say when I say it doesn't matter what you think or what I think—I obviously don't mean that literally—is that what happens to us is less important than what happens to our children, all our children. We can take care of ourselves, more or less. In my case, certainly, it's mainly less, but that's all right. I'm not profoundly concerned about your being a Jew or my being a Negro. We can take these facts as given. But our being American—that's something else, which is yet to be achieved. Or defined.

All that jazz, *Negro, Jewish*—it's pure bullshit. These terms are used to hide from every one of us, including, at this moment, you and me, the *real* disaster in this country—the failure of morality that is produced by a failure of identity.

SCHULBERG: Jimmy, if I follow you, when you speak about a failure of identity, I think you're reaching for something I was hoping we could get around to—I mean Negritude and the positive aspects of black nationalism and the new call for black power, which doesn't seem to panic me as much as it may some other people. It may not necessarily mean the Mau Mau screaming for "white blood" in frightened and prejudiced suburbia; it may simply be the search for self-esteem, self-respect, dignity, and pride, and the Negro's fair share of the total power. After all, the Irish were once awfully low on the racist totem pole. There used to be signs that read NO IRISH ALLOWED, but in New York they built up a full head of steam of Irish power through Tammany Hall. "Black power" is an emotional phrase that represents an emotional movement that is still groping for its own definition. It may even be that through black power and a period of frus-

155

tration, confusion, and rejection on the part of the would-be white ally, we meet together again on a higher plane of integration.

Now if I say I can see positive aspects to black nationalism, in which the black man goes searching back to his African roots in order to find out who he is—an identity which you say the Jew brought with him intact from Europe but which has been denied the Afro-American—and if I say that I can understand the appeal of black power to young black people who have felt their identity crushed and denied in a world of white power— if I can see how qualities of leadership and self-respect can be developed under the new flag of black power even if the honest feelings of sympathetic whites are hurt or even trampled in the process—then it may seem as if I am arguing not only with you but with myself, that I am arguing for an interracial struggle against the persistent, virulent bigotry, and at the same time being too permissive toward the recent phenomenon called, but not yet clearly understood as, black power. I am inclined to say, if that be ambivalence, make the most of it. I want to see an America that lives up to its promises, not its lies and hypocrisies. I want, for my own preservation as well as yours, an America joyously color-blind. But it may be that the new generation of Negroes, who even reject the term "Negro" and follow the charismatic Malcolm X in calling themselves black men or Afro-Americans, must find themselves through their own religions, societies, organizations, as the Jews and the Irish and the other minorities did, in order to cope with white America from a stronger position. That is what I mean by the possibility of meeting together on a higher plane of integration.

BALDWIN: For many years, aided by what can only be described, alas, as a handful of whites, who are looked on with great suspicion and hostility by the majority of whites, Negroes have been attempting to awaken the sleeping conscience of this unhappy nation. They have not succeeded. When a movement realizes that its tactics have failed, it is forced to evolve new tactics. As for racism in reverse, the hatred and bitterness to which this phrase has reference is felt most deeply by those who consider themselves helpless, who see no way of changing their condition. Also, it is worth pointing out, this racism in reverse, unlike the other, is absolutely impotent, and does not bother white people at all—until, of course, the ghetto explodes and they once again uneasily wonder, *What does the Negro want?* But when people have a sense that they *can* change their situation, and are really trying to do so, the need for hatred, which is always, after all, a more or less disguised self-hatred, is very sharply reduced.

The panic is really caused by the fact that, as some of us have always known, a change in the Negro situation implies a radical change in the country. It is not a matter of placing a few well-scrubbed darkies in a few strategically located windows. It is not a matter of so many black clerks or so many black cops. It is not a matter of supplying sprinklers for the ghetto streets. It is a matter of altering all our institutions in the direction of a greater freedom, recognizing that the Negro is an integral part of this nation, has also paid for it with his blood, and is here to stay. He can't go back to wherever he came from any more than anyone else can. And this demands— which is as difficult as it is obvious—that we begin to look at ourselves in another way; as part of the human race, in fact; and evolve a new ethic, an ethic which will transcend, for example, the profit motive which has made chaos of our cities and made bewildered rebels or demoralized monsters of our children.

The Negro assault impresses itself on the American

mind as anarchy: whereas, in fact, anarchy lies on the road one takes in flight from this assault. For let us also face the fact that the Negro's experience, his untapped vitality—and I think that you can bear witness to this—is absolutely indispensable for this transformation and, in many ways, in many areas, will be the only hope of this transformation. If we can release ourselves from the deeply held concept of a master race, we will no longer need an inferior one. Without an inferior race, racism in reverse cannot exist. But those people who are already weeping about racism in reverse may very well help create the evil they decry. The Negro simply wants to be dealt with as another human being. No more. And no less.

If we are not able to accept this, if we are not able to change, then the lives we lead in America will become so unbearable that we will surrender any remote attempt to become responsible for our lives, and at that moment anarchy and tyranny have come. We really must conquer our tremendous delusion that what has happened to others cannot happen to us. This presupposes that Americans are not capable of the evil which others have done. But there are witnesses, above and below the ground, whose testimony denies this.

We are trapped in massive moral contradiction. We will perish if we cannot resolve it. I cannot believe that we are fighting in Vietnam for freedom, for example. There are many, many reasons that I find myself unable to believe this, but, to get down to the nitty-gritty, I don't believe it because freedom, it seems to me, is precisely what Americans fear most. It is preposterous, at least, to suppose that a nation which cannot give *me* free elections, and which has not yet learned to live with me, even though we speak the same language, live in the same cities, read the same books, and even though I am toilet-trained and know how to use a shower, is, by some miracle of transcendence, able to free millions of exotic peasants. And one of the things that has happened, and which will continue to happen, to the real horror of the American government and the anger of the American people, is that many Negroes, especially the young, are aware of this and consider the struggle they are waging in America to be analogous to, indissoluble from, the struggle of the dispossessed all over the world. Even if the economy had the wherewithal—which it doesn't— to buy the American Negro, multitudes of Negroes would refuse the bargain. A prominent Negro is reported as having said that he wanted a U.S. victory in Vietnam because otherwise the U.S. would be weakened, and he wanted to be part of a great nation. Well, in this hard world, one must make *choices*, and I prefer to be part of a *just* nation.

SCHULBERG: Jimmy, the hour is late, both literally and figuratively. I agree that you and I, as abstractions, as symbols, either become responsible for this country or we let it go by default. And we cannot build an honest definition of America until we accept the "ferocious complexity" as its foundation. But once we accept this precondition, "ferocious complexity," can you still accuse all Americans of fearing freedom? That's much too sweeping—I can't agree. But tell me that "too many Americans fear freedom" and I would give you my ferociously complex assent. A revolution that we began in the eighteenth century, we seem too selfish, too corrupted, or too timid to fight through to its logical conclusion.

BALDWIN: If your "logical conclusion" includes the slogan "black power." I hate to think what those words do to the wholesome, simple, pious, go-getting American family who have always been terrified of Negroes anyway. But why should the word "power" when coupled with the word "black" strike such panic in the American breast? No one seems to be frightened of the white power which, after all, rules the country and is responsible for a corruption as stunning in its extent as it is deadly in its effects, which has already murdered millions of Negroes and which, at this very moment, hangs like the most menacing of clouds over the lives of all black men and women and all black boys and girls.

SCHULBERG: Jimmy, if we fail to turn ourselves inside out, if we are unable to live with and not merely wax rhetorical about liberty and justice for all, if we fail to resolve our massive contradictions, then I agree with you that we could go under. But before we go our fatal, separate ways, I think we must try once and for all the unprecedented social experiment of living together. The clock is ticking.

17

At the University of
California at Berkeley in 1979.

18

With Toni Morrison.

19

20

With Verta Mae Grosvenor (*far right*) and artist Romare Bearden.

James Baldwin (*above*)
and David Baldwin.

With Chinua Achebe,
(*left*).

26

*F*rom the left: Taj MaHal, Carmen DeLavallade, Gordon Parks, Sidney Poitier, James Baldwin, Paul Robeson, Jr.

27

With J. Saunders Redding, critic.

28

Left to right: T. J. Baldwin (a nephew), James Baldwin, and his mother viewing his sister Paula's fashion show.

29

With Quincy Troupe (*at Baldwin's immediate left*) and friends at a party in St. Louis in 1985.

AN INTERVIEW WITH JOSEPHINE BAKER AND JAMES BALDWIN (1973)

▪ by Henry Louis Gates, Jr. ▪

Henry Louis Gates, Jr., is W. E. B. DuBois Professor of Literature at Cornell University. He is the author of Figures in Black: Words, Signs, and the Racial Self *(Oxford, 1987); the editor of* The Slave's Narrative *and* In the House of Osubgo: Critical Essays on Wole Soyinka *(both by Oxford); the recipient of a prestigious MacArthur Foundation grant; the General Editor of the* Norton Anthology of Afro-American Literature; *and editor of Oxford's 30-volume series* The Schomburg Library of Nineteenth-Century Black Women Writers. *His most recent book is* The Signifying Monkey *(Oxford, 1988).*

S o many questions that I should have asked that night, but did not! I was so captivated by the moment: under the widest star-filled evening sky that I can remember, in the backyard of Baldwin's villa at St. Paul, drunk on conversation, burgundy, and a peasant stew, drunk on the fact that James Baldwin and Josephine Baker were seated on my right and left. It was my twenty-second summer; a sublime awe, later that evening, led me to tears.

Those few days in the south of France probably had more to do with my subsequent career as a literary critic than any other single event. At the time, I was a correspondent at the London bureau of *Time* magazine, a training that is, probably, largely responsible for the quantity of my later critical writing, and for its anecdotal opening paragraphs. I had just graduated from Yale College in June, as a Scholar of the House in History. *Time,* to even my great surprise, had hired me to work as a correspondent during the six-month collective vacations at Cambridge University. I figured that I would "read" philosophy or literature at Cambridge, take the M.A. degree, then join permanently the staff at *Time*.

So, I sailed to Southampton from New York on the *France* in June 1973. After a week of pure fright and anxiety—after all, what *does* a *Time* correspondent *do*, and *how?*—I decided to go for my fantasy. I proposed doing a story on "Black Expatriates," perhaps every young Afro-American would-be-intellectual's dream. To my astonishment, the story suggestion was approved. So, off we (Sharon Adams, to whom I am married, and I) went by boat, train, and automobile to Europe, in search of blackness and black people.

In the Paris bureau of *Time*—Paris was the only logical point of departure, after all—I dialed Jo Baker's phone number. (*Time* can get to virtually *anyone*.) She answered her own phone! Stumbling around, interrupting my tortured speech with loads of "uh's" and "um's," I asked her if she would allow me to interview her. On one condition, she responded: "Bring Jimmy Baldwin with you to Monte Carlo." Not missing a beat, I promised that I would bring him with me.

Baldwin agreed to see me, after I had begged one of his companions and told him that I was heading south anyway to see Jo Baker. Cecil Brown, the companion told me, was living there as well, so maybe I could interview him as well? Cecil Brown, I thought. Def-i-nite-ly! (*Jive-ass Nigger* had been a cult classic among us younger nationalists in the early seventies.) So, off we went.

Imagine sitting on a train, from Paris to Nice, on the hottest night of August 1973, wondering how I could drag Baldwin from St. Paul to Monte Carlo, and scared to death of Baldwin in the first place. It was a thoroughly Maalox evening; to top everything else, our train broke down in a tunnel. We must have lost twenty pounds in that tunnel. Finally, just after dawn, we arrived at Nice, rented a car, then drove the short distance to St. Paul.

After the best midday meal that I had ever eaten, before or since, I trekked with great trepidation over to Baldwin's "house." "When I grow up . . . ," I remember thinking as I walked through the gate. I won't bore you with details; suffice it to say that if you ever get the chance to have dinner with Jimmy Baldwin at his house at St. Paul, then *do* it. "Maybe *I* could write *Notes of a Native Son* if I lived here," I thought.

I am about to confess something that literary critics should not confess: James Baldwin *was* literature for me, especially the essay. No doubt like everyone who is reading these pages, I started reading "black books" avidly, voraciously, at the age of thirteen or fourteen. I read *everything* written by black authors that could be ordered from Red Bowl's paper store in Piedmont, West Virginia. Le Roi Jones's *Home* and *Blues People*, Malcolm's *Autobiography*, and *Invisible Man* moved me beyond words—beyond my own experience, which is even a further piece, I would suppose. But nothing could surpass my love for the Complete Works of James Baldwin. In fact, I have never before written about Baldwin just because I cannot read his words outside of an extremely personal nexus of adolescent sensations and emotions. "Poignancy" only begins to describe those feelings. I learned to love written literature, of any sort, through the language of James Baldwin.

When Baldwin came into the garden to be interviewed, I was so excited that I could not blink back the tears. That probably explains why he suggested that we begin with wine. Well into that first (of several) bottles, I confessed to him my promise to Jo Baker. Not missing a beat, he told me to bring Jo *here*. Did he think that she would drive back from Monte Carlo with me? Just tell her that dinner is served at nine.

And she did, after a warm and loving lunch with her family (we met *eleven* of the legendary twelve children), at her favorite restaurant overlooking Cape Martin. She had recently returned from a pilgrimage to Israel, and was looking foward to her return to the stage, her marvelous comeback. She was tall, as gracious and as warm as she was elegant, sensuous at sixty-five. Pablo this; Robeson that; Salvador so and so: she had been friends with the Western tradition, and its modernists. Everywhere we drove, people waved from the sidewalks or ran over to the car. She was so very *thoughtful*, so intellectual, and so learned of the sort of experience that, perhaps, takes six decades or so to ferment. I cannot drink a glass of Cantenac Brown without recreating her in its bouquet.

How did all of this lead to my present career? *Time* would not print the story, because, they said, "Baldwin is passé, and Baker a memory of the thirties and forties." . . . When I went "up" to Cambridge from *Time* and London in October 1973, I was so angered by the idiocy of that decision that I threw myself into the B.A. curriculum for English Language and Literature. A year later, I was admitted into the Ph.D. program, and four years later, I was awarded my degree.

That evening was the very last time that my two heroes saw each other, and the last time that Jo Baker would be interviewed at her home. She would die, on the stage, too soon thereafter. One day I hope to be forced to write about my other hero, James Baldwin.

GATES: Mrs. Baker, why did you leave the United States?

BAKER: I left in 1924, but the roots extend long before that. One of the first things I remember was the East St. Louis race riots (1906). I was hanging on to my mother's skirts, I was so little. All the sky was red with people's houses burning. On the bridge, there were people running with their tongues cut out. There was a woman who'd been pregnant with her insides cut out. That was the beginning of my feeling.

One day I realized I was living in a country where I was afraid to be black. It was only a country for white people, not black, so I left. I had been suffocating in the United States. I can't live anywhere that I can't breathe freedom. I must be free. Haven't I that right? I was created free. No chains did I wear when I came here. A lot of us left, not because we wanted to leave, but because we couldn't stand it anymore. Branded, banded, cut off. Canada Lee, Dr. DuBois, Paul Robeson, Marcus Garvey—all of us, forced to leave.

GATES: Did the French people offer you a respite from race prejudice?

BAKER: The French adopted me immediately. They all went to the beaches to get dark like Josephine Baker. They had a contest to see who could be the darkest, like Josephine Baker, they said. The French got sick, trying to get black—*café au lait*—you weren't anything unless you were *café au lait*.

I felt liberated in Paris. People didn't stare at me. But when I heard an American accent in the streets of Paris, I became afraid. I would tremble in my stomach. I was afraid they'd humiliate me.

I was afraid to go into prominent restaurants in Paris. Once, I dined in a certain restaurant with friends. An American lady looked at our table and called the waiter. "Tell her to get out," the lady said. "In my country, she is belonging only in the kitchen." The French management asked the American lady to leave. To tell the truth, I was afraid of not being wanted.

GATES: Mr. Baldwin, when did you leave the United States and for what reasons?

BALDWIN: It was November 1948, Armistice Day as a matter of fact. I left because I was a writer. I had discovered writing and I had a family to save. I had only one weapon to save them, my writing. And I couldn't write in the United States.

GATES: But why did you flee to France?

BALDWIN: I had to go somewhere where I could learn that it was possible for me to thrive as a writer. The French, you see, didn't see me; on the other hand, they watched me. Some people took care of me. Else I would have died. But the French left me alone.

GATES: Was it important for you to be left alone?

BALDWIN: The only thing standing between my writing had to be me: was I, it was me—I had to see that. Because the French left me alone I was freed of crutches, the crutches of race. That's a scary thing.

GATES: Did you find any basic differences between Americans and Europeans, since you said that you could at least be left alone in Paris?

BALDWIN: There was a difference, but now the difference is a superficial one. When I first came to Paris, it was poor—everybody was broke. Now, Europe thinks it has something again, that it has regained the material things it lost. So Europeans are becoming Americans. The irony, of course, is that Europe began the trend even before America was formed. The price of becoming "American" is beating the hell out of everybody else.

GATES: Mrs. Baker, you said you felt "liberated" in France. Did the freedom you found here in France sour you toward the United States?

BAKER: I love the country within which I was born. These people are my people. I don't care what color they are—we are all Americans. We must have the application to stand up again.

Once I fought against the discriminatory laws in America but America was strong then. Now, she is weak. I only want to extend my fingers to pull it out of the quicksand, because that's where it is. I have all the hope in the world, though. The storm will come; we can't stop it. But that's all right. America will still be—but it will be the America it was intended to be. We were a small train on the track. We fell off. We'll get on again.

GATES: Where do you think the United States is heading, with distrust in government so apparent, with Watergate attracting worldwide attention?

BAKER: America was the promised land. I just want to give them my spirit; they've lost the path. That makes me suffer. I was so unhappy in the United States; I saw my brothers and sisters so afraid. The problem is deep—it has long roots. It is basic. The soil must be purified, not only must the root be pruned. It makes me unhappy to think that— I wouldn't be human if I weren't made unhappy by that. Needlessly, people will suffer. They need someone who can give them more than money. Someone to offer his hand, not just his money.

GATES: Mr. Baldwin, do you think that Watergate is a new, a significant departure in American history, or do you think it is the logical extension of policies begun long before Nixon, before this century even?

BALDWIN: Simply stated, Watergate was a bunch of incompetent hoods who got caught in the White House in the name of law and order.

GATES: Do you think the public hearings, indictments, and possible convictions could purge America, could allow it to change those things which you do not like about it?

BALDWIN: America is my country. Not only am I fond of it, I love it. America would change itself if it could, if that change didn't hurt, but people rarely change. Take the German people, for example. The German experiment during the war was catastrophic. It was a horror not to be believed. But they haven't changed: the German nation is basically the same today as it was before the war.

In a different sense, it is easy to be a rebel at age eighteen; it is harder to be one at age twenty-five. A nation may change when it realizes it has to. But people don't give up things. They have things taken away from them. One does not give up a lover; you lose her.

GATES: What do you see as the significance of Vietnam to America?

BAKER: I won't criticize America today. She is weak. I said all this years ago. It all came true. But it is never too late. It can be saved, but we Americans are so proud—false dignity, though. It's nothing to be ashamed about to acknowledge

167

our mistakes; Vietnam was a mistake. All that money for no progress, that turned the whole world against America.

But actually, My Lai happened first with the Indians. We brought on our own enemies—nobody, no matter how powerful, needs enemies.

GATES: Did you ever reget that you had left the United States, or did you ever feel guilty, particularly during the civil rights era, for not being there to participate?

BAKER: Some of my own people called me an Uncle Tom; they said I was more French than the French. I've thought often about your question, about running away from the problem. At first, I wondered if it was cowardice, wondered whether I should have stayed to fight. But I couldn't have done anything. I would have been thwarted in ways in which I was free in France. I probably would have been killed.

But really, I belong to the world now. You know, America represented that: people coming from all over to make a nation. But America has forgotten that. I love all people at the same time. Our country is people of all countries. How else could there have been an America? And they made a beautiful nation. Each one depositing a little of his own beauty.

It's a sad thing to leave your country. How very often I've felt like the Wandering Jew with my twelve children on my arms. I've been able to bear it, though. It might be a mistake to love my country when my brothers are humiliated, where they kill each other, but I do love it. We are a wealthy people, a cultivated people. I wish people there would love. They can't go on like that. There's going to be a horrible storm. It's going to be a disaster. They'll torture each other through hate. It's ironic: people ran from slavery in Europe to find freedom in America and now . . .

GATES: Why don't you return to live in America now; aren't things a lot better for blacks?

BAKER: I don't think I could help America. I want to be useful, when I can help. America is desperate. In New York last year, I regretted for the first time not being young again. Young Americans need understanding and love. Children don't want to hear words; they want to see examples, not words—not blah, blah, blah—profound love, without malice, without hate.

GATES: When did you eventually return to the United States and why?

BAKER: It was in 1963. I kept reading about the "March on Washington," about preparations for the march. I so much wanted to attend. But I was afraid they wouldn't let me.

You see, for years I was not allowed to enter the United States. They said I was a Communist, during President Eisenhower's administration. They would make a black soldier—to humiliate me—they would make a black soldier lead me from a plane to a private room. It was so terrible, so painful. But I survived.

Then, in 1963, we applied to President Kennedy for permission to go to the March on Washington. He issued me a permanent visa. I wore the uniform I went through the war with, with all its medals. Thank God for John Kennedy for helping me get into America.

They had humiliated me so much; but still, I love them as if nothing happened. They didn't know what they were doing—digging their own grave through their hate. Then came Vietnam.

GATES: So you were actually forbidden to return to the United States between 1924 and 1963?

BAKER: Yes. They said I was a Communist because I dared love— thrown out for preferring freedom to riches, feelings to gold. I am not to be sold; no one can buy me. I lost America; I had nothing in my pockets, but I had my soul. I was so rich. For all this, they called me a Communist. America drives some of its most sensitive people away. Take Jimmy Baldwin: he had to leave the States to say what he felt.

GATES: And what were your first impressions of life in "exile"?

BALDWIN: I was no longer a captive nigger. I was the exotic attraction of the beast no longer in the cage. People paid attention. Of course you must realize that I am remembering the impression years later.

GATES: Did life abroad give you any particular insight into American society?

BALDWIN: I realized that the truth of American history was not and had never been in the White House. The truth is what had happened to black people, since slavery.

GATES: What do you think characterized Europeans to make them more ready to accept you at a time when you felt uncomfortable living in America?

BAKER: America has only been around for less than four hundred years; that's not a long time, really. Apparently it takes more than that to realize that a human being is a human being. Europeans are more basic. They see colors of the skin as colors of nature, like the flowers, for example.

GATES: Did you find any difference between the manner in which French men and women viewed you as a black man?

BALDWIN: That's a very important question. Before the Algerian war, and that's crucial in this, the black man did not exist in the French imagination; neither did the Algerian. After Dien Bien Phu, and after the "Civil War," as the French persist in calling it, there began to be a discernible difference between the way women and police had treated you before and after the war.

GATES: But were black Americans treated like Algerians were during their quest for independence?

BALDWIN: Of course I was removed, but you became a personal threat as a black American. You were a threat because you were visible. The French became conscious of your visibility because of the Algerians. You see, the French did not and don't know what a black man is. They'd like to put the blacks against the Algerians, to divide and rule, but the Arabs and black Americans were both slaves, one group was the slaves in Europe, the other back in America.

GATES: But surely you must believe that social change can come, that great men can effect change?

BALDWIN: Change does come, but not when or in the ways we want it to come. George Jackson, Malcolm X—now people all over the world were changed by them. Because they told the secret; now, the secret was out.

GATES: And the secret?

BALDWIN: Put it this way. In 1968, along with Lord Caradon (British delegate to the United Nations then), I addressed an assembly of the World Council of Churches in Switzerland on "White racism or world community?" When Lord Caradon was asked why the West couldn't break relations with South Africa, he brought out charts and figures that showed that the West would be bankrupt if they did that: the prosperity of the West is standing on the back of the South African miner. When he stands up, the whole thing will be over.

GATES: How do you assess the results of the war in Vietnam on the American people?

BALDWIN: Americans are terrified. For the first time they know that they are capable of genocide. History is built on genocide. But they can't face it. And it doesn't make any difference what Americans think that they think—they are terrified.

171

GATES: From your vantage point, where do you think not only America but Western civilization is heading?

BALDWIN: The old survivals of my generation will be wiped out. Western civilization is heading for an apocalypse.

"GO THE WAY YOUR BLOOD BEATS":
An Interview with James Baldwin
(1984)

▪ by Richard Goldstein ▪

Richard Goldstein is a senior editor of The Village
Voice *and the author of a forthcoming collection
of journalism from the 1960s.*

In the early 1980s I read a long interview with James Baldwin in
The New York Times Book Review, which didn't include a whisper
about its subject's sexuality. Since I belong to the generation of gay
men for whom Baldwin's fiction was an early vector of self-discovery,
I decided to broach the subject for myself. So I tracked Baldwin down
and badgered him with politics and personal charm until he agreed
to meet me at the Riviera Café in the Village, an old hangout for
him. When I arrived, Baldwin was sitting at an outside table, watching
the exotica with that faintly distracted look Europeans cultivate. I
proceeded to "orient" him for the interview that would follow, only
to discover that he knew very little about the state of American gay
life today: What's a "clone," he wanted to know, and how is AIDS
transmitted? What transpired over the next few days was one of the
most powerful experiences of my professional life—an insight into the

paradoxical nature of gay culture from a man who traced much of his acuity and pain to the nexus of racism and homophobia. But what I remember most about that afternoon is the sight of Baldwin, gnomelike and far from serene, surrounded by passersby who recognize him, and just wanted to say, as I did, how full of him our lives will always be.

GOLDSTEIN: Do you feel like a stranger in gay America?

BALDWIN: Well, first of all I feel like a stranger in America from almost every conceivable angle except, oddly enough, as a black person. The word "gay" has always rubbed me the wrong way. I never understood exactly what is meant by it. I don't want to sound distant or patronizing because I don't really feel that. I simply feel it's a world that has very little to do with me, with where I did my growing up. I was never at home in it. Even in my early years in the Village, what I saw of that world absolutely frightened me, bewildered me. I didn't understand the necessity of all the role playing. And in a way I still don't.

GOLDSTEIN: You never thought of yourself as being gay?

BALDWIN: No. I didn't have a word for it. The only one I had was "homosexual" and that didn't quite cover whatever it was I was beginning to feel. Even when I began to realize things about myself, began to suspect who I was and what I was likely to become, it was still very personal, absolutely personal. It was really a matter between me and God. I would have to live the life he had made me to live. I told him quite a long, long time ago there would be two of us at the Mercy Seat. He would not be asking all the questions.

GOLDSTEIN: When did you first begin to think of yourself in those terms?

BALDWIN: It hit me with great force while I was in the pulpit. I must have been fourteen. I was still a virgin. I had no idea what you were supposed to do about it. I didn't really understand any of what I felt except I knew I loved one boy, for example. But it was private. And by the time I left home, when I was seventeen or eighteen and still a virgin, it was like everything else in my life, a problem which I would have to resolve myself. You know, it never occurred to me to join a club. I must say I felt very, very much alone. But I was alone on so many levels and this was one more aspect of it.

GOLDSTEIN: So when we talk about gay life, which is so group-oriented, so tribal . . .

BALDWIN: And I am not that kind of person at all.

GOLDSTEIN: . . . do you feel baffled by it?

BALDWIN: I feel remote from it. It's a phenomenon that came along much after I was formed. In some sense, I couldn't have afforded it. You see, I am not a member of anything. I joined the Church when I was very, very young, and haven't joined anything since, except for a brief stint in the Socialist Party. I'm a maverick, you know. But that doesn't mean I don't feel very strongly for my brothers and sisters.

GOLDSTEIN: Do you have a special feeling of responsibility toward gay people?

BALDWIN: Toward that phenomenon we call gay, yeah. I feel special responsibility because I would have to be a kind of witness to it, you know.

GOLDSTEIN: You're one of the architects of it by the act of writing about it publicly and elevating it into the realm of literature.

BALDWIN: I made a public announcement that we're private, if you see what I mean.

GOLDSTEIN: When I consider what a risk it must have been to write about homosexuality when you did . . .

BALDWIN: You're talking about *Giovanni's Room*. Yeah, that was rough. But I had to do it to clarify something for myself.

GOLDSTEIN: What was that?

BALDWIN: Where I was in the world. I mean, what I'm made of. Anyway, *Giovanni's Room* is not really about homosexuality. It's the vehicle through which the book moves. *Go Tell It on the Mountain*, for example, is not about a church and *Giovanni* is not really about homosexuality. It's about what happens to you if you're afraid to love anybody. Which is much more interesting than the question of homosexuality.

GOLDSTEIN: But you didn't mask the sexuality.

BALDWIN: No.

GOLDSTEIN: And that decision alone must have been enormously risky.

BALDWIN: Yeah. The alternative was worse.

GOLDSTEIN: What would that have been?

BALDWIN: If I hadn't written that book I would probably have had to stop writing altogether.

GOLDSTEIN: It was that serious.

BALDWIN: It *is* that serious. The question of human affection, of integrity, in my case, the question of trying to become a writer, are all linked with the question of sexuality. Sexuality is only a part of it. I don't know even if it's the most important part. But it's indispensable.

GOLDSTEIN: Did people advise you not to write the book so candidly?

BALDWIN: I didn't ask anybody. When I turned the book in, I was told I shouldn't have written it. I was told to bear in mind that I was a young Negro writer with a certain audience, and I wasn't supposed to alienate that audience. And if I published the book, it would wreck my career. They wouldn't publish the book, they said, as a favor to me. So I took the book to England and I sold it there before I sold it here.

GOLDSTEIN: Do you think your unresolved sexuality motivated you, at the start, to write?

BALDWIN: Yeah. Well, everything was unresolved. The sexual thing was only one of the things. It was for a while the most tormenting thing and it could have been the most dangerous.

GOLDSTEIN: How so?

BALDWIN: Well, because it frightened me so much.

GOLDSTEIN: I don't think straight people realize how frightening it is to finally admit to yourself that this is going to be you forever.

BALDWIN: It's very frightening. But the so-called straight person is no safer than I am really. Loving anybody and being loved by anybody is a tremendous danger, a tremendous responsibility. Loving of children, raising of children. The terrors homosexuals go through in this society would not be so great if the society itself did not go through so many terrors which it doesn't want to admit. The discovery of one's sexual preference doesn't have to be a trauma. It's a trauma because it's such a traumatized society.

GOLDSTEIN: Have you got any sense of what causes people to hate homosexuals?

BALDWIN: Terror, I suppose. Terror of the flesh. After all, we're supposed to mortify the flesh, a doctrine which has led to untold horrors. This is a very biblical culture; people believe the wages of sin is death. In fact, the wages of sin *is* death, but not the way the moral guardians of this time and place understand it.

GOLDSTEIN: Is there a particularly American component of homophobia?

BALDWIN: I think Americans are terrified of feeling anything. And homophobia is simply an extreme example of the American terror that's concerned with growing up. I never met a people more infantile in my life.

GOLDSTEIN: You sound like Leslie Fiedler.

BALDWIN: I hope not. [Laughter]

GOLDSTEIN: Are you as apocalyptic about the prospects for sexual reconciliation as you are about racial reconciliation?

BALDWIN: Well, they join. The sexual question and the racial question have always been entwined, you know. If Americans can mature on the level of racism, then they have to mature on the level of sexuality.

GOLDSTEIN: I think we would agree there's a retrenchment going on in race relations. Do you sense that happening also in sex relations?

BALDWIN: Yeah. There's what we would have to call a backlash which, I'm afraid, is just beginning.

GOLDSTEIN: I suspect most gay people have fantasies about genocide.

BALDWIN: Well, it's not a fantasy exactly since the society makes its will toward you very, very clear. Especially the police, for example, or truck drivers. I know from my own experience that the macho men—truck drivers, cops, football players—these people are far more complex than they want to realize. That's why I call them infantile. They have needs which, for them, are literally inexpressible. They don't dare look into the mirror. And that is why they need faggots. They've created faggots in order to act out a sexual fantasy on the body of another man and not take any responsibility for it. Do you see what I mean? I think it's very important for the male homosexual to recognize that he is a sexual target for other men, and that is why he is despised, and why he is called a faggot. He is called a faggot because other males need him.

GOLDSTEIN: Why do you think homophobia falls so often on the right of the political spectrum?

BALDWIN: It's a way of controlling people. Nobody really cares who goes to bed with whom, finally. I mean, the State doesn't really care, the Church doesn't really care. They care that you should be frightened of what you do. As long as you feel guilty about it, the State can rule you. It's a way of exerting control over the universe, by terrifying people.

GOLDSTEIN: Why don't black ministers need to share in this rhetoric?

BALDWIN: Perhaps because they're more grown-up than most white ministers.

GOLDSTEIN: Did you never hear antigay rhetoric in church?

BALDWIN: Not in the church I grew up in. I'm sure that's still true. Everyone is a child of God, according to us.

GOLDSTEIN: Didn't people ever call you "faggot" uptown?

BALDWIN: Of course. But there's a difference in the way it's used. It's got less venom, at least in my experience. I don't know of anyone who has ever denied his brother or his sister because they were gay. No doubt it happens. It must happen. But in the generality, a black person has got quite a lot to get through the day without getting entangled in all the American fantasies.

GOLDSTEIN: Do black gay people have the same sense of being separate as white gay people do? I mean, I feel distinct from other white people.

BALDWIN: Well, that I think is because you are penalized, as it were, unjustly; you're placed outside a certain safety to which you think you were born. A black gay person who is a sexual conundrum to society is already, long before the question of sexuality comes into it, menaced and marked because he's black or she's black. The sexual question comes after the question of color; it's simply one more aspect of the danger in which all black people live. I think white gay people feel cheated because they were born, in principle, into a society in which they were supposed to be safe. The anomaly of their sexuality puts them in danger, unexpectedly. Their reaction seems to me in direct proportion to the sense of feeling cheated of the advantages which accrue to white people in a white society. There's an element, it has always seemed to me, of bewilderment and complaint. Now that may sound very harsh, but the gay world as such is no more prepared to accept black people than anywhere else in society. It's a very hermetically sealed world with very unattractive features, including racism.

GOLDSTEIN: Are you optimistic about the possibilities of blacks and gays forging a political coalition? Do you see any special basis for empathy between us?

BALDWIN: Yeah. Of course.

GOLDSTEIN: What would that be?

BALDWIN: Well, the basis would be shared suffering, shared perceptions, shared hopes.

GOLDSTEIN: What perceptions do we share?

BALDWIN: I supposed one would be the perception that love is where you find it. If you see what I mean.

GOLDSTEIN: [Laughter] Or where you lose it, for that matter.

BALDWIN: Uhm-hmm.

GOLDSTEIN: But are gay people sensitized by the perceptions we share with blacks?

BALDWIN: Not in my experience, no.

GOLDSTEIN: So I guess you're not very hopeful about that kind of coalition as something that could make a difference in urban politics.

BALDWIN: It's simply that the whole question has entered my mind another way. I know a great many white people, men and women, straight and gay, whatever, who are unlike the majority of their countrymen. On what basis we could form a coalition is still an open question. The idea of basing it on sexual preference strikes me as somewhat dubious, strikes me as being less than a firm foundation. It seems to me that a coalition has to be based on the grounds of human dignity. Anyway, what connects us, speaking about the private life, is mainly unspoken.

GOLDSTEIN: I sometimes think gay people look to black people as healing them . . .

BALDWIN: Not only gay people.

GOLDSTEIN: . . . healing their alienation.

BALDWIN: That has to be done, first of all, by the person and then you will find your company.

GOLDSTEIN: When I heard Jesse Jackson speak before a gay audience, I wanted him to say there wasn't any sin, that I was forgiven.

BALDWIN: Is that a question for you still? That question of sin?

GOLDSTEIN: I think it must be, on some level, even though I am not a believer.

BALDWIN: How peculiar. I didn't realize you thought of it as sin. Do many gay people feel that?

GOLDSTEIN: I don't know. [Laughter] I guess I'm throwing something at you, which is the idea that gays look to blacks as conferring a kind of acceptance by embracing them in a coalition. I find it unavoidable to think in those terms. When I fantasize about a black mayor or a black president, I think of it as being better for gay people.

BALDWIN: Well, don't be romantic about black people. Though I can see what you mean.

GOLDSTEIN: Do you think black people have heightened capacity for tolerance, even acceptance, in its truest sense?

BALDWIN: Well, there is a capacity in black people for experience, simply. And that capacity makes other things possible. It dictates the depth of one's acceptance of other people. The capacity for experience is what burns out fear. Because the homophobia we're talking about really is a kind of fear. It's a terror of flesh. It's really a terror of being able to be touched.

GOLDSTEIN: Do you think about having children?

BALDWIN: Not any more. It's one thing I really regret, maybe the only regret I have. But I couldn't have managed it then. Now it's too late.

GOLDSTEIN: But you're not disturbed by the idea of gay men being parents.

BALDWIN: Look, men have been sleeping with men for thousands of years—and raising tribes. This is a Western sickness, it really is. It's an artificial division. Men will be sleeping with each other when the trumpet sounds. It's only this infantile culture which has made such a big deal of it.

GOLDSTEIN: So you think of homosexuality as universal?

BALDWIN: Of course. There's nothing in me that is not in everybody else, and nothing in everybody else that is not in me.

We're trapped in language, of course. But homosexual is not a noun. At least not in my book.

GOLDSTEIN: What part of speech would it be?

BALDWIN: Perhaps a verb. You see, I can only talk about my own life. I loved a few people and they loved me. It had nothing to do with these labels. Of course, the world has all kinds of words for us. But that's the world's problem.

GOLDSTEIN: Is it problematic for you, the idea of having sex only with other people who are identified as gay?

BALDWIN: Well, you see, my life has not been like that at all. The people who were my lovers were never, well, the word gay wouldn't have meant anything to them.

GOLDSTEIN: That means that they moved in the straight world.

BALDWIN: They moved in the world.

GOLDSTEIN: Do you think of the gay world as being a false refuge?

BALDWIN: I think perhaps it imposes a limitation which is unnecessary. It seems to me simply a man is a man, a woman is a woman, and who they go to bed with is nobody's business but theirs. I suppose what I am really saying is that one's sexual preference is a private matter. I resent the interference of the State, or the Church, or any institution in my only journey to whatever it is we are journeying toward. But it has been made a public question by the institutions of this country. I can see how the gay world comes about in response to that. And to contradict myself, I suppose, or more precisely, I hope that it is easier for the transgressor to become reconciled with himself or herself than it was for many people in my generation—and it was difficult for me. It is difficult to be despised, in short. And if the so-called gay movement can cause men and women, boys and girls, to come to some kind of terms with themselves more speedily and

183

with less pain, then that's a very great advance. I'm not sure it can be done on that level. My own point of view, speaking out of black America, when I had to try to answer that stigma, that species of social curse, it seemed a great mistake to answer in the language of the oppressor. As long as I react as a "nigger," as long as I protest my case on evidence or assumptions held by others, I'm simply reinforcing those assumptions. As long as I complain about being oppressed, the oppressor is in consolation of knowing that I know my place, so to speak.

GOLDSTEIN: You will always come forward and make the statement that you're homosexual. You will never hide it, or deny it. And yet you refuse to make a life out of it?

BALDWIN: Yeah. That sums it up pretty well.

GOLDSTEIN: That strikes me as a balance some of us might want to look to, in a climate where it's possible.

BALDWIN: One has to make that climate for oneself.

GOLDSTEIN: Do you have good fantasies about the future?

BALDWIN: I have good fantasies and bad fantasies.

GOLDSTEIN: What are some of the good ones?

BALDWIN: Oh, that I am working toward the New Jerusalem. That's true, I'm not joking. I won't live to see it but I do believe in it. I think we're going to be better than we are.

GOLDSTEIN: What do you think gay people will be like then?

BALDWIN: No one will have to call themselves gay. Maybe that's at the bottom of my impatience with the term. It answers a false argument, a false accusation.

GOLDSTEIN: Which is what?

BALDWIN: Which is that you have no right to be here, that you have to prove your right to be here. I'm saying I have nothing to prove. The world also belongs to me.

GOLDSTEIN: What advice would you give a gay man who's about to come out?

BALDWIN: Coming out means to publicly say?

GOLDSTEIN: I guess I'm imposing these terms on you.

BALDWIN: Yeah, they're not my terms. But what advice can you possibly give? Best advice I ever got was an old friend of mine, a black friend, who said you have to go the way your blood beats. If you don't live the only life you have, you won't live some other life, you won't live any life at all. That's the only advice you can give anybody. And it's not advice, it's an observation.

THE LAST INTERVIEW
(1987)

▪ by Quincy Troupe ▪

BALDWIN: It all comes back now.

TROUPE: When did you first meet Miles?

BALDWIN: Oh, a long time ago, on West Seventy-seventh Street at his house.

TROUPE: What were the circumstances?

BALDWIN: I'm trying to remember. I was living on West End Avenue then, early sixties. What was I doing at his home? I hadn't met him, but I admired him very much. But I think I met him before that. Yes, I remember. I first met him in the Village, when he was playing at the Café Bohemia. Then I met him at Club Beverly, on Seventy-fifth Street. But that was a long time ago, too. But, I'm trying to remember

186

what I was doing at Miles's house. I don't remember. Anyway, it was a Sunday afternoon and Miles had invited me, he was having a kind of brunch. So there I was, there in Miles's presence. It was, at first, overwhelming, because I'm really shy. I remember there being a whole lot of people. Miles was at the other end of the room. At first he was upstairs, invisible. Then he was downstairs talking to someone he knew as Moonbeam. Still, he was visible, but barely. Finally he was standing in the room, visible, and so I went over to him. Miles looked like a little boy at the time, he looked about ten. So there I was trying to figure out what to say. Finally I told him how much I liked and admired him. I told him I liked his music very much and he said something like, "Are you sure?" He kind of smiled. Then he talked with me. Then we sort of knew each other. So the ice had been broken, so that ah, you know, how it is with friends, though I don't know if he thinks of me as a friend. I don't know what other people see. But I could see that there was something in Miles and me which was very much alike. I can see much of myself in Miles. And yet, I don't know what it is, can't explain it, but I think it has something to do with extreme vulnerability.

TROUPE: Extreme vulnerability? In what sense?

BALDWIN: First of all, you know, with what we look like, being black, which means that in special ways we've been maltreated. See, we evolve a kind of mask, a kind of persona, you know, to protect us from, ah, all these people who are carnivorous and they think you're helpless. Miles does it one way, I do it another.

TROUPE: How do you do it?

BALDWIN: I keep people away by seeming not to be afraid of them, by moving fast.

TROUPE: And how does he do it?

BALDWIN: In his language, by saying "bitch." Miles said when he saw me signing an autograph, "Why don't you tell the motherfuckers to get lost? What the fuck makes you think I think you can read?" I never saw him very often, but there was always a kind of shorthand between us, that nothing would ever change between us. Like Miles has come to visit me, here in St. Paul on a number of occasions when he's over here in France, playing. And you know Miles doesn't visit people. And even when he visits, he never says much, he doesn't say anything. Not all the time, however; it depends on how the spirit moves him.

TROUPE: So he just shows.

BALDWIN: He just shows up here, knocks at the door. Sometimes he calls, but he may just show.

TROUPE: When was the last time?

BALDWIN: A couple of summers ago.

TROUPE: He called and said, "I'm coming."

BALDWIN: No. I think what happened, he was staying in Nice, so his French manager called and asked me to come and have dinner and cocktails. It was a nice night. And afterwards, he came back here.

TROUPE: He came out here?

BALDWIN: Yeah. We sat around and talked about nothing.

TROUPE: You think he came because he feels safe with you.

BALDWIN: Yeah. We talked about nothing and everything and we would have a little sip and we would talk about whatever. But I do the same with some people I know.

TROUPE: Why do you think he feels this way with you, since he's afraid of writers?

BALDWIN: I don't think Miles thinks of me as a writer. He knows I'm a writer, but he doesn't look at me that way. He doesn't look at me that way at all. I think hc thinks of me as a brother, you know? In many ways I have the same difficulty as he has, in terms of the private and public life. In terms of the legend. It's difficult to be a legend. It's hard for me to recognize *me*. You spend a lot of time trying to avoid it. A lot of the time I've been through so many of the same experiences Miles has gone through. It's really something, to be a legend, unbearable. I could see it had happened to Miles. Again, it's unbearable, the way the world treats you is unbearable, and especially if you're black.

TROUPE: What is that?

BALDWIN: It's unbearable because time is passing and you are not your legend, but you're trapped in it. Nobody will let you out of it. Except other people who know what it is. But very few people have experienced it, know about it, and I think that can drive you mad; I know it can. It had a terrible effect on him and it had a terrible effect on me. And you don't see it coming.

TROUPE: You don't see it coming? Explain why?

BALDWIN: No way to see it.

TROUPE: How do you realize it?

BALDWIN: You have to be lucky. You have to have friends. I think at bottom you have to be serious. No one can point it out to you; you have to see it yourself. That's the only way you can act on it. And when it arrives it's a great shock.

TROUPE: To find out?

BALDWIN: It's a great shock to realize that you've been so divorced. So divorced from who you think you are—from who you really are. Who you think you are, you're not at all. The only thing is that Miles has got his horn and I've got my typewriter. We are both angry men.

TROUPE: I want to ask you what you were trapped in and how did you come to see it. I mean, did you come through friends?

BALDWIN: I know what you're saying but it's hard to answer, it's hard.

TROUPE: I know it's hard.

BALDWIN: I don't know how to answer that.

TROUPE: But you saw yourself trapped?

BALDWIN: I saw myself trapped. I think it happened to Miles, too.

TROUPE: What did you think you were, before you knew?

BALDWIN: Ah, that's even more interesting. I don't know who I thought I was. I was a witness, I thought. I was a very despairing witness, though, too. What I was actually doing was trying to avoid a certain estrangement, perhaps, an estrangement between myself and my generation. It was virtually complete, the estrangement was, in terms of what I might have thought and expected—my theories. About what I might have hoped—I'm talking now in terms of one's function as an artist. And the country itself being black and trying to deal with that.

TROUPE: Why do you think it occurred. That estrangement between your generation and the country?

BALDWIN: Well, because I was right. That's a strange way to put it.

TROUPE: That's not strange, at least not to me.

BALDWIN: I *was* right. I was right about what was happening in the country. What was about to happen to all of us really, one way or the other. And the choices people would have to make. And watching people make them and denying them at the same time. I began to feel more and more homeless in terms of the whole relationship between France and me and America, and *me* has always been a little painful, you know. Because my family's in America I will always go back. It couldn't have been a question in my mind unless it absolutely really came to that. But in the meantime you keep the door open and the price of keeping the door open was to actually be, in a sense, victimized by my own legend. You know, I was trying to tell the truth and it takes a long time to realize that you can't—that there's no point in going to the mat, so to speak, no point in going to Texas again. There's no point in saying this again. It's been said, and it's been said, and it's been said. It's been heard and not heard. You are a broken motor.

TROUPE: A broken motor?

BALDWIN: Yes. You're a running motor and you're repeating, you're repeating, you're repeating, and it causes a breakdown, lessening of will power. And sooner or later your will gives out, it has to. You're lucky if it is a physical matter. Most times it's spiritual. See, all this involves hiding from something else—not dealing with how lonely you are. And of course, at the very bottom it involves the terror of every artist confronted with what he or she has to do, you know, the next work. And everybody, in one way or another, and to some extent, tries to avoid it. And you avoid it more when you get older than you do when you're younger; still there's something terrifying about it, about doing the work. Something like that. But it happened to Miles sooner than it happened to me. I think for me it was lucky that it was physical, because it could have been mental.

TROUPE: It could have been mental?

BALDWIN: Yes. It could have been mental debilitation instead of my present physical one. I prefer the physical to the mental. Does that make sense?

TROUPE: It makes good sense, it makes fantastic sense. Now let me ask you something else. Now with Miles, you both were born close to each other?

BALDWIN: Just about. I think I'm a year older. I was born in '24.

TROUPE: He was born in '26. So then, probably both of you, black men, genuises, born close together, probably see the world very similar—you through your typewriter and him through his horn. Both vulnerable. So when you met you were brothers because you expected to meet each other or were you looking for each other?

BALDWIN: Yes. We were looking for each other. Neither he nor I would have said it that way but we were; we knew that the moment we saw each other.

TROUPE: You were hoping?

BALDWIN: Oh yes. That's why I was watching him before he watched me, you know.

TROUPE: But he knew you.

BALDWIN: He knew about me. Yes.

TROUPE: He knew you when he saw you.

BALDWIN: There's no question about that at all. We knew each other at once.

TROUPE: That's wonderful.

BALDWIN: Yes it is, discovering someone very much like yourself. It was wonderful.

TROUPE: And that's a wonderful connection. Because he's also estranged somewhat from his musical generation.

BALDWIN: He has to be, at least it makes sense to me that he would be, because he's always trying to be on the cutting edge of his art. That's certainly true for me.

TROUPE: In the windows of your eyes, you and Miles remind me of each other. It's a certain distinctive juju.

BALDWIN: Shit, I love that.

TROUPE: It's a certain distinctive juju that in Miles you recognize and you see a face that you have not seen before. And when I look at you and since I've always looked at you, I've always felt that. A certain juju, witch doctor, priest, high priest look of timelessness or representative of a certain tribe, point of view, mysticism, magic.

BALDWIN: That would cover my father certainly. He was not really my father, because I was born out of wedlock, but that's the difference, my father. He did give me something. Don't you see, he taught me how to fight. He taught me how to fight. But it would be better to say he taught me what to fight for. I was only fighting for safety, or for money at first. Then I fought to make you look at me. Because I was not born to be what someone said I was. I was not born to be defined by someone else, but by myself, and myself only.

TROUPE: So when you were younger, you didn't have the pen as a weapon, as a defense, a shield. How did you fight then?

BALDWIN: Any way I could.

TROUPE: What would you do?

BALDWIN: It's hard to remember. The pulpit was part of it, but that came later.

TROUPE: Before the pulpit.

BALDWIN: It was the streets.

TROUPE: How did you fight? Any way you could?

BALDWIN: Well, if you wanted to beat me up, okay. And, say, you were bigger than I was, you could do it, you could beat me, but you gonna have to do it every day.

TROUPE: Every day? Because you would fight to the death.

BALDWIN: You'd have to beat me up every single day. So then the question becomes which one of us would get tired first. And I knew it wouldn't be me.

TROUPE: You would always fight.

BALDWIN: Oh, yes, indeed. So then the other person would have to begin to think, and to be bugged by this kid he had to beat up every day. And some days perhaps he just didn't feel like doing it. But he would have to, yeah, because he said he was going to do it. So then come beat me up. But of course something happened to him, something has to happen to him—because someone beating someone else up is not so easy either. Because I would be standing in the schoolyard with a lead pipe as a deterrent. So, you know, eventually, it was just too dangerous. People began to leave me alone. Some of the big boys who were my friends got together and decided that they had to protect me, you know? So that after that I was really protected. Because it was funny to them after a while. But that's what happened. That was the beginning of it and then later on it was cops, you know. It became just a nightmare. Especially cops. I knew that they knew that I was seven or eight or nine and they were just having fun with me. They wanted me to beg. And I couldn't beg, so I got my ass kicked. But I learned a lot, a lot about them. I learned there were very few who were humane; they just wanted you to say what they wanted you to say. They wanted to be confirmed in something by you. By your face, by your terror of them.

TROUPE: What about the pulpit, the idea of the pulpit? Would you talk about it as an idea?

BALDWIN: That's a very complex idea really. I joined the Church, but my joining it was very complex, though I meant it, the purely religious part that is, the spiritual part. In a way that was very important to me, that whole time in the pulpit, because it gave me a kind of distance that was kind of respected; that was the reason I was in the pulpit, to put distance between people and myself. I began to see my people, so to speak, both ethnically and otherwise. And in the time that I was in the pulpit I learned a lot about my father. And later on, I thought, perhaps, I'd moved into the pulpit in order to arrest him. Because I thought that he had to be arrested, had to be stopped. He was having a terrible effect on everybody in the family. I could go as far as to say I thought he was crazy. But I knew with myself and the pulpit I cut out a lot of his power. He couldn't fight me in that arena. He fought me, but he couldn't fight me in that arena. And I say during that time that it taught me a lot about him and myself and about the people who were in the congregation, whom I couldn't lie to. And that was why I left the pulpit.

TROUPE: Is that where you started to learn about the truth? I mean you knew about the truth when you were talking about when you knew you weren't going to give in.

BALDWIN: I couldn't.

TROUPE: So then in the pulpit you learned another truth. And in the writing you take it . . .

BALDWIN: I knew that was where I had to go. That I was not going to become another fat preacher, you know? I was not going to, ah, lie to my congregation. I was not allowed to do that. I couldn't believe in what I had anymore. I didn't believe in the Christian Church anymore, not the way I had; I no longer believed in its spirituality, its healing powers.

TROUPE: Oh? Was it the Christian Church that disturbed you?

195

BALDWIN: The way people treated each other. In the Church and outside, but especially in the Church.

TROUPE: How did they treat each other?

BALDWIN: Well, they were so self-righteous. They didn't come with real deep love, for example. The people in the Church were very cruel about many things.

TROUPE: How old were you when you were involved in the Church?

BALDWIN: Fourteen, fifteen.

TROUPE: Okay. I want you now to talk about two extraordinary women that your brother David told me about. Jeanne Fauré, who used to own the house you live in now, and Tintine. I want you, at first, if you can, to talk to me about how you came to this house. And how you came to receive the medal of honor.

BALDWIN: Oh, that's a long story.

TROUPE: I know. But can you talk about it, if you can, how she came to accept you, why she accepted you, and what it was that you saw in each other?

BALDWIN: I came here to St. Paul in 1970. It was after Malcolm X's and Martin Luther King's death really. After Martin's death I sort of wandered and indeed didn't know where to go. I was in Turkey for a while, then I ended up here. I didn't want to leave; I had to. I ended up across the street from this house in a hotel. I came in the wintertime, nineteen years ago. Anyway, I and a friend of mine came down to St. Paul from Paris. We didn't have anything because it was terribly expensive at the hotel and so we settled here because at the time it also served as a roominghouse. Later I got sick, you know, and much of my family came over to see me. I rented almost all of the house. So I thought why not buy it. It was forty-three, forty-six thousand and I had been very ill so I didn't know how much longer I had to live. So I bought it. But Madame Fauré had offered to sell it to me.

TROUPE: This was earlier?

BALDWIN: Yes. When I first came, nineteen-some odd years ago.

TROUPE: What was wrong with you, can you remember what was the illness?

BALDWIN: Nobody knew. Nobody knew. But anyway, I needed some money to buy the house. That occupied me for a while, that occupied me considerably. But I was just busy working. And I got to know Jeanne Fauré, who was a very strange lady, solitary, very strange.

TROUPE: How would you describe her strangeness?

BALDWIN: In her solitude. She was a kind of legend, she was very old, you know, quite. And anyway, she and I had very little in common, it seemed to me, except I liked her very much. She was a refugee from Algeria, raised in Algeria, I believe, and then the French had to leave. And she was very bitter about that. That meant we had very little in common politically. And very little in common in what I could see in any other way. And yet there was something else beneath that made her my friend. She decided to sell the house to me; she refused to sell it to anybody else.

TROUPE: She decided to sell the house to you? Why do you think she picked you? Do you know to this day?

BALDWIN: No.

TROUPE: Was it spiritual?

BALDWIN: Yes.

TROUPE: Cosmic.

BALDWIN: I wasn't the best candidate; in fact, I was the worst. Something in her, I don't know. We also had a very stormy relationship.

TROUPE: Stormy?

BALDWIN: Politically speaking we did. In many other ways we did, too. She knew something I didn't know. She knew about Europe, she knew about civilization, she knew about responsibility. A million things that I as an American would not know, that were alien to me. And I was very slow to learn these things. In fact, it was a very expensive lesson, one that I haven't learned entirely just yet. But she was a valuable kind of guide and a kind of protection. And Tintine Roux was the old lady that ran La Colombe D'Or, which is a world-famous restaurant and inn. She became my guardian. I never lived in a small town before, which is not so easy, and she protected me. I could come in and have lunch at her restaurant. And I didn't realize it at first, that she had picked herself to be my protector.

TROUPE: What do you think she saw in you?

BALDWIN: I don't know.

TROUPE: What do you think?

BALDWIN: I knew Tintine liked me. Still she must have thought I was crazy, you know, at least a little strange, in any event. But both these women liked me. It was as though they recognized where I came from. That I was a peasant, and I am. But I've only found this out over time.

TROUPE: Why do you say that?

BALDWIN: I'm a peasant because of where I really come from, you know. My background, my father, my mother, the line. Something of the peasant must be in all of my family. And that's where Madame Fauré and Tintine come from, too. And the color of my skin didn't add into it at all. Both these women were watching something else besides my color. And they protected me and loved me. They're both dead now and I miss them both terribly. Because with

Jeanne I truly learned a lot from her, from her European optic in regard to others; but she also had an optic that came from Algeria. What I liked about it was that she was willing to be my guide; willing and unwilling: in fact, she was a hard guide. But mostly she was willing. And so it seemed like she was my guide to something else.

TROUPE: What?

BALDWIN: To a way of life, to a potential civilization she had seen only from a height.

TROUPE: Didn't they know about your fame?

BALDWIN: No, not really. They'd heard of me. But beyond that, nothing.

TROUPE: You were comfortable with that.

BALDWIN: Yes. Because my fame did not get in the way because by the time they knew it didn't make any difference. It was just one more aspect of this crazy kid. That's the best way to put it. They were my guides, and they were very good guides.

TROUPE: David told me a story about an incident that happened when her brother died, and Madame Fauré picked you to be at the head of the funeral procession.

BALDWIN: He told you that? Well, she was the last of kin and she made me lead her brother Louis's funeral procession. Yes she did. She put her arm in mine and I had to lead. I had to. It was an incredible scene. I had to lead the funeral procession with her or she with me. It was fascinating.

TROUPE: I think it's a great image. Tell me about it. How did you feel?

BALDWIN: I was in a state of shock. I didn't know what to do. And of course the people of St. Paul were shocked, too. This was in either 1974 or '75. But I was in a state of shock. I didn't quite know what to think; in fact, the town was in a state of shock.

TROUPE: What was the reason?

BALDWIN: Well, they knew who I was by then, of course, but they couldn't understand why I was representing the family. When we were at the cemetery everybody had to say good-bye to me, too. Because I was standing there with her at the head of the family, under the gates of the cemetery. Because what it meant, symbolically speaking, is that I was the next in line, when she died. That's what it meant.

TROUPE: Do you think that could have happened in America?

BALDWIN: I can't imagine where. I really cannot imagine where.

TROUPE: So in a sense that was a comforting, human experience. A remarkable spiritual connection, bond.

BALDWIN: A very great thing, very great. At least for me. I want to write about it one day. Yes, sometime I'll have to talk about it.

TROUPE: When you received the Legion of Honor of France? Who did you take with you to the ceremony?

BALDWIN: David came over. Jeanne Fauré was there and my house-keeper Valerie was there too.

TROUPE: Why did you pick them?

BALDWIN: Because they had seen me through so much and I'd prom-ised to take Jeanne and Valerie to Paris one day. Jeanne had been to Paris but she hadn't been there for a long time. I thought that would be nice for her to go. So I took them and because I owed it to them, but especially to Jeanne Fauré. Because she'd seen me through.

TROUPE: And how did she feel?

BALDWIN: She was very proud. She didn't say anything to me; she never said much to me about it. But I could see it—how proud she was—in her face, in her eyes.

TROUPE: What year was this?

BALDWIN: Last year, 1986.

TROUPE: Was that right before she died?

BALDWIN: Yes. She died in the winter of 1987.

TROUPE: What month was that?

BALDWIN: I received the award in June, and she died in January 1987.

TROUPE: And how did you feel with her being there?

BALDWIN: I was very pleased. It was very nice. It was something that gave her a great pleasure and that meant a lot to me.

TROUPE: I thought that was a great story when he told me. I said I was definitely going to ask you about that. Because I thought that was fundamentally fantastic and so fundamentally, in a sense, spiritually right; but it's something which you don't expect to happen.

BALDWIN: No, you don't, not at all.

TROUPE: Who gave you the award?

BALDWIN: The president, the president of France, François Mitterrand. The ceremony was at the Élysée in Paris.

TROUPE: What other people received the award that year?

BALDWIN: Leonard Bernstein. Leonard Bernstein and me. It was a very nice ceremony, very nice.

TROUPE: Okay. Let's change the subject and talk about some writers. What is your opinion of Amiri Baraka?

BALDWIN: I remember the first time I met Amiri Baraka, who was then Le Roi Jones. I was doing *The Amen Corner* and he was a student at Howard University. I liked him right away. He was a pop-eyed little boy, a poet. He showed me a couple of his poems. I liked them very much. And then he came to New York a couple of years later. He came to New York when I came back to New York from Paris. And by this time I knew the business. I'd been through the fucking business by that time. I was a survivor. And I remember telling him that his agent wanted him to become the young James Baldwin. But I told him, "You're not the young James Baldwin. There's only one James Baldwin and you are Le Roi Jones and there's only one Le Roi Jones. Don't let them run this game on us, you know? You're Le Roi Jones, I'm James Baldwin. And we're going to need each other." That's all I said. He didn't believe it then but time took care of that.

TROUPE: He believes it now.

BALDWIN: Yes, he knows it now.

TROUPE: What person has hurt you the most recently?

BALDWIN: Ishmael Reed.

TROUPE: Why?

BALDWIN: Because he is a great poet and it seemed to be beneath him, his anger and his contempt for me, which were both real and not real. He ignored me for so long and then he called me a cocksucker, you know what I mean? It's boring. But I always did say he was a great poet, a great writer. But that does not mean I can put up with being insulted by him every time I see him, which I won't.

TROUPE: What do you think about Toni Morrison?

BALDWIN: Toni's my ally and it's really probably too complex to get into. She's a black woman writer, which in the public domain makes it more difficult to talk about.

TROUPE: Have you read *Beloved*?

BALDWIN: Not yet. She sent it to me but I haven't read it yet.

TROUPE: What do you think are her gifts?

BALDWIN: Her gift is in allegory. *Tar Baby* is an allegory. In fact all her novels are. But they're hard to talk about in public. That's where you get in trouble because her books and allegory are not always what it seems to be about. I was too occupied with my recent illness to deal with *Beloved*. But in general she's taken a myth, or she takes what seems to be a myth, and turns it into something else. I don't know how to put this—*Beloved* could be about the story of truth. She's taken a whole lot of things and turned them upside down. Some of them—you recognize the truth in it. I think that Toni's very painful to read.

TROUPE: Painful?

BALDWIN: Yes.

TROUPE: Why?

BALDWIN: Because it's always or most times a horrifying allegory; but you recognize that it works. But you don't really want to march through it. Sometimes people have a lot against Toni, but she's got the most believing story of everybody— this rather elegant matron, whose intentions really are serious and, according to some people, lethal.

TROUPE: I remember you saying that Alex Haley's *Roots* had another title. What was it called first?

BALDWIN: It was called *Before the Anger*. But let me change the subject and just say this. It's very important for white Americans to believe their version of the black experience. That's why they have white and black commentators telling all those lies about us. You see, it's very important for the nigger to suffer. Therefore, they, white people, can feel guilty.

Therefore, they can do something about it in their own good time. Let me again explain further. Once, after I published *Go Tell It on the Mountain* and *Giovanni's Room,* my publisher, Knopf, told me I was a "Negro writer" and that I "reached a certain audience." So, they told me, "you cannot afford to alienate that audience. This new book will ruin your career because you're not writing about the same things and in the same manner as you were before and we won't publish this book as a favor to you."

TROUPE: As a favor to you?

BALDWIN: So I told them fuck you. My editor, whose name I won't mention here, is dead now, poor man. Later on, Bennett Cerf and I tangled too, but that was about a Christmas boycott of books we were planning.

TROUPE: So what did they say after you told them "fuck you"?

BALDWIN: I told them that I needed a boat ticket. So I took a boat to England with my book and I sold it in England before I sold it in America. You see whites want black writers to mostly deliver something as if it were an official version of the black experience. But the vocabulary won't hold it, simply. No true account really of black life can be held, can be contained in the American vocabulary. As it is, the only way that you can deal with it is by doing great violence to the assumptions on which the vocabulary is based. But they won't let you do that. And when you go along, you find yourself very quickly painted into a corner; you've written yourself into a corner. Because you can't compromise as a writer. By the time I left America in 1948 I had written myself into a corner as I perceived it. The book reviews and the short essays had led me to a place where I was on a collision course totally with the truth; it was the way I was operating. It was only a matter of time before I'd simply be destroyed by it. And no amount of manipulation of vocabulary or part would have spared me. It's like I think that Al Murray and Ralph Ellison are totally trapped. It's sad, because they're both trapped in the same way, and they're both very gifted writers. Ralph certainly, and Al, I thought. But you can't do anything with America unless you are willing to dissect it. You certainly cannot hope to fit yourself into it; nothing fits into it, not your past, not your present. The *Invisible Man* is fine as far as it goes until you ask yourself who's invisible to whom? You know, what is this dichotomy supposed to do? Are we invisible before each other? And invisible why, and by what system can one hope to be invisible? I don't know how anything in American life is worthy of this sacrifice. And further, I don't see anything in American life—for myself—to aspire to. Nothing at all. It's all so very false. So shallow, so plastic, so morally and ethically corrupt.

TROUPE: We were talking once about the claustrophobia among writers. You said you prefer actors and painters to writers.

BALDWIN: Yes. Well, first of all when I was coming up there weren't any writers that I knew. Langston Hughes was far away. The first writer I met was Richard Wright and he was much older than me. And the people I knew were people like Beauford Delaney and the women who hung out with him; it was a whole world that was not literary. That came later; then it wasn't literary. It came later in Paris, with Sartre and others. But there was something else. And in Paris it had nothing whatsoever to do with race for one thing. It was another kind of freedom there altogether. It had nothing to do with literature. But we can't talk about that. But when I looked back on it years and years later, looked back at myself on the American literary scene, I could see that what almost happened to me was an attempt to make myself fit in, so to speak, to wash myself clean for the American literary academy.

TROUPE: You mean they wanted you scrubbed and squeaky clean?

BALDWIN: Exactly. You have to be scrubbed and squeaky clean and then there's nothing left of you. Let me tell you a story. When Ralph Ellison won the National Book Award in 1953 for *Invisible Man*, I was up for it the next year, in 1954, for *Go Tell It on the Mountain*. But at the time I was far from scrubbed. I didn't win. Then, years later, someone who was on the jury told me that since Ralph won it the year before they couldn't give it to a Negro two years in a row. Now, isn't that something?

TROUPE: A judge told you that? Can you tell us his name?

BALDWIN: No, I wouldn't want to do that.

TROUPE: Okay. Do you have any comments on Norman Mailer?

BALDWIN: Well the answer to that question is very short and very simple. Not simple, but short. Norman decided not to be a writer. He decided to be a celebrity instead and that's what he is now. Now let me tell you a story about Norman. Out of my father's first marriage there is a sister and a couple of sons, you know, a few sons. My sister had a brother who lives in California. He's a senior citizen now. But he lived with Norman Mailer when Norman was writing *The White Negro*. He was taking the pages out of Norman's typewriter, changing his clothes—they wore the same clothes, exchanged cars, and his car was better than Norman's at the time. He was like the second husband in a way. They lived together. They lived close together. Norman doesn't know I know this. No one knows this. This story took place in the forties, the early forties, in California. I've kept quiet about this all these years that Norman was living with one of my step-brothers when he wrote the book. No one knows it, though. You're the first one, outside of the family, that I have mentioned it to. His name is Osby Mitchell. Osby did something in show business, hung out with Frank Sinatra, Charlie Chaplin, that crowd.

TROUPE: Okay. That's something. Now, what do you think of the great praise you have received in France for *Just Above My Head*, that it has gotten in translation. How does that make you feel?

BALDWIN: As you know the French call the book *Harlem Quartet*. I don't know how to answer that, Quincy, because it was written here almost ten years ago. It was the hardest book I'd ever written until then.

TROUPE: Why?

BALDWIN: I had to face my own legends, too.

TROUPE: Which were?

BALDWIN: It had something to do about my brothers, my relationship to my brothers. And that implied relationship to my whole life really. The key to one's life is always in a lot of unexpected places. I tried to deal with what I was most afraid of. That's why the vehicle of the book is music. Because music was and is my salvation. And when the book was done, I was glad it was over. It got the usual stormy reception in America, but by that time I was used to it. In any case, by that time I was in a different kind of trouble altogether. The reception of *Harlem Quartet* here in France didn't mean as much as it might have meant if I had gotten the praise earlier. I never thought I'd see the book again. But its translation came about after my book on the Atlanta murders was published here in France. It was hard to get the Atlanta book published in America for complex and political reasons.

TROUPE: Can you talk about them?

BALDWIN: I don't quite know what they are. It's difficult for me to talk about a book that involves a possible lawsuit. It's just another example of American business, the ways in which Americans, the American publishers, attempt to control and to demolish the American writer, regardless of color, but especially a black one. I had to fight that, so I brought the book here. And it was published by Stock. And it did better than anyone thought it would do in France. So Stock already had a contract for *Just Above My Head* (*Harlem Quartet*). And so they published it. Stock had gone through all kinds of publishing problems—it had gone through a breakup and a reorganization. The Atlanta book won a couple of awards, and a German writer and I won the Human Rights Award of France two years ago, in 1985. But the German writer, poor man, had to leave Germany. Anyway, behind all of this came this book *Just Above My Head*, or *Harlem Quartet*. And I think that the French for the first time really looked at my writing; the Atlanta book was something of a shock to them.

TROUPE: Why?

BALDWIN: Because it demolishes, so to speak, the American myth of integration, you know, by using Atlanta, which is supposed to be the model of integration in the Deep South and exposes it for what it is; shit, you know? So the French reader goes through all of that in terms of those twenty-eight dead black children. And so it was a shock, you know. And it sort of set up, I don't know what, exactly, but it did set up expectations, or fears, whatever for the novel. It may have set up an audience for the novel. And so *Just Above My Head* turns out to be somewhat of a revelation for the French. So you know, I'm considered somewhat of an intellectual in Paris. I mean in France. For a black writer, you know? Essentially as an essayist. But the novel was a great revelation; it gave me another kind of reputation altogether. Because now, instead of an essayist, what they saw in me was a novelist. I'm much better known as an essayist in France and elsewhere, too, than I am as a novelist. Before, the translations of my novels in France have been so bad. But this was a good translation, a marvelous translation, which makes a tremendous difference. And the subject, my handling of the subject, they liked. So it's simply a matter of something happening at the right time, and that can never be foreseen, you know.

TROUPE: What's the award *Harlem Quartet* is up for now?

BALDWIN: The best foreign novel published in France, the Prix Femina. We will know about that in a week.

TROUPE: Let me ask you about the difficulty the American press and critics might have had in getting into your fiction.

BALDWIN: Well, probably the American legend of black life. It's one thing to be aware of a Miles Davis and quite another thing to know where he comes from and what sustains him. Hollywood should be sued for libel, it's true. So that the book, my book, and others come as a direct opposition of the myth by Americans of black life and black music. It's not like what they, the press and critics, say it is, not at all. But the books prove them wrong, so they ignore the books. You see what I mean? Like I very much liked the film *'Round Midnight*, which is a very important film. It fills in something that is important in our lives, a gap that was once there, that one might have thought about but didn't know about.

TROUPE: Why do you say it's important?

BALDWIN: Well, first of all the personality of Dexter Gordon, he gives at least a reading of what happens to the musician. The black musician inside the music industry in Paris, you know? The ruin that they met which they brought with them and which wasn't brought about by Paris.

TROUPE: You mean the black musicians brought the ruin with them?

BALDWIN: Yes, that's precisely what I mean. And *'Round Midnight* makes that point in some ways very clearly.

TROUPE: Can you talk about the neglect of the black painter Beauford Delaney?

BALDWIN: That's hard to do because people are still lying about Beauford. Let's talk about that over supper.

TROUPE: Okay. You said something to me once about how people shouldn't be jealous of someone's success. Do you recall that?

BALDWIN: Well, what I was really trying to say was that people don't know what it is sometimes to be very successful. Don't know what it is. What I meant to say was that you can't be jealous of somebody else's success because you have no idea what it means, you know? It looks like success to you, but you're not the one that's paying for it.

TROUPE: And there's a price?

BALDWIN: Of course there's a price, are you kidding? It's definitely not easy. It's rough. But for most great black writers in general, "they"—meaning white and black Americans— won't read us until they have nothing else to read.

TROUPE: Why do you think that is?

BALDWIN: Well, because of the entire way of American life, the marrow of the American bone. Now today it's a *fait accompli*. There's nothing to be done about it. The whole American optic in terms of reality is based on the necessity of keeping black people out of it. We are nonexistent. Except according to their terms, and their terms are unacceptable.

TROUPE: Let me ask you this, since you said that. How do you look at the American society as it was during Dr. King's time and now? Any changes? Do you think it is worse, or what?

BALDWIN: Certainly, in my opinion, it's worse. I'm not sure it's the society, I don't know what it is now.

TROUPE: What do you think that Ronald Reagan represents to white America?

BALDWIN: Ronald Reagan represents the justification of their history, their sense of innocence. He means the justification of *Birth of a Nation*. The justification, in short, of being white.

TROUPE: How do you think white Americans feel now that they're in this economic crisis?

BALDWIN: They're not thinking about it.

TROUPE: What?

BALDWIN: They're not thinking about it. Americans don't think of such things. They try and get out of it. They hope it'll go away. And luckily they began to realize that maybe Reagan has to go, too. But they hope it all goes away. Because it's like a bad dream for them.

TROUPE: Won't they do anything to help it go away?

BALDWIN: No. Because they don't know how. They don't know how they got into it or, worse, won't recognize how. I don't know. They don't know how they got into the chaos of their cities, for example. But they did it. Now how and why did they do it? They did it because they wanted their children to be safe, to be raised safely. So they set up their communities so that they wouldn't have to go to school with black children, whom they fear, and that dictates the structure of their cities, the chaos of their cities and the danger in which they live.

TROUPE: "They" being white.

BALDWIN: "They" being white and their believing that they're white. But they did it; niggers didn't do it. They did it. Inch by inch, stone by stone, decree by decree. Now their kids are deeply lost and they can't even blame it now on the nigger, you know what I mean?

TROUPE: Yes.

BALDWIN: That's what happened, I don't care who says what. I watched it happen, I know because I watched it happen. And all this, because they want to be white. And why do they want to be white? Because it's the only way to justify the slaughter of the Indians and enslaving the blacks—they're trapped. And nothing, nothing will spring the trap, nothing. Now they're really trapped because the world is present. And the world is not white and America is not the symbol of civilization. Neither is England. Neither is France. Something else is happening which will engulf them by and by. You, Quincy, will be here, but I'll be gone. It's the only hope the world has, that the notion of the supremacy of Western hegemony and civilization be contained.

TROUPE: Do you have any feelings about yuppies?

BALDWIN: I saw them coming. I knew them. They can't, I'm afraid, be taught anything.

TROUPE: You don't think they can be taught anything?

BALDWIN: No. Because you can't be taught anything if you think you know everything already, that something else—greed, materialism, and consuming—is more important to your life. You know, I taught the yuppies before they were called yuppies. And then what happened to them, really? Perfectly sound young men came out of college, went to work for Nixon, and were hardened criminals on Wall Street before you knew it. Now, is it true or not?

TROUPE: It's true.

BALDWIN: And here I've only mentioned Nixon. But it's true for Reagan, too. So that's that. It's the fiber of the nation, unfortunately.

JAMES BALDWIN

• by Chinua Achebe •

*Chinua Achebe was brought up in Ogidi, Eastern
Nigeria. He graduated from University College,
Ibadan, and after a brief career in broadcasting,
he became Senior Research Fellow and later Professor at the University of Nigeria Nsukka. He
became Professor Emeritus in 1985. He has been
Professor of English at the University of Massachusetts, Amherst, and the University of Connecticut, Storrs.*

Achebe has published five novels, including
Things Fall Apart *and his latest,* Anthills of the
Savannah; *short stories; essays; and children's
books. He has been the recipient of eleven honorary doctorates.*

THE many and varied tributes to
Jimmy Baldwin, like the blind men's versions of the elephant, are
consistent in one detail—the immensity, the sheer prodigality of endowment.

When my writing first began to yield small rewards in the way of
free travel, UNESCO came along and asked where I would like to
go. Without hesitation I said, "U.S.A. and Brazil." And so I came to
the Americas for the first time in 1963.

My intention, which was somewhat nebulous to begin with, was
to find out how the Africans of the diaspora were faring in the two
largest countries of the New World. In UNESCO files, however, it
was stated with greater precision. I was given a fellowship to enable
me to study literary trends and to meet and exchange ideas with writers.

I did indeed make very many useful contacts: John O. Killens,

Langston Hughes, Ralph Ellison, Paule Marshall, Le Roi Jones (now Amiri Baraka), and so on; and for good measure, Arthur Miller. They were all wonderful to me. And yet there was no way I could hide from myself or my sponsors my sense of disappointment that one particular meeting could not happen because the man concerned was away in France. And that was the year of *The Fire Next Time*.

Before I came to America I had discovered and read *Go Tell It on the Mountain*, and been instantly captivated. For me it combined the strange and the familiar in a way that was entirely new. I went to the United States Information Service Library in Lagos to see what other material there might be *by* or *on* this man. There was absolutely nothing. So I offered a couple of suggestions and such was the persuasiveness of newly independent Africans in those days that when next I looked in at the library they had not only Baldwin but Richard Wright as well.

I had all my schooling in the educational system of colonial Nigeria. In that system Americans, when they were featured at all, were dismissed summarily by our British administrators as loud and vulgar. Their universities, which taught such subjects as dishwashing, naturally produced half-baked noisy political agitators, some of whom were now rushing up and down the country because they had acquired no proper skills.

But there was one American book which the colonial educators considered of sufficient value to be exempted from the general censure of things American and actually to be prescribed reading in my high school. It was the autobiography of Booker T. Washington: *Up from Slavery*.

This bizarre background probably explains why my first encounter with Baldwin's writing was such a miraculous experience. Nothing that I had heard or read or seen quite prepared me for the Baldwin phenomenon. Needless to say, my education was entirely silent about W. E. B. DuBois, who, as I later discovered, had applied *his* experience of what he called "the strange meaning of being black" in America to ends and insights radically different from Washington's.

A major aspect of my reeducation was to see (and what comfort it gave me!) that Baldwin was neither an aberration nor likely to be a flash in the pan. He brought a new sharpness of vision, a new energy of passion, a new perfection of language to battle the incubus of race which DuBois had prophesied would possess our century—which prophecy itself had a long pedigree through the slave revolts back into Africa where, believe it or not, a seventeenth-century Igbo priest-king, Eze Nri, had declared slavery an abomination. I say *believe it or not* because this personage and many others like him in different parts of Africa do not fit the purposes of your history books.

When at last I met Jimmy in person in the jungles of Florida in 1980, I actually greeted him with "Mr. Baldwin, I presume!" You should have seen his eyes dancing, his remarkable face working in ripples of joyfulness. During the four days we spent down there I saw how easy it was to make Jimmy smile, and how the world he was doomed to inhabit would remorselessly deny him that simple benediction.

Baldwin and I were invited by the African Literature Association to open its annual conference in Gainesville with a public conversation. As we stepped into a tremendous ovation in the packed auditorium of the Holiday Inn, Baldwin was in particularly high spirits. I thought the old preacher in him was reacting to the multitude.

He went to the podium and began to make his opening statements. Within minutes a mystery voice came over the public address system and began to hurl racial insults at him and me. I will see that moment to the end of my life: the happiness brutally wiped off Baldwin's face; the genial manner gone; the eyes flashing in defiant combativeness; the voice incredibly calm and measured. And the words of remorseless prophecy began once again to flow.

One of the few hopeful examples of leadership in Africa was terminated abruptly when Captain Thomas Sankara, leader of Burkina Faso, was murdered in his fourth year of rule by his second-in-command. The world did not pay too much attention to yet another round of musical chairs by power-hungry soldiers in Africa. In any event Sankara was a brash young man with Marxist leanings who recently had the effrontery to read a lecture to a visiting head of state who happened to be none other than President Mitterrand of France himself. According to press reports of the incident, Mitterrand, who is a socialist veteran in his own right, rose to the occasion. He threw away his prepared speech and launched into an hour-long counter-attack in which he must have covered much ground. But the sting was in the tail: "Sankara is a disturbing person. With him it is impossible to sleep in peace. He does not leave your conscience alone" (*New York Times*, August 23, 1987, p. 10).

I have no doubt that Mitterrand meant his comment as some kind of praise for his young and impatient host. But it was also a deadly arraignment and even conviction. Principalities and powers do not tolerate those who interrupt the sleep of their consciences. That Baldwin got away with it for forty years was a miracle. Except, of course, that he didn't get away; he paid dearly every single day of those years, every single hour of those days.

What was his crime that we should turn him into a man of sadness, this man inhabited by a soul so eager to be loved and to smile? His demands were so few and so simple.

His bafflement, childlike—which does not mean simpleminded but deeply profound and saintly—comes across again and again and nowhere better perhaps than in his essay "Fifth Avenue, Uptown": "Negroes want to be treated like men: a perfectly straightforward statement containing seven words. People who have mastered Kant, Hegel, Shakespeare, Marx, Freud and the Bible find this statement impenetrable." This failure to comprehend turns out to be, as one might have suspected, a willful, obdurate refusal. And for good reason. For let's face it, that sentence, simple and innocent-looking though it may seem, is in reality a mask for a profoundly subversive intent to reorder the world. And the world, viewed from the high point of the pyramid where its controllers reside, is working perfectly well and sitting firm.

Egypt's Pharaoh, according to the myth of the Israelites, faced the same problem when a wild-eyed man walked up to him with a simple demand, four words long: "Let my people go!" We are not told that he rushed off to his office to sign their exit visa. On the contrary.

So neither history nor legend encourages us to believe that a man who sits on his fellow will some day climb down on the basis of sounds reaching him from below. And yet we must consider how so much more dangerous our already very perilous world would become if the oppressed everywhere should despair altogether of invoking reason and humanity to arbitrate their cause. This is the value and the relevance, into the foreseeable future, of James Baldwin.

As long as injustice exists, whether it be within the American nation itself or between it and its neighbors; as long as a tiny cartel of rich, creditor nations can hold the rest in iron chains of usury; so long as one third or less of mankind eat well and often to excess while two-thirds and more live perpetually with hunger; as long as white people who constitute a mere fraction of the human race consider it natural and even righteous to dominate the rainbow majority whenever and wherever they are thrown together; and—the oldest of them all—as long as the discrimination by men against women persists, the words of James Baldwin will be there to bear witness and to inspire and elevate the struggle for human freedom.

· V ·

SELECTED WRITINGS

Truth *is* a two-edged sword—and if one is not willing to be pierced by that sword, even to the extreme of dying on it, then all of one's intellectual activity is a masturbatory delusion and a wicked and dangerous fraud.

—JAMES BALDWIN

NOTES OF A NATIVE
SON (1955)

• by James Baldwin •

• ONE •

On the twenty-ninth of July, in 1943, my father died. On the same day, a few hours later, his last child was born. Over a month before this, while all our energies were concentrated in waiting for these events, there had been, in Detroit, one of the bloodiest race riots of the century. A few hours after my father's funeral, while he lay in state in the undertaker's chapel, a race riot broke out in Harlem. On the morning of the third of August, we drove my father to the graveyard through a wilderness of smashed plate glass.

The day of my father's funeral had also been my nineteenth birthday. As we drove him to the graveyard, the spoils of injustice, anarchy, discontent, and hatred were all around us. It seemed to me that God himself had devised, to mark my father's end, the most sustained and brutally dissonant of codas. And it seemed to me, too, that the violence which rose all about us as my father left the world had been devised as a corrective for the pride of his eldest son. I had declined to believe in that apocalypse which had been central to my father's vision; very well, life seemed to be saying, here is something that will certainly pass for an apocalypse until the real thing comes along. I had inclined to be contemptuous of my father for the conditions of his life, for the conditions of our lives. When his life had ended I began to wonder about that life and also, in a new way, to be apprehensive about my own.

I had not known my father very well. We had got on badly, partly because we shared, in our different fashions, the vice of stubborn pride. When he was dead I realized that I had hardly ever spoken to him. When he had been dead a long time I began to wish I had. It seems to be typical of life in America, where opportunities, real and fancied, are thicker than anywhere else on the globe, that the second generation has no time to talk to the first. No one, including my father, seems to have known exactly how old he was, but his mother had been born during slavery. He was of the first generation of free men. He, along with thousands of other Negroes, came North after 1919 and I was part of that generation which had never seen the landscape of what Negroes sometimes call the Old Country.

He had been born in New Orleans and had been a quite young man there during the time that Louis Armstrong, a boy, was running errands for the dives and honky-tonks of what was always presented to me as one of the most wicked of cities—to this day, whenever I think of New Orleans, I also helplessly think of Sodom and Gomorrah. My father never mentioned Louis Armstrong, except to forbid us to play his records; but there was a picture of him on our wall for a long time. One of my father's strong-willed female relatives had placed it there and forbade my father to take it down. He never did, but he eventually maneuvered her out of the house and when, some years later, she was in trouble and near death, he refused to do anything to help her.

He was, I think, very handsome. I gather this from photographs and from my own memories of him, dressed in his Sunday best and on his way to preach a sermon somewhere, when I was little. Handsome, proud, and ingrown, "like a toenail," somebody said. But he looked to me, as I grew older, like pictures I had seen of African tribal chieftains: he really should have been naked, with warpaint on and barbaric mementos, standing among spears. He could be chilling in the pulpit and indescribably cruel in his personal life and he was certainly the most bitter man I have ever met; yet it must be said that there was something else in him, buried in him, which lent him his tremendous power and, even, a rather crushing charm. It had something to do with his blackness, I think—he was very black—with his blackness and his beauty, and with the fact that he knew that he was black but did not know that he was beautiful. He claimed to be proud of his blackness but it had also been the cause of much humiliation and it had fixed bleak boundaries to his life. He was not a young man when we were growing up and he had already suffered many kinds of ruin; in his outrageously demanding and protective way he loved his children, who were black like him and menaced, like him; and all these things sometimes showed in his face when he tried, never to my knowledge with any success, to establish contact with any of us. When he took one of his children on his knee to play, the child always became fretful and began to cry; when he tried to help one of us with our homework the absolutely unabating tension which emanated from him caused our minds and our tongues to become paralyzed, so that he, scarcely knowing why, flew into a rage and the child, not knowing why, was punished. If it ever entered his head to bring a surprise home for his children, it was, almost unfailingly, the wrong surprise and even the big watermelons he often brought home on his back in the summertime led to the most appalling scenes. I do not remember, in all those years, that one of his children was ever glad to see him come home. From what I was able to gather of his early life, it seemed that this inability to establish contact with other people had always marked him and had been one of the things which had driven him out of New Orleans. There was something in him, therefore, groping and tentative, which was never expressed and which was buried with him. One saw it most clearly when he was facing new people and hoping to impress them. But he never did, not for long. We went from church to smaller and more improbable church, he found himself in less and less demand as a minister, and by the time he died none of his friends had come to see him for a long time. He had lived and died in an intolerable bitterness of spirit and it frightened me, as we drove him to the graveyard through those unquiet, ruined streets, to see how powerful and overflowing this bitterness could be and to realize that this bitterness now was mine.

When he died I had been away from home for a little over a year. In that year I had had time to become aware of the meaning of all my father's bitter warnings, had discovered the secret of his proudly pursed lips and rigid carriage: I had discovered the weight of white people in the world. I saw that this had been for my ancestors and now would be for me an awful thing to live with and that the bitterness which had helped to kill my father could also kill me.

He had been ill a long time—in the mind, as we now realized, reliving instances of his fantastic intransigence in the new light of his affliction and endeavoring to feel a sorrow for him which never, quite, came true. We had not known that he was being eaten up by paranoia, and the discovery that his cruelty, to our bodies and our minds, had been one of the symptoms of his illness was not, then, enough to enable us to forgive him. The younger children felt, quite simply, relief that he would not be coming home anymore. My mother's observation that it was he, after all, who had kept them alive all these years meant nothing because the problems of keeping children alive are not real for children. The older children felt, with my father gone, that they could invite their friends to the house without fear that their friends would be insulted or, as had sometimes happened with me, being told that their friends were in league with the devil and intended to rob our family of everything we owned. (I didn't fail to wonder, and it made me hate him, what on earth we owned that anybody else would want.)

His illness was beyond all hope of healing before anyone realized that he was ill. He had always been so strange and had lived, like a prophet, in such unimaginably close communion with the Lord that his long silences which were punctuated by moans and hallelujahs and snatches of old songs while he sat at the living room window never seemed odd to us. It was not until he refused to eat because, he said, his family was trying to poison him that my mother was forced to accept as a fact what had, until then, been only an unwilling suspicion. When he was committed, it was discovered that he had tuberculosis and, as it turned out, the disease of his mind allowed the disease of his body to destroy him. For the doctors could not force him to eat, either, and, though he was fed intravenously, it was clear from the beginning that there was no hope for him.

In my mind's eye I could see him, sitting at the window, locked up in his terrors; hating and fearing every living soul including his children who had betrayed him, too, by reaching toward the world which had despised him. There were nine of us. I began to wonder what it could have felt like for such a man to have had nine children whom he could barely feed. He used to make little jokes about our poverty, which never, of course, seemed very funny to us; they could not have seemed very funny to him, either, or else our all too feeble response to them would never have caused such rages. He spent great energy and achieved, to our chagrin, no small amount of success in keeping us away from the people who surrounded us, people who had all-night rent parties to which we listened when we should have been sleeping, people who cursed and drank and flashed razor blades on Lenox Avenue. He could not understand why, if they had so much energy to spare, they could not use it to make their lives better. He treated almost everybody on our block with a most uncharitable asperity and neither they, nor, of course, their children were slow to reciprocate.

The only white people who came to our house were welfare workers and bill collectors. It was almost always my mother who dealt with them, for my father's temper, which was at the mercy of his pride, was never to be trusted. It was clear that he felt their very presence in his home to be a violation: this was conveyed by his carriage, almost ludicrously stiff, and by his voice, harsh and vindictively polite. When I was around nine or ten I wrote a play which was directed by a young, white schoolteacher, a woman, who then took an interest in me, and gave me books to read and, in order to corroborate my theatrical bent, decided to take me to see what she somewhat tactlessly referred to as "real" plays. Theater-going was forbidden in our house, but, with the really cruel intuitiveness of a child, I suspected that the color of this woman's skin would carry the day for me. When, at school, she suggested taking me to the theater, I did not, as I might have done if she had been a Negro, find a way of discouraging her, but agreed that she should pick me up at my house one evening. I then, very cleverly, left all the rest to my mother, who suggested to my father, as I knew she would, that it would not be very nice to let such a kind woman make the trip for nothing. Also, since it was a schoolteacher, I imagine that my mother countered the idea of sin with the idea of "education," which word, even with my father, carried a kind of bitter weight.

Before the teacher came my father took me aside to ask *why* she was coming, what *interest* she could possibly have in our house, in a boy like me. I said I didn't know but I, too, suggested that it had something to do with education. And I understood that my father was waiting for me to say something—I didn't quite know what; perhaps that I wanted his protection against this teacher and her "education." I said none of these things and the teacher came and we went out. It was clear, during the brief interview in our living room, that my father was agreeing very much against his will and that he would have refused permission if he had dared. The fact that he did not dare caused me to despise him: I had no way of knowing that he was facing in that living room a wholly unprecedented and frightening situation.

Later, when my father had been laid off from his job, this woman became very important to us. She was really a very sweet and generous woman and went to a great deal of trouble to be of help to us, particularly during one awful winter. My mother called her by the highest name she knew: she said she was a "Christian." My father could scarcely disagree but during the four or five years of our relatively close association he never trusted her and was always trying to surprise in her open, midwestern face the genuine, cunningly hidden, and hideous motivation. In later years, particularly when it began to be clear that this "education" of mine was going to lead me to perdition, he became more explicit and warned me that my white friends in high school were not really my friends and that I would see, when I was older, how white people would do anything to keep a Negro down. Some of them could be nice, he admitted, but none of them were to be trusted and most of them were not even nice. The best thing was to have as little to do with them as possible. I did not feel this way and I was certain, in my innocence, that I never would.

But the year which preceded my father's death had made a great change in my life. I had been living in New Jersey, working in defense plants, working and living among southerners, white and black. I knew about the South, of course, and about how southerners treated Negroes and how they expected them to behave, but it had never entered my mind that anyone would look at me and expect *me* to behave that way. I learned in New Jersey that to be a Negro meant, precisely, that one was never looked at but was simply at the mercy of the reflexes the color of one's skin caused in other people. I acted in New Jersey as I had always acted, that is as though I thought a great deal of myself—I had to *act* that way—with results that were, simply, unbelievable. I had scarcely arrived before I had earned the enmity, which was extraordinarily ingenious, of all my superiors and nearly all my co-workers. In the beginning, to make matters worse, I simply did not know what was happening. I did not know what I had done, and I shortly began to wonder what *anyone* could possibly do, to bring about such unanimous, active, and unbearably vocal hostility. I knew about Jim Crow but I had never experienced it. I went to the same self-service restaurant three times and stood with all the Princeton boys before the counter, waiting for a hamburger and coffee; it was always an extraordinarily long time before anything was set before me; but it was not until the fourth visit that I learned that, in fact, nothing had ever been set before me: I had simply picked something up. Negroes were not served there, I was told, and they had been waiting for me to realize that I was always the only Negro present. Once I was told this, I determined to go there all the time. But now they were ready for me and, though some dreadful scenes were subsequently enacted in that restaurant, I never ate there again.

It was the same story all over New Jersey, in bars, bowling alleys, diners, places to live. I was always being forced to leave, silently, or with mutual imprecations. I very shortly became notorious and children giggled behind me when I passed and their elders whispered or shouted—they really believed that I was mad. And it did begin to work

227

on my mind, of course; I began to be afraid to go anywhere and to compensate for this I went places to which I really should not have gone and where, God knows, I had no desire to be. My reputation in town naturally enhanced my reputation at work and my working day became one long series of acrobatics designed to keep me out of trouble. I cannot say that these acrobatics succeeded. It began to seem that the machinery of the organization I worked for was turning over, day and night, with but one aim: to eject me. I was fired once, and contrived, with the aid of a friend from New York, to get back on the payroll; was fired again, and bounced back again. It took awhile to fire me for the third time, but the third time took. There were no loopholes anywhere. There was not even any way of getting back inside the gates.

That year in New Jersey lives in my mind as though it were the year during which, having an unsuspected predilection for it, I first contracted some dread, chronic disease, the unfailing symptom of which is a kind of blind fever, a pounding in the skull and fire in the bowels. Once this disease is contracted, one can never be really carefree again, for the fever, without an instant's warning, can recur at any moment. It can wreck more important things than race relations. There is not a Negro alive who does not have this rage in his blood—one has the choice, merely, of living with it consciously or surrendering to it. As for me, this fever has recurred in me, and does, and will until the day I die.

My last night in New Jersey, a white friend from New York took me to the nearest big town, Trenton, to go to the movies and have a few drinks. As it turned out, he also saved me from, at the very least, a violent whipping. Almost every detail of that night stands out very clearly in my memory. I even remember the name of the movie we saw because its title impressed me as being so patly ironical. It was a movie about the German occupation of France, starring Maureen O'Hara and Charles Laughton and called *This Land Is Mine*. I remember the name of the diner we walked into when the movie ended: it was the "American Diner." When we walked in the counterman asked what we wanted and I remember answering with the casual sharpness which had become my habit: "We want a hamburger and a cup of coffee, what do you think we want?" I do not know why, after a year of such rebuffs, I so completely failed to anticipate his answer, which was, of course, "We don't serve Negroes here." This reply failed to discompose me, at least for the moment. I made some sardonic comment about the name of the diner and we walked out into the streets.

This was the time of what was called the "brownout," when the lights in all American cities were very dim. When we reentered the streets something happened to me which had the force of an optical illusion, or a nightmare. The streets were very crowded and I was facing north. People were moving in every direction but it seemed to me, in that instant, that all of the people I could see, and many more than that, were moving toward me, against me, and that everyone was white. I remember how their faces gleamed. And I felt, like a physical sensation, a *click* at the nape of my neck as though some interior string connecting my head to my body had been cut. I began to walk. I heard my friend call after me, but I ignored him. Heaven only knows what was going on in his mind, but he had the good sense not to touch me—I don't know what would have happened if he had—and to keep me in sight. I don't know what was going on in my mind, either; I certainly had no conscious plan. I wanted to do something to crush these white faces, which were crushing me. I walked for perhaps a block or two until I came to an enormous, glittering, and fashionable restaurant in which I knew not even the intercession of the Virgin would cause me to be served. I pushed through the doors and took the first vacant seat I saw, at a table for two, and waited.

I do not know how long I waited and I rather wonder, until today, what I could possibly have looked like. Whatever I looked like, I frightened the waitress who shortly appeared, and the moment she appeared all of my fury flowed toward her. I hated her for her white face, and for her great, astounded, frightened eyes. I felt that if she found a black man so frightening I would make her fright worthwhile.

She did not ask me what I wanted, but repeated, as though she had learned it somewhere, "We don't serve Negroes here." She did not say it with the blunt, derisive hostility to which I had grown so accustomed, but, rather, with a note of apology in her voice, and fear. This made me colder and more murderous than ever. I felt I had to do something with my hands. I wanted her to come close enough for me to get her neck between my hands.

So I pretended not to have understood her, hoping to draw her closer. And she did step a very short step closer, with her pencil poised incongruously over her pad, and repeated the formula: ". . . don't serve Negroes here."

Somehow, with the repetition of that phrase, which was already ringing in my head like a thousand bells of a nightmare, I realized that she would never come any closer and that I would have to strike from a distance. There was nothing on the table but an ordinary water mug half full of water, and I picked this up and hurled it with all my strength at her. She ducked and it missed her and shattered against the mirror behind the bar. And, with that sound, my frozen blood abruptly thawed, I returned from wherever I had been, I *saw*, for the first time, the restaurant, the people with their mouths open, already, as it seemed to me, rising as one man, and I realized what I had done, and where I was, and I was frightened. I rose and began running for the door. A round, potbellied man grabbed me by the nape of the neck just as I reached the doors and began to beat me about the face. I kicked him and got loose and ran into the streets. My friend whispered, *"Run!"* and I ran.

My friend stayed outside the restaurant long enough to misdirect my pursuers and the police, who arrived, he told me, at once. I do not know what I said to him when he came to my room that night. I could not have said much. I felt, in the oddest, most awful way, that I had somehow betrayed him. I lived it over and over and over again, the way one relives an automobile accident after it has happened and one finds oneself alone and safe. I could not get over two facts, both equally difficult for the imagination to grasp, and one was that I could have been murdered. But the other was that I had been ready to commit murder. I saw nothing very clearly but I did see this: that my life, my *real* life, was in danger, and not from anything other people might do but from the hatred I carried in my own heart.

▪ TWO ▪

I had returned home around the second week in June—in great haste because it seemed that my father's death and my mother's confinement were both but a matter of hours. In the case of my mother, it soon became clear that she had simply made a miscalculation. This had always been her tendency and I don't believe that a single one of us arrived in the world, or has since arrived anywhere else, on time. But none of us dawdled so intolerably about the business of being born as did my baby sister. We sometimes amused ourselves, during those endless, stifling weeks, by picturing the baby sitting within in the safe, warm dark, bitterly regretting the necessity of becoming a part of our chaos and stubbornly putting it off as long as possible. I understood her perfectly and congratulated her on showing such good sense so soon. Death, however, sat as purposefully at my father's bedside as life stirred within my mother's womb and it was harder to understand why he so lingered in that long shadow. It seemed that he had bent, and for a long time, too, all of his energies toward dying. Now death was ready for him but my father held back.

All of Harlem, indeed, seemed to be infected by waiting. I had never before known it to be so violently still. Racial tensions throughout this country were exacerbated during the early years of the war, partly because the labor market brought together hundreds of thousands of ill-prepared people and partly because Negro soldiers, regardless of where they were born, received their military training in the South. What happened in defense plants and army camps had repercussions, naturally, in every Negro ghetto. The situation in Harlem had grown bad enough for clergymen, policemen, educators, politicians, and social workers to assert in one breath that there was no "crime wave" and to offer, in the very next breath, suggestions as to how to combat it. These suggestions always seemed to involve playgrounds, despite the fact that racial skirmishes were occurring in the playgrounds, too. Playground or not, crime wave or not, the Harlem police force had been augmented in March, and the unrest grew—perhaps, in fact, partly as a result of the ghetto's instinctive hatred of policemen. Perhaps the most revealing news item, out of the steady parade of reports of muggings, stabbings, shootings, assaults, gang wars, and accusations of police brutality, is the item concerning six Negro girls who set upon a white girl in the subway because, as they all too accurately put it, she was stepping on their toes. Indeed she was, all over the nation.

I had never before been so aware of policemen, on foot, on horseback, on corners, everywhere, always two by two. Nor had I ever been so aware of small knots of people. They were on stoops and on corners and in doorways, and what was striking about them, I think, was that they did not seem to be talking. Never, when I passed these groups, did the usual sound of a curse or a laugh ring out and neither did there seem to be any hum of gossip. There was certainly, on the other hand, occurring between them communication extraordinarily intense. Another thing that was striking was the unexpected diversity of the people who made up these groups. Usually, for example, one would see a group of sharpies standing on the street corner, jiving the passing chicks; or a group of older men, usually, for some reason, in the vicinity of a barber shop, discussing baseball scores, or the numbers, or making rather chilling observations about women they had known. Women, in a general way, tended to be seen less often together— unless they were church women, or very young girls, or prostitutes met together for an unprofessional instant. But that summer I saw the strangest combinations: large, respectable, churchly matrons standing on the stoops or the corners with their hair tied up, together with a girl in sleazy satin whose face bore the marks of gin and the razor, or heavy-set, abrupt, no-nonsense older men, in company with the most disreputable and fanatical "race" men, or these same "race" men with the sharpies, or these sharpies with the churchly women. Seventh-Day Adventists and Methodists and Spiritualists seemed to be hobnobbing with Holy Rollers and they were all, alike, entangled with the most flagrant disbelievers; something heavy in their stance seemed to indicate that they had all, incredibly, seen a common vision, and on each face there seemed to be the same strange, bitter shadow.

The churchly women and the matter-of-fact, no-nonsense men had children in the Army. The sleazy girls they talked to had lovers there, the sharpies and the "race" men had friends and brothers there. It would have demanded an unquestioning patriotism, happily as uncommon in this country as it is undesirable, for these people not to have been disturbed by the bitter letters they received, by the newspaper stories they read, not to have been enraged by the posters, then to be found all over New York, which described the Japanese as "yellow-bellied Japs." It was only the "race" men, to be sure, who spoke ceaselessly of being revenged—how this vengeance was to be exacted was not clear—for the indignities and dangers suffered by Negro boys in uniform; but everybody felt a directionless, hopeless bitterness, as well as that panic which can scarcely be suppressed when one knows that a human being one loves is beyond one's reach, and in danger. This helplessness and this gnawing uneasiness does something, at length, to even the toughest mind. Perhaps the best way to sum all this up is to say that the people I knew felt, mainly, a peculiar kind of relief when they knew that their boys were being shipped out of the South, to do battle overseas. It was, perhaps, like feeling that the most dangerous part of a dangerous journey had been passed and that now, even if death should come, it would come with honor and without the complicity of their countrymen. Such a death would be, in short, a fact with which one could hope to live.

It was on the twenty-eighth of July, which I believe was a Wednesday, that I visited my father for the first time during his illness and for the last time in his life. The moment I saw him I knew why I had put off this visit so long. I had told my mother that I did not want to see him because I hated him. But this was not true. It was only that I *had* hated him and I wanted to hold on to this hatred. I did not want to look on him as a ruin: it was not a ruin I had hated. I imagine that one of the reasons people cling to their hates so stubbornly is because they sense, once hate is gone, that they will be forced to deal with pain.

We traveled out to him, his older sister and myself, to what seemed to be the very end of a very Long Island. It was hot and dusty and we wrangled, my aunt and I, all the way out, over the fact that I had recently begun to smoke and, as she said, to give myself airs. But I knew that she wrangled with me because she could not bear to face the fact of her brother's dying. Neither could I endure the reality of her despair, her unstated bafflement as to what had happened to her brother's life, and her own. So we wrangled and I smoked and from time to time she fell into a heavy reverie. Covertly, I watched her face, which was the face of an old woman; it had fallen in, the eyes were sunken and lightless; soon she would be dying, too.

In my childhood—it had not been so long ago—I had thought her beautiful. She had been quick-witted and quick-moving and very generous with all the children and each of her visits had been an event. At one time one of my brothers and myself had thought of running away to live with her. Now she could no longer produce out of her handbag some unexpected and yet familiar delight. She made me feel pity and revulsion and fear. It was awful to realize that she no longer caused me to feel affection. The closer we came to the hospital the more querulous she became and at the same time, naturally, grew more dependent on me. Between pity and guilt and fear I began to feel that there was another me trapped in my skull like a jack-in-the-box who might escape my control at any moment and fill the air with screaming.

She began to cry the moment we entered the room and she saw him lying there, all shriveled and still, like a little black monkey. The great, gleaming apparatus which fed him and would have compelled him to be still even if he had been able to move brought to mind, not beneficence, but torture; the tubes entering his arm made me think of pictures I had seen when a child, of Gulliver, tied down by the pygmies on that island. My aunt wept and wept, there was a whistling sound in my father's throat; nothing was said; he could not speak. I wanted to take his hand, to say something. But I do not know what I could have said, even if he could have heard me. He was not really in that room with us, he had at last really embarked on his journey; and though my aunt told me that he said he was going to meet Jesus, I did not hear anything except that whistling in his throat. The doctor came back and we left, into that unbearable train again, and home. In the morning came the telegram saying that he was dead. Then the house was suddenly full of relatives, friends, hysteria, and confusion and I quickly left my mother and the children to the care of those impressive women, who, in Negro communities at least, automatically appear at times of bereavement armed with lotions, proverbs, and patience, and an ability to cook. I went downtown. By the time I returned, later the same day, my mother had been carried to the hospital and the baby had been born.

▪ THREE ▪

For my father's funeral I had nothing black to wear and this posed a nagging problem all day long. It was one of those problems, simple, or impossible of solution, to which the mind insanely clings in order to avoid the mind's real trouble. I spent most of that day at the downtown apartment of a girl I knew, celebrating my birthday with whisky and wondering what to wear that night. When planning a birthday celebration one naturally does not expect that it will be up against competition from a funeral and this girl had anticipated taking me out that night, for a big dinner and a night club afterwards. Sometime during the course of that long day we decided that we would go out anyway, when my father's funeral service was over. I imagine I decided it, since, as the funeral hour approached, it became clearer and clearer to me that I would not know what to do with myself when it was over. The girl, stifling her very lively concern as to the possible effects of the whisky on one of my father's chief mourners, concentrated on being conciliatory and practically helpful. She found a black shirt for me somewhere and ironed it and, dressed in the darkest pants and jacket I owned, and slightly drunk, I made my way to my father's funeral.

The chapel was full, but not packed, and very quiet. There were, mainly, my father's relatives, and his children, and here and there I saw faces I had not seen since childhood, the faces of my father's one-time friends. They were very dark and solemn now, seeming somehow to suggest that they had known all along that something like this would happen. Chief among the mourners was my aunt, who had quarreled with my father all his life; by which I do not mean to suggest that her mourning was insincere or that she had not loved him. I suppose that she was one of the few people in the world who had, and their incessant quarreling proved precisely the strength of the tie that bound them.

The only other person in the world, as far as I knew, whose relationship to my father rivaled my aunt's in depth was my mother, who was not there.

It seemed to me, of course, that it was a very long funeral. But it was, if anything, a rather shorter funeral than most, nor, since there were no overwhelming, uncontrollable expressions of grief, could it be called—if I dare to use the word—successful. The minister who preached my father's funeral sermon was one of the few my father had still been seeing as he neared his end. He presented to us in his sermon a man whom none of us had ever seen—a man thoughtful, patient, and forbearing, a Christian inspiration to all who knew him, and a model for his children. And no doubt the children, in their disturbed and guilty state, were almost ready to believe this; he had been remote enough to be anything and, anyway, the shock of the incontrovertible, that it was really our father lying up there in that casket, prepared the mind for anything. His sister moaned and this grief-stricken moaning was taken as corroboration. The other faces held a dark, noncommittal thoughtfulness. This was not the man they had known, but they had scarcely expected to be confronted with *him*; this was, in a sense deeper than questions of fact, the man they had not known, and the man they had not known may have been the real one. The real man, whoever he had been, had suffered and now he was dead: this was all that was sure and all that mattered now. Every man in the chapel hoped that when his hour came he, too, would be eulogized, which is to say forgiven, and that all of his lapses, greeds, errors, and strayings from the truth would be invested with coherence and looked upon with charity. This was perhaps the last thing human beings could give each other and it was what they demanded, after all, of the Lord. Only the Lord saw the midnight tears, only He was present when one of His children, moaning and wringing hands, paced up and down the room. When one slapped one's child in anger the recoil in the heart reverberated through heaven and became part of the pain of the universe. And when the children were hungry and sullen and distrustful and one watched them, daily, growing wilder, and further away, and running headlong into danger, it was the Lord who knew what the charged heart endured as the strap was laid to the backside; the Lord alone who knew what one *would* have said if one had had, like the Lord, the gift of the living word. It was the Lord who knew of the impossibility every parent in that room faced: how to prepare the child for the day when the child would be despised and how to *create* in the child—by what means?—a stronger antidote to this poison than one had found for oneself. The avenues, side streets, bars, billiard halls, hospitals, police stations, and even the playgrounds of Harlem— not to mention the houses of correction, the jails, and the morgue— testified to the potency of the poison while remaining silent as to the efficacy of whatever antidote, irresistibly raising the question of whether or not such an antidote existed; raising, which was worse, the question of whether or not an antidote was desirable; perhaps poison should be fought with poison. With these several schisms in the mind and with more terrors in the heart than could be named, it was better not to judge the man who had gone down under an impossible burden. It was better to remember: *Thou knowest this man's fall; but thou knowest not his wrassling.*

While the preacher talked and I watched the children—years of changing their diapers, scrubbing them, slapping them, taking them to school, and scolding them had had the perhaps inevitable result of making me love them, though I am not sure I knew this then—my mind was busily breaking out with a rash of disconnected impressions. Snatches of popular songs, indecent jokes, bits of books I had read, movie sequences, faces, voices, political issues—I thought I was going mad; all these impressions suspended, as it were, in the solution of the faint nausea produced in me by the heat and liquor. For a moment I had the impression that my alcoholic breath, inefficiently disguised with chewing gum, filled the entire chapel. Then someone began singing one of my father's favorite songs and, abruptly, I was with him, sitting on his knee, in the hot, enormous, crowded church which was the first church we attended. It was the Abyssinian Baptist Church on 138th Street. We had not gone there long. With this image, a host of others came. I had forgotten, in the rage of my growing up, how proud my father had been of me when I was little. Apparently, I had had a voice and my father had liked to show me off before the members of the church. I had forgotten what he had looked like when he was pleased but now I remembered that he had always been grinning with pleasure when my solos ended. I even remembered certain expressions on his face when he teased my mother—had he loved her? I would never know. And when had it all begun to change? For now it seemed that he had not always been cruel. I remembered being taken for a haircut and scraping my knee on the footrest of the barber's chair and I remembered my father's face as he soothed my crying and applied the stinging iodine. Then I remembered our fights, fights which had been of the worst possible kind because my technique had been silence.

I remembered the one time in all our life together when we had really spoken to each other.

It was on a Sunday and it must have been shortly before I left home. We were walking, just the two of us, in our usual silence, to or from church. I was in high school and had been doing a lot of writing and I was, at about this time, the editor of the high school magazine. But I had also been a Young Minister and had been preaching from the pulpit. Lately, I had been taking fewer engagements and preached as rarely as possible. It was said in the church, quite truthfully, that I was "cooling off."

My father asked me abruptly, "You'd rather write than preach, wouldn't you?"

I was astonished at his question—because it was a real question. I answered, "Yes."

That was all we said. It was awful to remember that that was all we had *ever* said.

The casket now was opened and the mourners were being led up the aisle to look for the last time on the deceased. The assumption was that the family was too overcome with grief to be allowed to make this journey alone and I watched while my aunt was led to the casket and, muffled in black, and shaking, led back to her seat. I disapproved of forcing the children to look on their dead father, considering that the shock of his death, or, more truthfully, the shock of death as a reality, was already a little more than a child could bear, but my judgment in this matter had been overruled and there they were, bewildered and frightened and very small, being led, one by one, to the casket. But there is also something very gallant about children at such moments. It has something to do with their silence and gravity and with the fact that one cannot help them. Their legs, somehow, seem *exposed*, so that it is at once incredible and terribly clear that their legs are all they have to hold them up.

I had not wanted to go to the casket myself and I certainly had not wished to be led there, but there was no way of avoiding either of these forms. One of the deacons led me up and I looked on my father's face. I cannot say that it looked like him at all. His blackness had been equivocated by powder and there was no suggestion in that casket of what his power had or could have been. He was simply an old man dead, and it was hard to believe that he had ever given anyone either joy or pain. Yet, his life filled that room. Further up the avenue his wife was holding his newborn child. Life and death so close together, and love and hatred, and right and wrong, said something to me which I did not want to hear concerning man, concerning the life of man.

After the funeral, while I was downtown desperately celebrating my birthday, a Negro soldier, in the lobby of the Hotel Braddock, got into a fight with a white policeman over a Negro girl. Negro girls, white policemen, in or out of uniform, and Negro males—in or out of uniform—were part of the furniture of the lobby of the Hotel Braddock and this was certainly not the first time such an incident had occurred. It was destined, however, to receive an unprecedented publicity, for the fight between the policeman and the soldier ended with the shooting of the soldier. Rumor, flowing immediately to the streets outside, stated that the soldier had been shot in the back, an instantaneous and revealing invention, and that the solider had died protecting a Negro woman. The facts were somewhat different—for example, the soldier had not been shot in the back, and was not dead, and the girl seems to have been as dubious a symbol of womanhood as her white counterpart in Georgia usually is, but no one was interested in the facts. They preferred the invention because this invention expressed and corroborated their hates and fears so perfectly. It is just as well to remember that people are always doing this. Perhaps many of those legends, including Christianity, to which the world clings began their conquest of the world with just some such concerted surrender to distortion. The effect, in Harlem, of this particular legend was like the effect of a lit match in a tin of gasoline. The mob gathered before the doors of the Hotel Braddock simply began to swell and to spread in every direction, and Harlem exploded.

The mob did not cross the ghetto lines. It would have been easy, for example, to have gone over Morningside Park on the West Side or to have crossed the Grand Central railroad tracks at 125th Street on the East Side, to wreak havoc in white neighborhoods. The mob seems to have been mainly interested in something more potent and real than the white face, that is, in white power, and the principal damage done during the riot of the summer of 1943 was to white business establishments in Harlem. It might have been a far bloodier story, of course, if, at the hour the riot began, these establishments had still been open. From the Hotel Braddock the mob fanned out, east and west along 125th Street, and for the entire length of Lenox, Seventh, and Eighth avenues. Along each of these avenues, and along each major side street—116th, 125th, 135th, and so on—bars, stores, pawnshops, restaurants, even little luncheonettes had been smashed open and entered and looted—looted, it might be added, with more haste than efficiency. The shelves really looked as though a bomb had struck them. Cans of beans and soup and dog food, along with toilet paper, corn flakes, sardines, and milk, tumbled every which way, and abandoned cash registers and cases of beer leaned crazily out of the splintered windows and were strewn along the avenues. Sheets, blankets, and clothing of every description formed a kind of path, as though people had dropped them while running. I truly had not realized that Harlem *had* so many stores until I saw them all smashed open; the first time the word "wealth" ever entered my mind in relation to Harlem was when I saw it scattered in the streets. But one's first, incongruous impression of plenty was countered immediately by an impression of waste. None of this was doing anybody any good. It would have been better to have left the plate glass as it had been and the goods lying in the stores.

It would have been better, but it would also have been intolerable, for Harlem had needed something to smash. To smash something is the ghetto's chronic need. Most of the time it is the members of the ghetto who smash each other, and themselves. But as long as the ghetto walls are standing there will always come a moment when these outlets do not work. That summer, for example, it was not enough to get into a fight on Lenox Avenue, or curse out one's cronies in the barber shops. If ever, indeed, the violence which fills Harlem's churches, pool halls, and bars erupts outward in a more direct fashion, Harlem and its citizens are likely to vanish in an apocalyptic flood. That this is not likely to happen is due to a great many reasons, most hidden and powerful among them the Negro's real relation to the white American. This relation prohibits, simply, anything as uncomplicated and satisfactory as pure hatred. In order really to hate white people, one has to blot so much out of the mind—and the heart—that this hatred itself becomes an exhausting and self-destructive pose. But this does not mean, on the other hand, that love comes easily: the white world is too powerful, too complacent, too ready with gratuitous humiliation, and, above all, too ignorant and too innocent for that. One is absolutely forced to make perpetual qualifications and one's own reactions are always canceling each other out. It is this, really, which has driven so many people mad, both white and black. One is always in the position of having to decide between amputation and gangrene. Amputation is swift but time may prove that the amputation was not necessary—or one may delay the amputation too long. Gangrene is slow, but it is impossible to be sure that one is reading one's symptoms right. The idea of going through life as a cripple is more than one can bear, and equally unbearable is the risk of swelling up slowly, in agony, with poison. And the trouble, finally, is that the risks are real even if the choices do not exist.

"But as for me and my house," my father had said, "we will serve the Lord." I wondered, as we drove him to his resting place, what this line had meant for him. I had heard him preach it many times. I had preached it once myself, proudly giving it an interpretation different from my father's. Now the whole thing came back to me, as though my father and I were on our way to Sunday school and I were memorizing the golden text: *And if it seem evil unto you to serve the Lord, choose you this day whom you will serve; whether the gods which your father served that were on the other side of the flood, or the gods of the Amorites, in whose land ye dwell: but as for me and my house, we will serve the Lord*. I suspected in these familiar lines a meaning which had never been there for me before. All of my father's texts and songs, which I had decided were meaningless, were arranged before me at his death like empty bottles, waiting to hold the meaning which life would give them for me. This was his legacy: nothing is ever escaped. That bleakly memorable morning I hated the unbelievable streets and the Negroes and whites who had, equally, made them that way. But I knew that it was folly, as my father would have said, this bitterness was folly. It was necessary to hold on to the things that mattered. The dead man mattered, the new life mattered; blackness and whiteness did not matter; to believe that they did was to acquiesce in one's own destruction. Hatred, which could destroy so much, never failed to destroy the man who hated and this was an immutable law.

It began to seem that one would have to hold in the mind forever two ideas which seemed to be in opposition. The first idea was acceptance, the acceptance, totally without rancor, of life as it is, and men as they are: in the light of this idea, it goes without saying that injustice is a commonplace. But this did not mean that one could be complacent, for the second idea was of equal power: that one must never, in one's own life, accept these injustices as commonplace but must fight them with all one's strength. This fight begins, however, in the heart and it now had been laid to my charge to keep my own heart free of hatred and despair. This intimation made my heart heavy and, now that my father was irrecoverable, I wished that he had been beside me so that I could have searched his face for the answers which only the future would give me now.

INTRODUCTION TO *THE PRICE OF THE TICKET* (1985)

• by James Baldwin •

$\mathbf{M}$Y soul looks back and wonders how I got over—indeed: but I find it unexpectedly difficult to remember, in detail, how I got started. I will never, for example, forget Saul Levitas, the editor of *The New Leader*, who gave me my first book review assignment sometime in 1946, nor Mary Greene, a wonderful woman, who was his man Friday: but I do not remember exactly how I met them.

I *do* remember how my life in Greenwich Village began—which is, essentially, how my career began—for it began when I was fifteen.

One day, a DeWitt Clinton H. S. running buddy, Emile Capouya, played hookey without me and went down to Greenwich Village and made the acquaintance of Beauford Delaney. The next day, he told me about this wonderful man he had met, a black—then, Negro, or Colored—painter and said that I must meet him: and he gave me Beauford Delaney's address.

I had a Dickensian job, after school, in a sweat shop on Canal Street, and was getting on so badly at home that I dreaded going home: and, so, sometime later, I went to 181 Greene Street, where Beauford lived then, and introduced myself.

I was terrified, once I had climbed those stairs and knocked on that door. A short, round brown man came to the door and looked at me. He had the most extraordinary eyes I'd ever seen. When he had completed his instant X-ray of my brain, lungs, liver, heart, bowels, and spinal column (while I had said, usefully, "Emile sent me") he smiled and said, "Come in," and opened the door.

He opened the door all right.

Lord, I was to hear Beauford sing, later, and for many years, *open the unusual door*. My running buddy had sent me to the right one, and not a moment too soon.

I walked through that door into Beauford's colors—on the easel, on the palette, against the wall—sometimes turned to the wall—and sometimes (in limbo?) covered by white sheets. It was a small studio (but it didn't seem small) with a black potbellied stove somewhere near the two windows. *I* remember two windows, there may have been only one: there *was* a fire escape which Beauford, simply by his presence, had transformed, transmuted into the most exclusive terrace in Manhattan or Bombay.

I walked into music. I had grown up with music, but, now, on Beauford's small black record player, I began to hear what I had never dared or been able to hear. Beauford never gave me any lectures. But, in his studio and because of his presence, I really began to *hear* Ella Fitzgerald, Ma Rainey, Louis Armstrong, Bessie Smith, Ethel Waters, Paul Robeson, Lena Horne, Fats Waller. He could inform me about Duke Ellington and W. C. Handy, and Josh White, introduce me to Frankie Newton and tell tall tales about Ethel Waters. And these people were not meant to be looked on by me as celebrities, but as a part of Beauford's life and as part of my inheritance.

I may have been with Beauford, for example, the first time I saw Paul Robeson, in concert, and in *Othello*: but I know that he bought tickets for us—really, for me—to see and hear Miss Marian Anderson, at Carnegie Hall.

Because of her color, Miss Anderson was not allowed to sing at the Met, nor, as far as the Daughters of the American Revolution were concerned, anywhere in Washington where white people might risk hearing her. Eleanor Roosevelt was appalled by this species of patriotism and arranged for Marian Anderson to sing on the steps of the Lincoln Memorial. This was a quite marvelous and passionate event in those years, triggered by the indignation of one woman who had, clearly, it seemed to me, married beneath her.

By this time, I was working for the Army—or the Yankee dollar!—in New Jersey. I hitchhiked, in sub-zero weather, out of what I will always remember as one of the lowest and most obscene circles of Hell, into Manhattan: where both Beauford and Miss Anderson were on hand to inform me that I had no right to permit myself to be defined by so pitiful a people. Not only was I not born to be a slave: I was not born to hope to become the equal of the slave-master. They had, the masters, incontestably, the rope—in time, with enough, they would hang themselves with it. They were not to hang *me: I* was to see to that. If Beauford and Miss Anderson were a part of my inheritance, I was a part of their hope.

I still remember Miss Anderson, at the end of that concert, in a kind of smoky yellow gown, her skin copper and tan, roses in the air about her, roses at her feet. Beauford painted it, an enormous painting, he fixed it in time, for me, forever, and he painted it, he said, for me.

Beauford was the first walking, living proof, for me, that a black man could be an artist. In a warmer time, a less blasphemous place, he would have been recognized as my Master and I as his Pupil. He became, for me, an example of courage and integrity, humility and passion. An absolute integrity: I saw him shaken many times and I lived to see him broken but I never saw him bow.

His example operated as an enormous protection: for the Village, then, and not only for a boy like me, was an alabaster maze perched above a boiling sea. To lose oneself in the maze was to fall into the sea. One saw it around one all the time: a famous poet of the twenties and thirties grotesquely, shamelessly, cadging drinks, another relic living in isolation on opium and champagne, someone your own age suddenly strung out or going under a subway train, people you ate with and drank with suddenly going home and blowing their brains out or turning on the gas or leaping out of the window. And, racially, the Village was vicious, partly because of the natives, largely because of the tourists, and absolutely because of the cops.

Very largely, then, because of Beauford and Connie Williams, a beautiful black lady from Trinidad who ran the restaurant in which I was a waiter, and the jazz musicians I loved and who referred to me, with a kind of exasperated affection, as "the kid," I was never entirely at the mercy of an environment at once hostile and seductive. They knew about dope, for example—I didn't: but the pusher and his product were kept far away from me. I needed love so badly that I could as easily have been hit with a needle as persuaded to share a joint of marijuana. And, in fact, Beauford and the others let me smoke with them from time to time. (But there were people they warned me *not* to smoke with.)

The only real danger with marijuana is that it can lead to rougher stuff, but this has to do with the person, not the weed. In my own case, it could hardly have become a problem, since I simply could not write if I were "high." Or, rather, I could, sometimes all night long, the greatest pages the world had ever seen, pages I tore up the moment I was able to read them.

Yet, I learned something about myself from these irredeemable horrors: something which I might not have learned had I not been forced to know that I was valued. I repeat that Beauford never gave me any lectures, but he didn't have to—he expected me to accept and respect the value placed upon me. Without this, I might very easily have become the junky which so many among those I knew were becoming then, or the Bellevue or Tombs inmate (instead of the visitor) or the Hudson River corpse which a black man I loved with all my heart was shortly to become.

Shortly: I was to meet Eugene sometime between 1943 and 1944 and "run" or "hang" with him until he hurled himself off the George Washington Bridge, in the winter of 1946. We were never lovers: for what it's worth, I think I wish we had been.

When he was dead, I remembered that he had, once, obliquely,

246

suggested this possibility. He had run down a list of his girlfriends: those he liked, those he *really* liked, one or two with whom he might really be in love, and, then, he said, "I wondered if I might be in love with you."

I wish I had heard him more clearly: an oblique confession is always a plea. But I was to hurt a great many people by being unable to imagine that anyone could possibly be in love with an ugly boy like me. To be valued is one thing, the recognition of this assessment demanding, essentially, an act of the will. But love is another matter: it is scarcely worth observing what a mockery love makes of the will. Leaving all that alone, however: when he was dead, I realized that I would have done anything whatever to have been able to hold him in this world.

Through him, anyway, my political life, insofar as I can claim, formally, to have had one, began. He was a Socialist—a member of the Young People's Socialist League (YPSL)—and urged me to join, and I did. I, then, outdistanced him by becoming a Trotskyite—so that I was in the interesting position (at the age of nineteen) of being an anti-Stalinist when America and Russia were allies.

My life on the Left is of absolutely no interest. It did not last long. It was useful in that I learned that it may be impossible to indoctrinate me; also, revolutionaries tend to be sentimental and I hope that I am not. This was to lead to very serious differences between myself and Eugene, and others: but it was during this period that I met the people who were to take me to Saul Levitas, of *The New Leader*; Randall Jarrell, of *The Nation*; Elliott Cohen and Robert Warshow, of *Commentary*; and Philip Rahv, of *Partisan Review*.

These men are all dead, now, and they were all very important to my life. It is not too much to say that they helped to save my life. (As Bill Cole, at Knopf, was later to do when the editor assigned *Go Tell It on the Mountain* had me on the ropes.) And their role in my life says something arresting concerning the American dilemma, or, more precisely, perhaps, the American torment.

I had been to two black newspapers before I met these people and had simply been laughed out of the office: I was a shoeshine boy who had never been to college. I don't blame these people, God knows that I was an unlikely cub reporter: yet, I still remember how deeply I was hurt.

On the other hand, around this time, or a little later, I landed a job as messenger for New York's liberal newspaper, *PM*. It is perhaps worth pointing out that *PM* had a man of about my complexion (dark) in the tower, under whom I worked, a coal-black Negro in the cellar, whom nobody ever saw, and a very fair Negro on the city desk, in the window. My career at *PM* was very nearly as devastating as my career as a civilian employee of the U.S. Army, except that *PM* never (as far as I know) placed me on a blacklist. If the black newspapers had considered me absolutely beyond redemption, *PM* was determined to save me: I cannot tell which attitude caused me the more bitter anguish.

Therefore, though it may have cost Saul Levitas nothing to hurl a book at a black boy to see if he could read it and be articulate concerning what he had read, I took it as a vote of confidence and swore that I would give him my very best shot. And I loved him— the old man, as I sometimes called him (to his face) and I think—I know—that he was proud of me, and that he loved me, too.

It was a very great apprenticeship. Saul required a book review a week, which meant that I had to read and write all the time. He paid me ten or twenty dollars a shot: Mary Greene would sometimes coerce him into giving me a bonus. Then he would stare at her, as though he could not believe that she, his helper, could be capable of such base treachery and look at me more tragically than Julius Caesar looked at Brutus and sigh—and give me another five or ten dollars.

As for the books I reviewed—well, no one, I suppose, will ever read them again. It was after the war, and the Americans were on one of their monotonous conscience "trips": be kind to niggers, for Christ's sake, be kind to Jews! A high, or turning point of some kind was reached when I reviewed Ross Lockridge's sunlit and fabulously successful *Raintree County*. The review was turned in and the author committed suicide before the review was printed. I was very disagreeably shaken by this, and Saul asked me to write a postscript—which I did. That same week I met the late Dwight Macdonald, whom I admired very much because of his magazine, *Politics*, who looked at me with wonder and said that I was "very smart." This pleased me, certainly, but it frightened me more.

But no black editor could or would have been able to give me my head, as Saul did then: partly because he would not have had the power, partly because he could not have afforded—or needed—Saul's politics, and partly because part of the price of the black ticket is involved—fatally—with the dream of becoming white.

This is not possible, partly because white people are not white: part of the price of the white ticket is to delude themselves into believing that they are. The political position of *my old man*, for example, whether or not he knew it, was dictated by his (in his case) very honorable necessity not to break faith with the Old World. One may add, in passing, that the Old World, or Europe, has become nothing less than an American superstition, which accounts, if anything can, for an American vision of Russia so Talmudic and self-serving that it has absolutely nothing to do with any reality occurring under the sun.

But the black American must find a way to keep faith with, and to excavate, a reality much older than Europe. Europe has never been, and cannot be, a useful or valid touchstone for the American experience because America is not, and never can be, white.

My father died before Eugene died. When my father died, Beauford helped me to bury him and I then moved from Harlem to the Village.

This was in 1943. We were fighting the Second World War.

We: who was this *we*?

For this war was being fought, as far as I could tell, to bring freedom to everyone with the exception of Hagar's children and the "yellow-bellied Japs."

This was not a matter, merely, of my postadolescent discernment. It had been made absolutely clear to me by the eighteen months or so that I had been working for the Army, in New Jersey, by the anti-Japanese posters to be found, then, all over New York, and by the internment of the Japanese.

At the same time, one was expected to be "patriotic" and pledge allegiance to a flag which had pledged no allegiance to you: it risked becoming your shroud if you didn't know how to keep your distance and stay in your "place."

And all of this was to come back to me much later, when Cassius Clay, a.k.a. Muhammad Ali, refused to serve in Vietnam because he was a Muslim—in other words, for religious reasons—and was stripped of his title, while placards all over New York trumpeted *Be true to your faith!*

I have never been able to convey the confusion and horror and heartbreak and contempt which every black person I then knew felt. Oh, we dissembled and smiled as we groaned and cursed and did our duty. (And we *did* our duty.) The romance of treason never occurred to us for the brutally simple reason that you can't betray a country you don't have. (Think about it.) Treason draws its energy from the conscious, deliberate betrayal of a trust—as we were not trusted, we could not betray. And we did not wish to be traitors. We wished to be citizens.

We: the black people of this country, then, with particular emphasis on those serving in the armed forces. The way blacks were treated in, and by, an American army spreading freedom around the globe was the reason for the heartbreak and contempt. Daddy's youngest son, by his first marriage, came home, on furlough, to help with the funeral. When these young men came home, in uniform, they started talking: and one sometimes trembled, for their sanity and for one's own. One trembled, too, at another depth, another incoherence, when one wondered—as one could not fail to wonder—what *nation* they represented. My brother, describing his life in uniform, did not seem to be representing the America his uniform was meant to represent—: he had never seen the America his uniform was meant to represent. Had anyone? Did he know, had he met, anyone who had? Did anyone *live* there? Judging from the great gulf fixed between their conduct and their principles, it seemed unlikely.

Was it worth his life?

For he, certainly, on the other hand, represented something much larger than himself and something in him knew it: otherwise, he would have been broken like a match-stick and lost or have surrendered the power of speech. A *nation within a nation:* this thought wavered in my mind, I think, all those years ago, but I did not know what to make of it, it frightened me.

We: my family, the living and the dead, and the children coming along behind us. This was a complex matter, for I was not living with my family in Harlem, after all, but "downtown," in the "white world," in alien and mainly hostile territory. On the other hand, for me, then, Harlem was almost as alien and in a yet more intimidating way and risked being equally hostile, although for very different reasons. This truth cost me something in guilt and confusion, but it was the truth. It had something to do with my being the son of an evangelist and having been a child evangelist, but this is not all there was to it—that is, guilt is not all there was to it.

The fact that this particular child had been born when and where he was born had dictated certain expectations. The child does not really know what these expectations are—does not know how real they are—until he begins to fail, challenge, or defeat them. When it was clear, for example, that the pulpit, where I had made so promising a beginning, would not be my career, it was hoped that I would go on to college. This was never a very realistic hope and—perhaps because I knew this—I don't seem to have felt very strongly about it. In any case, this hope was dashed by the death of my father.

Once I had left the pulpit, I had abandoned or betrayed my role in the community—indeed, my departure from the pulpit and my leaving home were almost simultaneous. (I had abandoned the ministry in order not to betray myself by betraying the ministry.)

Once it became clear that I was not going to go to college, I became a kind of two-headed monstrosity of a problem. Without a college education, I could, clearly, never hope to become a writer: would never acquire the skills which would enable me to conquer what was thought of as an all-white world. This meant that I would become a half-educated handyman, a vociferous, bitter ruin, spouting Shakespeare in the bars on Saturday night and sleeping it off on Sunday.

I could see this, too. I saw it all around me. There are few things more dreadful than dealing with a man who knows that he is going under, in his own eyes, and in the eyes of others. Nothing can help that man. What is left of that man flees from what is left of human attention.

I fled. I didn't want my mama, or the kids, to see me like that.

And if all this seems, now, ridiculous and theatrical apprehension on the part of a nineteen-year-old boy, I can say only that it didn't seem remotely ridiculous then. A black person in this democracy is certain to endure the unspeakable and the unimaginable in nineteen years. It is far from an exaggeration to state that many, and by the deliberate will and action of the Republic, are ruined by that time.

White Americans cannot, in the generality, hear this, anymore than their European ancestors, and contemporaries, could, or can. If I say that my best friend, black, Eugene, who took his life at the age of twenty-four, had been, until that moment, a survivor, I will be told that he had "personal" problems. Indeed he did, and one of them was trying to find a job, or a place to live, in New York. If I point out that there is certainly a connection between his death (when I was twenty-two) and my departure for Paris (when *I* was twenty-four) I will be condemned as theatrical.

But I am really saying something very simple. The will of the people, or the State, is revealed by the State's institutions. There was not, then, nor is there, now, a single American institution which is not a racist institution. And racist institutions—the unions, for one example, the Church, for another, and the Army—or the military—for yet another, are meant to keep the nigger in his place. Yes: we have lived through avalanches of tokens and concessions but white power remains white. And what it appears to surrender with one hand it obsessively clutches in the other.

I know that this is considered to be heresy. Spare me, for Christ's *and* His Father's sake, any further examples of American white progress. When one examines the use of this word in this most particular context, it translates as meaning that those people who have opted for being white congratulate themselves on their generous ability to return to the slave that freedom which they never had any right to endanger, much less take away. For this dubious effort, and still more dubious achievement, they congratulate themselves and expect to be congratulated—: in the coin, furthermore, of black gratitude, gratitude not only that my burden is—(slowly, but it takes time) being made lighter but my joy that white people are improving.

My black burden has not, however, been made lighter in the sixty years since my birth or the nearly forty years since the first essay in this collection was published and my joy, therefore, as concerns the immense strides made by white people is, to say the least, restrained.

Leaving aside my friends, the people I love, who cannot, usefully, be described as either black or white, they are, like life itself, thank God, many, many colors, I do not feel, alas, that my country has any reason for self-congratulation.

If I were still in the pulpit which some people (and they may be right) claim I never left, I would counsel my countrymen to the self-confrontation of prayer, the cleansing breaking of the heart which precedes atonement. This is, of course, impossible. Multitudes are capable of many things, but atonement is not one of them.

A multitude is, I suppose, by definition, an anonymous group of people bound or driven together by fears (I wrote "tears") and hopes and needs which no individual member could face or articulate alone.

On the one hand, for example, mass conversions are notoriously transitory: within days, the reformed—"saved"—whore, whoremonger, thief, drunkard, have ventilated their fears and dried their tears and returned to their former ways. Nor do the quite spectacularly repentant "born again" of the present hour give up this world to follow Jesus. No, they take Jesus with them into the marketplace where He is used as proof of their acumen and as their Real Estate Broker, now, and, as it were, forever.

But it does not demand a mass conversion to persuade a mob to lynch a nigger or stone a Jew or mutilate a sexual heretic. It demands no conversion at all: in the very same way that the act demands no courage at all. That not one member of the mob could or would accomplish the deed alone is not merely, I think, due to physical cowardice but to cowardice of another order. To destroy a nigger, a kike, a dyke, or a faggot, by one's own act alone is to have committed a communion and, above all, to have made a public confession more personal, more total, and more devastating than any act of love: whereas the orgasm of the mob is drenched in the blood of the lamb.

A mob is not autonomous: it executes the real will of the people who rule the State. The slaughter in Birmingham, Alabama, for example, was not, merely, the action of a mob. That blood is on the hands of the state of Alabama: which sent those mobs into the streets to execute the will of the State. And, though I know that it has now become inconvenient and impolite to speak of the American Jew in the same breath with which one speaks of the American black (*I hate to say I told you so*, sings the right righteous Reverend Ray Charles, *but: I told you so*), I yet contend that the mobs in the streets of Hitler's Germany were in those streets not only by the will of the German State, but by the will of the Western world, including those architects of human freedom, the British, and the presumed guardian of Christian and human morality, the Pope. The American Jew, if I may say so—and I say so with love, whether or not you believe me—makes the error of believing that his Holocaust ends in the New World, where mine begins. My diaspora continues, the end is not in sight, and I certainly cannot depend on the morality of this panic-stricken consumer society to bring me out of—: Egypt.

A mob cannot afford to doubt: that the Jews killed Christ or that niggers want to rape their sisters or that anyone who fails to make it in the land of the free and the home of the brave deserves to be wretched. But these ideas do not come from the mob. They come from the state, which creates and manipulates the mob. The idea of black persons as property, for example, does not come from the mob. It is not a spontaneous idea. It does not come from the people, who knew better, who thought nothing of intermarriage until they were penalized for it: this idea comes from the architects of the American State. These architects decided that the concept of Property was more important—more real—than the possibilities of the human being.

In the church I come from—which is not at all the same church to which white Americans belong—we were counseled, from time to time, to do our first works over. Though the church I come from and the church to which most white Americans belong are both Christian churches, their relationship—due to those pragmatic decisions concerning Property made by a Christian State sometime ago—cannot be said to involve, or suggest, the fellowship of Christians. We do not, therefore, share the same hope or speak the same language.

To do your first works over means to reexamine everything. Go back to where you started, or as far back as you can, examine all of it, travel your road again and tell the truth about it. Sing or shout or testify or keep it to yourself: but *know whence you came.*

This is precisely what the generality of white Americans cannot afford to do. They do not know how to do it—: as I must suppose. They come through Ellis Island, where *Giorgio* becomes *Joe, Pappavasiliu* becomes *Palmer, Evangelos* becomes *Evans, Goldsmith* becomes *Smith* or *Gold,* and *Avakian* becomes *King.* So, with a painless change of name, and in the twinkling of an eye, one becomes a white American.

Later, in the midnight hour, the missing identity aches. One can neither assess nor overcome the storm of the middle passage. One is mysteriously shipwrecked forever, in the Great New World.

The slave is in another condition, as are his heirs: *I told Jesus it would be all right/ If He changed my name.*

If *He* changed my name.

The Irish middle passage, for but one example, was as foul as my own, and as dishonorable on the part of those responsible for it. But the Irish became white when they got here and began rising in the world, whereas I became black and began sinking. The Irish, therefore and thereafter—again, for but one example—had absolutely no choice but to make certain that I could not menace their safety or status or identity: and, if I came too close, they could, with the consent of the governed, kill me. Which means that we can be friendly with each other anywhere in the world, except Boston.

What a monumental achievement on the part of those heroes who conquered the North American wilderness!

The price the white American paid for his ticket was to become white—: and, in the main, nothing more than that, or, as he was to insist, nothing less. This incredibly limited not to say dim-witted ambition has choked many a human being to death here: and this, I contend, is because the white American has never accepted the real reasons for his journey. I know very well that my ancestors had no desire to come to this place: but neither did the ancestors of the people who became white and who require of my captivity a song. They require of me a song less to celebrate my captivity than to justify their own.

· BIBLIOGRAPHY ·

BOOKS BY BALDWIN

Perspectives: Angles of African Art [James Baldwin *et al.*]. Michael Weber, ed. New York: Center for African Art: H. N. Abrams, 1987.

The Evidence of Things Not Seen. New York: Henry Holt and Co., 1985.

The Price of the Ticket: Collected Nonfiction. New York: St. Martin's/Marek, 1985.

Jimmy's Blues: Selected Poems. London: Michael Joseph, 1983; New York: St. Martin's, 1986.

Just Above My Head. New York: Dial Press, 1979.

The Devil Finds Work. New York: Dial Press, 1976.

Little Man, Little Man: A Story of Childhood. Illustrated by Yoran Cazac. New York: Dial Press, 1976.

If Beale Street Could Talk. New York: Dial Press, 1974.

A Rap on Race. Margaret Mead and James Baldwin. Philadelphia: J. P. Lippincott, 1973.

No Name in the Street. New York: Dial Press, 1972.

One Day, When I Was Lost: A Scenario Based on Alex Haley's "The Autobiography of Malcolm X." London: Michael Joseph, 1972.

A Dialogue: James Baldwin and Nikki Giovanni. Philadelphia: J. P. Lippincott, 1971.

The Amen Corner. New York: Dial Press, 1968.

Tell Me How Long the Train's Been Gone. New York: Dial Press, 1968.

Going to Meet the Man. New York: Dial Press, 1965.

Blues for Mr. Charlie. New York: Dial Press, 1964.

Nothing Personal. Photographs by Richard Avedon and text by James Baldwin. New York: Atheneum Publishers, 1964.

The Fire Next Time. New York: Dial Press, 1963.

Another Country. New York: Dial Press, 1962.

Nobody Knows My Name: More Notes of a Native Son. New York: Dial Press, 1961.

Giovanni's Room. New York: Dial Press, 1956.

Notes of a Native Son. Boston: Beacon Press, 1955.

Go Tell It on the Mountain. New York: Alfred A. Knopf, 1953.

BALDWIN IN OTHER TITLES

"The Artist's Struggle for Integrity." In *Seeds of Liberation* by Paul Goodman. New York: Braziller, 1964, pp. 380–87.

"As Much Truth as One Can Bear." In *Opinions and Perspectives from The New York Times Book Review.* Edited and with an introduction by Francis Brown. Boston: Houghton Mifflin, 1964, pp. 207–15.

"Black Boys Look at White Boys." In *Smiling Through the Apocalypse.* Edited by Harold Hayes. New York: McCall Publishing Co., 1969, pp. 713–30.

"Come Out the Wilderness." In *Prize Stories, 1959.* Edited by Paul Engle. New York: Doubleday, 1959, pp. 208–33.

"Compressions: L'Homme et La Machine." In *César: Compression d'or* by César Baldaccini. Paris: Hachette, 1973, pp. 9–16.

"The Creative Process." In *Creative America.* The National Cultural Center. New York: Ridge Press, 1962, pp. 17–21.

"The Discovery of What It Means to Be an American." In *Opinions and Perspectives from The New York Times Book Review.* Edited and with an introduction by Francis Brown. Boston: Houghton Mifflin, 1964, pp. 320–26.

"East River Downtown." In *First Person Singular: Essays for the Sixties.* Edited with an introduction by Herbert Gold. New York: Dial Press, 1963, pp. 38–45.

"Easy Rider." In *The Dial: An Annual of Fiction.* New York: Dial Press, 1962, pp. 3–26. Excerpts from *Another Country.*

"Envoi." In A *Quarter Century of Unamericana 1938–63; A Tragico-Comical Memorabilia of HUAC.* Edited by Charlotte Pomerantz. Nieuw Amsterdam: Marzani and Munsell, 1963.

"Fifth Avenue, Uptown: A Letter from Harlem." In *First Person Singular: Essays for the Sixties.* Edited and with an introduction by Herbert Gold. New York: Dial Press, 1963, pp. 27–38. Also in *For Our Times: 24 Essays by 8 Contemporary Americans.* Edited by Barry Gross. New York: Dodd, Mead, 1970, pp. 33–42.

Foreword to *Freedom Ride* by Jim Peck. New York: Simon and Schuster, 1962.

Foreword to A *Lonely Rage: The Autobiography of Bobby Seale.* New York: Times Books, 1978.

"From Dreams of Love to Dreams of Terror." In *Natural Enemies: Youth and the Clash of Generations.* New York: Lippincott, 1969, pp. 274–79.

"Gabriel's Prayer." In *Black Insights: Significant Literature by Black Americans— 1760 to the Present.* Edited by Nick Aaron Ford. Waltham, Massachusetts: Ginn and Company, 1971, pp. 196–219. Excerpts from *Go Tell It on the Mountain.*

"The Highroad to Destiny." In *Martin Luther King, Jr.: A Profile.* Edited by C. Eric Lincoln. New York: Hill and Wang, 1970, pp. 90–112.

"In Search of a Basis for Mutual Understanding and Racial Harmony." In *The Nature of Human Society.* Edited by H. Ober Hesse. Philadelphia: Fortress Press, 1967, pp. 231–40.

Introduction to *The Chasm: The Life and Death of a Great Experiment in Ghetto Education* by Robert Campbell. Boston: Houghton Mifflin, 1974.

Introduction to *We Are Everywhere: Narrative Accounts of Rhodesian Guerrillas* by Michael Raeburn. New York: Random House, 1978.

"James Baldwin on the Negro Actor." In *Anthology of the American Negro in the Theatre.* Edited by Lindsay Patterson. New York: Publishers Company, 1967, pp. 127–30.

"The Language of the Streets." In *Literature and the Urban Experience: Essays on the City and Literature.* Edited by Chalmer Watts. New Brunswick, New Jersey: Rutgers University Press, 1981, pp. 133–37.

"Many Thousand Gone." In *Five Black Writers: Essays on Wright, Ellison, Baldwin, Hughes and Le Roi Jones.* New York: New York University Press; London: University of London Press Ltd.; 1970, pp. 230–42.

"Mass Culture and the Creative Artist: Some Personal Notes." In *Culture for the Millions?* Edited by Jacob Norman. Princeton, New Jersey: Van Nostrand, 1961, pp. 120–23.

"My Dungeon Shook." In *The Outnumbered: Stories, Essays, and Poems About Minority Groups by America's Leading Writers.* New York: Delacorte Press, pp. 148–53.

"Negroes Are Anti-Semitic Because They're Anti-White." In *Black Anti-Semitism and Jewish Racism.* Introduction by Nat Hentoff. New York: Baron, 1969, pp. 3–14.

"Notes of a Native Son." In *For Our Times: 24 Essays by 8 Contemporary Americans.* Edited by Barry Gross. New York: Dodd, Mead, 1970, pp. 2–21.

"A Report from Occupied Territory." In *Law and Resistance: American Attitudes Toward Authority.* New York: Harper and Row, 1970, pp. 318–28.

"Roy's Wound." In *New World Writing,* Vol. 2. New York: New American Library, 1952, pp. 109–16. Excerpts from *Go Tell It on the Mountain.*

"The Search for Identity." In *American Principles and Issues.* Edited by Oscar Handlin. New York: Holt, Rinehart and Winston, 1961, pp. 459–67.

"Sonny's Blues." In *Best American Short Stories, 1958 and the Yearbook of the American Short Story.* Edited by Martha Foley and David Burnett. Boston: Houghton Mifflin, 1958, pp. 21–53. Also in *New York, New York: The City as Seen by Masters of Art and Literature.* Edited by John Gordon and L. Rust Hills. New York: Shorecrest, 1965, pp. 365–93. Also in *The Loners: Short Stories About the Young and Alienated.* New York, Macmillan, 1970, pp. 160–202.

"Stranger in the Village." In *For Our Times: 24 Essays by 8 Contemporary Americans.* Edited by Barry Gross. New York: Dodd, Mead, 1970, pp. 21–33.

"A Talk to Harlem Teachers." In *Harlem U.S.A.,* rev. ed. Edited by John Henrik Clarke. New York: Collier Books, 1971, pp. 171–80.

"The Threshing Floor." In *Cavalcade: Negro American Writing from 1760 to the Present.* Edited by Arthur P. Davis and Saunders Redding. Boston: Houghton Mifflin Company, 1971, pp. 572–83. Excerpts from *Go Tell It on the Mountain.*

"Unnameable Objects, Unspeakable Crimes." In *The White Problem in America.* Edited by Ebony. Chicago: Johnson Publishing Company, 1966, pp. 173–81.

"The Uses of the Blues." In *The Twelfth Anniversary Playboy Reader.* Edited by Hugh Hefner. Chicago: Playboy Press, distributed by Trident Press, 1965, pp. 150–59.

"We Can Change the Country." In *Seeds of Liberation.* Edited by Paul Goodman. New York: Braziller, 1964, pp. 341–45.

"The White Problem." In *100 Years of Emancipation.* Edited by Robert A. Goodwin. Chicago: Rand McNally, 1964, pp. 80–88.

"A Word from Writer Directly to Reader." In *Fiction of the Fifties.* Edited by Herbert Gold. New York: Doubleday, 1959, pp. 18–19.

INTERVIEWS WITH BALDWIN

"James Baldwin: *The Art of Fiction,*" LXXVIII. Interview by Jordan Egrably. In *Paris Review* (91) Spring 1984.

"Disturber of the Peace: James Baldwin." Interview by Eve Auchincloss and Nancy Lynch. In *The Black American Writer*, Vol. I. Edited by C. W. E. Bigsby. Deland, Florida: Everett/Edwards, 1969, pp. 199–216.

"An Interview with a Negro Intellectual." In *The Negro Protest: Talks with James Baldwin, Malcolm X, Martin Luther King*. Edited by Kenneth B. Clark. Boston: Beacon Press, 1963, pp. 1–14, 49.

"James Baldwin . . . in Conversation." Interview by Dan Georgakas. In *Black Voices: An Anthology of Afro-American Literature*. Edited by Abraham Chapman. New American Library, 1968, pp. 660–68.

"James Baldwin." Interview by Kenneth B. Clark. In his *King, Malcolm, Baldwin: Three Interviews*. Middletown, Connecticut: Wesleyan University Press; Scranton, Pennsylvania: Distributed by Harper and Row, 1985.

"Are We on the Edge of Civil War?" In *The Americans*. Interviews by David Frost. New York: Stein and Day Publishers, 1970, pp. 145–50.

"Why I Left America. Conversations: Ida Lewis and James Baldwin." In *New Black Voices*. Edited by Abraham Chapman. New York: New American Library, 1972, pp. 409–19.

ABOUT BALDWIN

Bigsby, C. W. E. "James Baldwin." In his *Confrontation and Commitment: A Study of Contemporary American Drama 1959–66*. Columbia, Missouri: University of Missouri Press, 1968, pp. 126–37.

Bloom, Harold, ed. *James Baldwin*. New York: Chelsea House Publishers, 1986.

Bone, Robert. "The Novels of James Baldwin." In *Images of the Negro in American Literature*. Edited by Seymour Gross and John Edward Hardy. Chicago: University of Chicago Press, 1966, pp. 265–99. Also in *The Black Novelist*. Edited by Robert Hemenway. Columbus, Ohio: Charles E. Merrill Publishing Company, 1970, pp. 111–33.

Boyle, Kay. "Introducing James Baldwin." In *Contemporary American Novelists*. Edited by Harry T. Moore. Carbondale: Southern Illinois University Press, 1964, pp. 155–57.

Breit, Harvey. "James Baldwin and Two Footnotes." In *The Creative Present: Notes on Contemporary American Fiction*. Edited by Nona Balakian and Charles Simmons. New York: Doubleday, 1963, pp. 1–23.

Bruck, Peter. *Von der "Store-front Church" zum "American Dream": James Baldwin und der Amerikanische Rassenkonflikt*. Amsterdam: Verlag B. R. Grunner, 1975.

Brustein, Robert. "Everybody's Protest Play." In his *Season of Discontent: Dramatic Opinions, 1959–65*. New York: Simon and Schuster, 1965, pp. 161–65.

Butterfield, Stephen. "James Baldwin: The Growth of a New Radicalism." In his *Black Autobiography in America*. Amherst, Massachusetts: University of Massachusetts Press, 1974, pp. 183–200.

Clarke, John Henrik. "The Alienation of James Baldwin." In *Black Expression*. Edited by Addison Gayle. New York: Weybright and Talley, 1969, pp. 350–53. Also in his *Harlem U.S.A.* Revised edition. New York: Collier Books, 1971.

Cleaver, Eldridge. "Notes on a Native Son." In his *Soul on Ice*. New York: McGraw-Hill, Inc., 1968, pp. 97–111.

Cohn, Ruby. "James Baldwin." In her *Dialogue in American Drama*. Bloomington, Indiana: Indiana University Press, 1971, pp. 188–92.

Dance, Daryl C. "James Baldwin." In *Black American Writers: Bibliographical Essays*. Edited by M. Thomas Inge *et al*. New York: St. Martin's Press, 1978, pp. 73–120.

Davis, Arthur P. "Integrationist and Transitional Writers: James Baldwin." In his *From the Dark Tower: Afro-American Writers, 1900–60*. Washington, D.C.: Howard University Press, 1974, pp. 216–26.

Davis, Arthur P., and J. Saunders Redding. "James Baldwin." In their *Cavalcade: Negro American Writing from 1760 to the Present*. Boston: Houghton Mifflin, 1971, pp. 571–86.

Davis, Ursula Broschke. *Paris Without Regret: James Baldwin, Kenny Clarke, Chester Himes and Donald Byrd*. Iowa City: University of Iowa Press, 1986.

Dupee, F. W. "James Baldwin and 'the Man.' " In his *The King of the Cats and Other Remarks on Writers and Writing*. New York: Farrar, Straus and Giroux, 1965, pp. 208–14.

Eckman, Fern Marja. *The Furious Passage of James Baldwin*. New York: M. Evans, 1966.

Edwards, David Lawrence. *James Baldwin and North America*. London: S.C.M. Press, 1975.

Fabré, Michel. "Fathers and Sons in James Baldwin's *Go Tell It on the Mountain*." In *Modern Black Novelists: A Collection of Critical Essays*. Edited by M. G. Cooke. Englewood Cliffs, New Jersey: Prentice-Hall, 1971, pp. 88–104.

Finkelstein, S. W. "Existentialism and Social Demands: Norman Mailer and James Baldwin." In his *Existentialism and Alienation in American Literature*. New York: International Publishers, 1965, pp. 276–84.

Ford, Nick Aaron. *Black Insights: Significant Literature by Afro-Americans, 1760 to the Present*. Waltham, Massachusetts: Ginn and Company, 1971, pp. 192–219, 300–301.

Freese, Peter. "James Baldwin." In his *Die Amerikanische Kurzgeschichte nach 1945. Salinger, Malamud, Baldwin, Purdy, Barth*. Frankfurt: Athenaum Verlag, pp. 246–320.

Gayle, Addison, Jr. "The Function of Black Literature at the Present Time." In his *Black Aesthetic*. New York: Doubleday, 1971, pp. 383–400.

Gibson, Donald B., ed. In *Five Black Writers: Essays on Wright, Ellison, Baldwin, Hughes, and Le Roi Jones*. New York: New York University Press; London: University of London Press Ltd., 1970, pp. 11–28, 119–64, 243–70.

———. "Politics of Ellison and Baldwin." In *The Politics of Twentieth-Century Writers*. Edited by George Panichas. New York: Hawthorne Publishing Company, 1971, pp. 307–20.

Gross, Theodore L. "The Major Black Authors: Richard Wright, Ralph Ellison, James Baldwin." In his *Historic Ideals in American Literature*. New York: Free Press, 1971, pp. 148–80.

Harris, Trudier. *Black Women in the Fiction of James Baldwin*. Knoxville: University of Tennessee Press, 1985.

Harper, Howard M., Jr. "James Baldwin—Art or Propaganda." In his *Desperate Faith: A Study of Bellows, Salinger, Mailer, Baldwin and Updike*. Chapel Hill, North Carolina: University of North Carolina Press, 1967.

Hernton, Calvin C. "Blood of the Lamb: The Ordeal of James Baldwin." In his *White Papers for White Americans*. New York: Doubleday, 1966, pp. 105–21. Also in *Amistad I: Writings on Black History and Culture*. Edited by John A. Williams and Charles F. Harris. New York: Vintage Books, 1970, pp. 183–99.

———. "A Fiery Baptism: Postscript." *Ibid.* pp. 200–225.

Hicks, Granville. "Another Country." In his *Literary Horizons: A Quarter Century of American Fiction*. New York: New York University Press, 1970, pp. 84–105. "James Baldwin." In *Literary Horizons: A Quartet of American Fiction*. New York: New York University Press, 1970, pp. 85–105.

Howe, Irving. "Black Boys and Native Sons." In his *A World More Attractive: A View of Modern Literature and Politics*. New York: Horizon, 1963, pp. 98–122. New York: Books for Libraries Press, 1970, pp. 98–122.

Kazin, Alfred. "Essays of James Baldwin." In his *Contemporaries*. Boston: Little, Brown, 1962, pp. 254–58.

Kent, George E. "Baldwin and the Problem of Being." In his *Blackness and the Adventure of Western Culture*. Chicago: Third World Press, 1972, pp. 139–51.

Kinnamon, Keneth, ed. *James Baldwin: A Collection of Critical Essays*. Englewood Cliffs, New Jersey: Prentice-Hall, 1974.

Klein, Marcus. "James Baldwin: A Question of Identity." In his *After Alienation: American Novels in Mid-Century*. New York: World Publishing Company, 1962, pp. 147–95.

Lee, Brian. "James Baldwin: Caliban to Prospero." In *The Black American Writer*, Vol. I: Fiction. Edited by C. W. E. Bigsby. Deland, Florida: Everett/Edwards, 1969, pp. 169–79.

Littlejohn, David. *Black on White: A Critical Survey of Writing of American Negroes*. New York: Grossman, 1966, pp. 72–74, 110–37.

Long, Richard, and Eugenia W. Collier. "James Baldwin." In their *Afro-American Writings: An Anthology of Prose and Poetry*, Vol. II. New York: New York University Press, 1972, pp. 619–23.

Macebuh, Stanley. *James Baldwin: A Critical Study*. New York, Third World Press/Joseph Okpaku, 1973.

Major, Clarence. "James Baldwin: A Fire in the Mind." In his *The Dark and Feeling: Black American Writers and Their Work*. New York: Joseph Okpaku, pp. 73–83.

Margolies, Edward. "The Negro Church: James Baldwin and the Christian Vision." In his *Native Sons: A Critical Study of Twentieth-Century Negro American Authors*. New York: J. P. Lippincott, 1968, pp. 102–26.

May, John R. "Ellison, Baldwin, and Wright: Vestiges of Christian Apocalypse." In his *Toward a New Earth: Apocalypse in the American Novel*. Notre Dame, Indiana: University of Notre Dame Press, 1972, pp. 145–71.

Mayfield, Julian. "And Then Came Baldwin." In *Harlem, U.S.A*. Revised edition. Edited by John Henrik Clarke. New York: Collier Books, 1971, pp. 157–70.

Meserve, Walker. "James Baldwin's 'Agony Way.' " In *The Black American Writer*, Vol. II: Poetry and Drama. Edited by C. W. E. Bigsby. Deland, Florida: Everett/Edwards, 1969, pp. 171–86.

Moller, Karin. *The Theme of Identity in the Essays of James Baldwin: An Interpretation*. Goteborg, Sweden: Acta Universitatis Gothoburgensis, 1975.

Moore, John R. "An Embarrassment of Riches: Baldwin's *Going to Meet the Man*." in *The Sounder Few: Essays from the Hollins Critic*. Edited by R. H. W. Dillard, George Garrett, and John R. Moore. Athens, Georgia: University of Georgia Press, 1971, pp. 121–36.

Murray, Alber. "James Baldwin, Protest Fiction and the Blues Tradition." In his *The Omni-Americans: New Perspectives on Black Experience and American Culture*. New York: Outerbridge and Dienstfrey, 1970, pp. 142–70.

Nobel, David. "The Present: Norman Mailer, James Baldwin, Saul Bellow." In his *Eternal Adam and the New World Garden*. New York: George Braziller, 1968, pp. 195–224.

O'Daniel, Therman B., ed. *James Baldwin: A Critical Evaluation*. Washington, D.C.: Howard University Press, 1977.

Phillips, Louis. "The Novelist as Playwright: Baldwin, McCullers and Bellow." In *Modern American Drama: Essays in Criticism*. Edited by William E. Taylor. Deland, Florida: Everett/Edwards, 1968, pp. 145–62.

Podhoretz, Norman. "The Article as Art." In his *Doings or Undoings: The Fifties and After in American Writing*. New York: Farrar, Straus and Company, 1964, pp. 126–42. "In Defense of James Baldwin." In *Five Black Writers*. Edited by Donald B. Gibson. New York: New York University Press, 1970, pp. 143–47.

Prasad, Thakur Duru. "*Another Country*: The Tensions of Dream and Nightmare in the American Psyche." In *Indian Studies of American Fiction*. Edited by M. K. Naik, S. K. Desai, S. Mokashi-Punekar. Dharwar: Karnatak University; Delhi: Macmillan India, 1974, pp. 296–310.

Pratt, Louis. *James Baldwin*. Boston: Twayne Publishers, 1978.

Ro, Sigmund. "The Black Musician as Literary Hero: Baldwin's 'Sonny's Blues' and William Kelley's 'Cry for Me.' " In his *Rage and Celebration: Essays on Contemporary Afro-American Writing*. Solum Verlag, 1984, pp. 9–43.

Rupp, Richard H. "James Baldwin: The Search for Celebration." In his *Celebration in Postwar American Fiction: 1945–1967*. Coral Gables, Florida: University of Miami Press, 1970, pp. 133–49.

Sarotte, George Michel. *Like a Brother, Like a Lover: Male Homosexuality in the American Novel and Theatre from Herman Melville to James Baldwin*. Trans. by Richard Miller. New York: Anchor Press/Doubleday, 1978, pp. 27–29, 54–60, 96–103.

Sayre, Robert F. "James Baldwin's Other Country." In *Contemporary American Novelists*. Edited by Harry T. Moore. Carbondale: Southern Illinois University Press, 1964, pp. 158–69.

Standley and Standley, eds. *James Baldwin. A Reference Guide*. Boston: G. K. Hall, 1980.

Straumann, Heinrich. "The Power of Reality." In his *American Literature in the Twentieth Century*, 3rd revised edition. New York: Harper and Row, 1965, pp. 39–41.

Sylander, Carolyn W. *James Baldwin*. New York: Ungar, 1980.

Thelwell, Mike. "*Another Country*: Baldwin's New York Novel." In *The Black American Writer*, Vol. I: Fiction. Edited by C. W. E. Bigsby. Deland, Florida: Everett/Edwards, 1969, pp. 181–98.

Warren, Robert Penn. *Who Speaks for the Negro?* New York: Random House, 1965, pp. 160–61, 277–92, 293–98, 323–34.

Weatherby, W. J. *Squaring Off: Mailer vs. Baldwin*. New York: Mason/Charter; London: Robson Books, 1977.

· ACKNOWLEDGMENTS ·

Grateful acknowledgment is made for permission to reprint the following:

Foreword by Wole Soyinka, © 1988. By permission of the author.

I. Excerpt from *No Name in the Street* by James Baldwin. Copyright © 1972 by James Baldwin. Reprinted by permission of Doubleday, a division of Bantam, Doubleday, Dell Publishing Group, Inc.

"Celebrating Jimmy" by Clyde Taylor, © 1988. By permission of the author.

II. "James Baldwin, Friend and Brother." Citation from the Baldwin Family, funeral service December, 1987.

"A Brother's Love" by Maya Angelou, © 1987. From remarks delivered at James Baldwin funeral, also printed in *The New York Times Book Review*. By permission of the author.

"Jimmy in the House" by William Styron, © 1987, also printed in *The New York Times Book Review*. By permission of the author.

"Baldwin" by Mary McCarthy, © 1988. By permission of the author.

Quincy Troupe has published four volumes of poetry: *Embryo* (1972); *Snake-Back Solos* (1979), winner of the 1980 American Book Award for poetry; *Skulls Along the River* (1984); and *Weather Reports* (1989); and his poetry has been translated into several languages.

Troupe was editor of the anthology *Watts Poets and Writers* (1968) and co-editor of *Giant Talk: An Anthology of Third World Writing* (1975). He is also the author of *Soundings*, a book of essays (1989), and coauthor of *Miles: the Autobiography of Miles Davis* (1989). In 1978 he coauthored *The Inside Story of TV's "Roots"* with David L. Wolper, producer of that award-winning series. The founding editor of *Confrontation: A Journal of Third World Literature* and *The American Rag*, he currently serves as senior editor for the St. Louis–based literary quarterly, *River Styx*.

Troupe is professor of American and Third World Literature at the College of Staten Island (City University of New York) and teaches creative writing at Columbia University.

Wole Soyinka, winner of the 1986 Nobel Prize in Literature, is one of Africa's most prolific and influential writers. Educated at the Universities of Ibadan and Leeds, he was associated with the English Stage Company and the Royal Court Theatre before returning to Nigeria. His many notable works include the plays *Death and the King's Horseman* (1975) and *A Play of Giants* (1984); the volumes of poetry *Poems from Prison* (1969) and *Ogun Abibiman* (1976); and the novels *The Interpreters* (1965) and *The Season of Anomy* (1974). He edited the literary journal *Transition* and *Poems of Black Africa* (1974). His autobiography is entitled *Aké: The Years of Childhood* (1981).

· PHOTO CREDITS ·

3110